# The Leaders We Need

*And What Makes Us Follow*

Michael Maccoby
*with* Tim Scudder

PUBLISHED BY ARRANGEMENT WITH
HARVARD BUSINESS REVIEW PRESS

© Copyright 2018 Michael Maccoby and Tim Scudder

Printed in the United States of America

All rights reserved, including, but not limited to, the right to create, produce, and license training and development materials based on the content of this book. No part of this publication may be reproduced or transmitted in any form or by any means, electronic or mechanical, including photocopy, recording, or any information storage or retrieval system, without written permission from the publisher. Personal Strengths Publishing, 2701 Loker Avenue West, Suite 250, Carlsbad, CA 92010, USA.

Catalog-In-Publication Data

Maccoby, Michael, 1933-
   The Leaders We Need: and what makes us follow / Michael Maccoby, Tim Scudder—2nd ed.
      p. cm.
   Includes index, notes, and biographical references.
   ISBN-13: 978-1-932627-12-1
   1. Leadership. 2. Leadership—Psychological aspects. 3. Context effects (Psychology) 4. Transference (Psychology)

Printed in the United States of America

SECOND EDITION

Original work copyright © 2007 Michael Maccoby

Published by arrangement with Harvard Business Review Press

Cover art: Kent Mitchell

# Contents

*Preface to the Second Edition* — v

*Preface* — ix

1 Introduction — 1
   *Leadership in a New Context*

2 Revising Leadership Thinking — 15

3 Why We Follow — 37
   *The Power of Transference*

4 From Bureaucratic Followers
   to Interactive Collaborators — 53

5 Developing Personality Intelligence — 67

6 Applying Personality Intelligence — 87

7 Developing a Productive Social Character — 107

| 8 | Leaders for Knowledge Work | 129 |
| 9 | Becoming a Leader We Need | 139 |
|   | Notes | 157 |
|   | Index | 169 |
|   | Acknowledgments | 181 |
|   | About the Authors | 183 |

PREFACE TO THE SECOND EDITION

WE NEED LEADERS who can mobilize people to deal effectively and creatively with the threats and opportunities of the 21st century. But what kind of leaders are these? There are many definitions of leaders – and leadership – and as I've learned from Michael Maccoby, sometimes the simplest definitions are the most profound. A leader is, simply stated, someone people follow. Without followers, there is no leader. That implies that leadership is a relationship, a relationship that exists in a social, economic, and natural context. To have any hope of averting the serious threats facing us today and creating a better world for tomorrow's children, there is an urgent need to improve the relationships between the leaders we need and the followers essential for their success.

Michael and I have been motivated to update this book because of our practical experience leading workshops based on this book and the techniques for understanding self and others developed by SDI (Strength Deployment Inventory). We have met many leaders who struggle to fit some sort of ideal of a leader. They try to be like someone they admire, or try to follow advice from the most recent book, lecture, or workshop they attended. The problem with this is that the advice giver, or the idealized leader, does not operate in the same context, does not have the same personality, and does not have the same followers. We found that leaders become much more effective when they truly know themselves and the people they want to lead and when they develop a philosophy that guides them.

Some workshop participants initially scoffed at the idea of writing a leadership philosophy. But without a clear statement of purpose and values, followers will make up stories about leaders, saying they are self-interested, or play favorites, or don't keep their commitments. A philosophy that's communicated and practiced develops trust and can help leaders to transform followers into collaborators.

Workshop participants, from Cairo to Jakarta, from Napa Valley's bucolic vineyards to the Civil War Battlefield at Gettysburg's National Military Park, from the California School of Professional Psychology to Oxford University, and many places in between have benefited from these ideas, while challenging us to think more deeply about what it means to lead, and to make these ideas even more accessible. Leaders from all types of organizations have told us that the ability to understand systems at human, organizational, and societal levels has helped them to become better, more effective, and more fulfilled leaders.

This book owes a debt of gratitude to many people. Kevin Small for the original vision and encouragement to begin the second edition; Jim Meier for encouraging Michael to make the ideas from the first edition accessible through a training program; Cliff and Jane Norman for recruiting people into these early workshops, and introducing Michael and me; Maia Browning for allowing Michael, Richard Margolies and me to pilot our training program with leaders at the US National Park Service; Ginny Barnhill for making The Leaders We Need a cornerstone of a corporate university; Ray Hart, and Ron Palmieri for creating an environment at GEI Consultants where leaders are nourished and inviting us into the process; Tim Perlick, David Wong, and Rick Sciortino at CME Group for integrating concepts from The Leaders We Need into the organization's innovation and leadership development efforts; John McKissick for organizing workshops Michael led in Cairo, Amman, and Beirut; Elizabeth Howard and Marc Thompson for inviting Michael to lead workshops at Oxford; Erhard Friedberg for inviting Michael to give leadership workshops at Sciences Po in Paris, and for Tim at the School of Government and Public Policy in Jakarta; Mary Ann Castronovo Fusco for her skillful copy edits, which went beyond corrections to make the book more clear, concise, and compelling.

Leadership training is big business around the globe, but much of it is really management training, focused on skills without considering values or accounting for the complexities of individual differences and relationships. To understand leadership, it is essential to understand leaders and followers, their roles and values. We believe that leadership development requires that skills training be paired with a deep understanding of values and philosophy – individually and organizationally.

Our philosophy for this second edition starts with a purpose: to enrich leadership thought and improve the quality and humanity of work and the workplace. It is guided by humanistic concepts of human development, such as those described by Carol Dweck, Erik Erikson, Sigmund Freud, Erich Fromm, William James, Robert Kegan, and Carl Rogers. Development is more than a technique. Of course every author hopes to sell books. But we hope that sales of this book will indicate that people are putting these concepts to work, that these concepts are making a difference in the daily lives of people at work, and improving results in all types of teams, organizations, and communities.

To add a personal note, this book simultaneously grounds and advances the work I've been doing for the last 20 years. My passion for my work with the SDI has led me to explore the foundational psychological theories of Fromm and Freud. Working with Michael, who worked closely with Fromm, has deepened my understanding; we have found great joy in discovering and re-integrating concepts that diverged and developed along separate paths.

It is a privilege and honor to be able to contribute to this second edition, because the first has proven indispensable to me in my work. I hope you enjoy reading it and that you find the ideas as interesting, practical, and powerful as I have.

*Tim Scudder*
*Carlsbad, California*
*December 2017*

PREFACE

# Leadership is a Relationship in a Context

THE NEED FOR GOOD LEADERS is urgent—to mobilize human intelligence and energy to grapple with historic threats such as terrorism, climate changes, and the threat of weapons of mass destruction, and also to respond to vast opportunities to improve life on this planet. Only a persuasive national leader can gain support at home and abroad for policies that protect our society from its enemies, sustain a healthy environment and promote the common good. Only exceptional business and organizational leaders can provide employment and produce the goods and services essential for a strong economy and healthy population. Yet despite the thousands of books and articles on the subject, we haven't improved very much on classic writings about leadership. To start with, even the best recent writers on leadership stumble over the definition of a leader, and a good definition is the necessary start to understanding the kinds of leaders we need and how they'll gain followers in the context of our time.

John Gardner, a former secretary of Health and Human Services and noted leadership thinker, described very well what bureaucratic bosses do, but like a number of writers on the subject, his definition of a leader is inadequate. He defines a leader in terms of tasks: setting goals, motivating people, evaluating them.[1] This definition doesn't distinguish a leader from a manager or even from some leaderless teams that set their own goals and motivate each other. Other writers tell us the defining task of a leader is visioning.² Certainly, many leaders have been visionaries, but lots of people with visions have no followers; some of them have ended up isolated—and even in mental hospitals. Furthermore, artists, scientists and craftsman can be visionaries without being leaders.

James McGregor Burns's brilliant treatise on leadership is full of rich historical vignettes.³ Burns has given us the useful distinction of transactional versus transformational leaders. By his definition, a transformational leader raises people to higher moral levels, changing them in a positive way. But this definition implies that monsters like Hitler, Stalin, and Mao weren't transformational leaders—even though millions of people worshiped them and millions were changed by them, mostly for the worse. Even if a leader is just defined as someone who gets people to change, this wouldn't distinguish a leader from a manager who shakes up an organization by redesigning roles and incentives. It wouldn't even distinguish a leader from a skillful psychotherapist.

There is only one irrefutable definition of a leader, and that is someone people follow. This may seem too simple a definition for many academics, but once accepted it opens the door for plenty of hard thinking. Once we agree that anyone with followers—liberator or oppressor, transformational visionary or transactional problem solver—is a leader, then we have to answer two difficult, essential questions about leadership.

The first is: Why do people follow this person? Much is written about leaders, but much less about followers. This book is about the leaders we need particularly within organizations and also about the attitudes toward leaders and leadership that are being formed in a new historical context. How will leaders gain these followers? This is not just a question of using well-known techniques; we'll see in this book that many would-be followers are no longer moved by what worked in the past.

Of course, there are and always have been leaders who force people to follow them and make the alternative unpleasant—imprisonment or execution by despots; firing by managers. In fact, most of the organizational leaders we've met are followed grudgingly, without enthusiasm or trust. But those leaders won't inspire anyone to meet the challenges of our time.

The second question: How do people follow the leader? Do they follow blindly? Do they do what they are told to do? Do they imitate the leader? These are typical follower behaviors in the bureaucratic-industrial world. But in the emerging era of knowledge work in which technical and professional specialists work across organizational and national boundaries, we'll see that leaders are most effective when they and their followers become collaborators who share a common purpose.[4]

Leadership always implies a relationship between leader and led, and that relationship exists within a context. Leaders who gain followers in one context—which could be historical, cultural, or organizational—may not attract followers in a different context. A well-known example is Winston Churchill, the indispensable leader who was willingly followed when Britain was attacked by Germany, but was rejected by his countrymen before and after World War II. Before the war, the British public wanted peace and rejected Churchill because he urged the country to prepare for war against Hitler's Germany. After the war, the voters rejected Churchill's vision of sustaining empire in favor of turning inward to build the welfare state. Another example is the Confucian benevolent despot Lee Kwan Yu, who led Singapore, a poor city-state, to glittering prosperity. But he's not a leader who'd be followed in the democratic West.

In times of chaos and uncertainty, many people are attracted to leaders who promise to make things right. They can be demagogues who threaten liberty like Napoleon or Hitler, or they can be democratic visionaries like Abraham Lincoln or Nelson Mandela.

Then there are the entrepreneurs like Jerry Yang of Yahoo who are able to lead start-ups but lose their followers when the company becomes large and complex.

Who are the leaders we need now? They are the leaders motivated to achieve the common good who have the qualities required to gain willing followers in our culture, at a historical moment when leadership becomes essential to meet the challenges of that time and place. They are leaders who are able to transform tribalistic societies and organizations into collaborative communities. To understand leadership in our current context, we have to get inside the heads of the people a would-be leader is trying to mobilize (i.e., the followers) and understand the qualities needed by the leader.

Our leadership context for organizations has changed from that of fifty years ago, when corporate bureaucracies enjoyed stable, predictable markets. Then, managers were needed to plot a steady course; innovative leaders were often seen as disruptive and sidelined. Now, in the context of continual change brought about by technology, competition and knowledge workers, leadership is needed not only at the top, but also throughout companies. Furthermore, different types of leaders are needed to integrate projects and teams of technical professionals working across department and national borders: strategic, operational, and network or bridge-building:

- Strategic leaders communicate a vision with a compelling sense of purpose.

- Operational leaders build the organization and infuse the energy that transforms visions into results.

- Network/bridge-building leaders facilitate the understanding and trust that turns different types of specialists into collaborators.

These leadership roles are most effectively filled by different types of people in terms of their intellectual skills and personalities. Furthermore, these leaders need to understand each other in order to work together; and most importantly, they need to understand the diverse mix of people they want to follow or better yet, collaborate with them to achieve a common purpose.

Not only has the context of leadership changed, but also the relationships between leaders and their followers, especially among knowledge workers.[5] We'll explore this change and its implications for leadership in this book.

My approach to the study of leadership is shaped by my academic training and professional experience as a psychoanalyst and anthropologist who for over forty years has studied and counseled leaders in business, government, universities, non-profits, and unions. As an anthropologist, I view leadership within a cultural context, that weaves together modes of work, political institutions, family structure, and values. As a psychoanalyst, I focus on the way personality determines how we relate to others, especially at work. Erich Fromm's idea of social character, which integrates anthropological context with a psychoanalytic approach to personality, is an essential concept for developing what I call Personality Intelligence, the ability to understand people, both intellectually and emotionally, with both head and heart. In Chapter 6, Tim Scudder shows that Personality Intelligence can be a powerful aid for engaging people at work and avoiding disruptive conflicts. Leaders who are best able to develop this ability understand themselves and care about the well-being and development of the people they lead.

Although I don't subscribe to all of Freud's theories, in this book I do make extensive use of his concept of unconscious transference, and I build on his theory of personality types. Transference helps to explain why people sometimes idealize leaders, projecting onto them comforting childhood images of protective parents. And it also explains why they sometimes turn against these leaders, seeing them as inept or neglectful parents. In chapter 3, we'll examine how changes in the experience of childhood and a shift in the social character cause different perceptions of parents and peers resulting in dramatically different attitudes to leadership.

In my teaching and consulting work, I've met many inspiring young leaders with strong values and high aspirations for the common good. This book expands on what I have taught to and learned from them combined with what I've learned from Tim Scudder. It is the foundation book for three other books I've written on leadership in the twenty-first century. *Transforming Health Care Leadership, A Systems Guide to Improve Patient Care, Decrease Costs, and Improve Population Health*[6] describes the leaders we need for health care. *Strategic Intelligence, Conceptual Tools for Leading Change*[7] includes exercises for developing the qualities essential for creating great and good organizations. And *Narcissistic Leaders, Who Succeeds and Who Fails*[8] is a guidebook for analyzing visionary leaders, predicting which ones will succeed and understanding how to work with them. After I wrote the first edition of *The Leaders We Need*, Tim Scudder joined me in developing a workshop that combined the concepts presented here with the conceptual tools he has helped to develop at Personal Strengths Publishing. In his Preface, he describes some of the leadership workshops he and I have facilitated. Besides collaborating in the task of bringing the chapters up to date, Tim has contributed chapter 6, which describes how understanding personality can be applied to improve workplace relationships. His collaboration makes this book a better aid for developing the qualities essential to become a leader we need.

*Michael Maccoby*
*Washington, D.C.*
*December 2017*

CHAPTER 1

# Introduction

*Leadership in a New Context*

IN TIMES OF GREAT CULTURAL CHANGE, such as the present, people need leaders to take them to a positive future. But what makes leaders successful depends not only on their message and their skill in getting it across, but also on their understanding of followers and their grasp of what followers want from them. Throughout history, people have not always followed the leaders they needed. Sometimes they have been forced to follow oppressive dictators. Sometimes they have idealized and willingly followed seductive demagogues who have led them to disaster. This book is about why people follow leaders and what it takes to become the kind of leader we need today—a time of profound change in organizations, work, family life, and the social character—when both opportunities to improve life and threats to life have never been so great.

The cultural change we're experiencing is at least as far-reaching as the Industrial Revolution, which drove people from farms into factories and bureaucracies, and changed their work from handling tools to mastering machines. It can be compared to the chain of changes begun by Genghis Khan and his Mongol followers 900 years ago.[1] The Mongol invaders smashed feudal ties in Eastern Europe and built the foundations of a new culture in China. Innovative Chinese technologies—gunpowder, the compass, printing—spread to the West and became tools for an era of exploration and conquest, the rise of a new entrepreneurial class, the beginnings of capitalism, and profound changes in values and emotional attitudes. The writings of the era about leadership have had a profound influence on Western civilization. Descriptions of how leaders gain power in turbulent times by Niccolò Machiavelli and William Shakespeare in the 16th century still influence our thinking.

Our thinking about leadership has not kept up with events. Fast-moving currents of technology and social revolution move some people to a new practice of life and leave others in their wake. People relate to each other in new ways; they create personal identities that didn't exist in previous generations. Everyone is in some way touched by what happens in places that once seemed far away. Work moves to low-wage countries, but there is an even greater impact from the information and communication technology that wipes out millions of factory and transactional service jobs, replacing them with work that calls for more brainpower and interpersonal skills. Bureaucratic hierarchies are pulled and stretched into complex systems, and the new roles demand flexibility from employees.

Persistent tension and anxiety keep people on edge. Corporate executives who once felt invulnerable now need to worry that someone else's innovation will blindside them and send their companies into a tailspin. Alarming information and images about highly competitive international markets, global warming, terrorist threats, natural disasters, and weapons of mass destruction, all funneled through radio, television, and the Internet, and often filtered or distorted through social media, are instantaneously sent to people around the globe. Individuals now have information at the touch of a mouse that was previously available, if at all, only to privileged experts; yet they struggle to parse its meaning or to determine whether it is true or fake. At the same time that people yearn for protective and soothing leaders, they have become skeptical about leaders in general and distrustful of their motives and competence.[2]

Social changes have upset historic patterns of family relationships. The liberation and empowerment of women has transformed workplace, family, and the way men and women view each other. The whole experience of growing up has been shaken up and, with it, the dynamics that shape the deep-rooted emotional attitudes that form people's values—what we call the social character.

Social character is a key concept at the center of my research. It can be thought of as a kind of macro personality, describing the emotional attitudes and values shared by people whose personality has been formed in a particular culture or social class. It's a concept that clarifies how cultures shape human nature. In this age of globalization and cultural change, it's an essential concept for understanding the leaders we need and why people will follow them. Yes, we all share needs and strivings for self-protection, sustenance, and relatedness—love and work, self-expression and self-worth. But these needs play out differently, shaped by culture, acting through institutions of family, school, workplace, and religion. Yes, we each have a unique personality, and our genetic patterns are as different as snowflakes. Yes, we take on different identities, some of which are membership cards for interest groups. Despite these differences, however, most people who have grown up and adapted to the norms of similar institutions share ways of almost instinctually relating to their work and to others. We all think that the way we feel and act in social relationships is human nature, yet those in other cultures who feel and act differently think the same thing. They and we are both wrong; human nature is always formed and expressed through the social character.[3]

With such radical changes in the context in which people live and work and in the social character, it is not surprising that how people view their leaders—what they want and need from them—also has changed. Our theories of leadership were formed in other contexts. Leaders, especially those in the most advanced organizations, can no longer gain followers in the old ways. In particular, how we have been taught to think about organizational leadership—a one-size-fits-all manager in a bureaucratic hierarchy with uniform roles—is now misleading and grossly inadequate. The bureaucratic theory of leadership assumes a psychology of followers that no longer describes a growing number of working people, especially in our dominant organizations and global companies.

In the evolving knowledge organization, it's more useful to know how different personality types fit specific leadership roles, and how they can get people to collaborate with them. Changes in social character and the knowledge-creating workplace make it essential to raise our understanding of personality, not just intellectually but also experientially, and to develop *Personality Intelligence*.

4  *The Leaders We Need*

To describe the leadership we need, we can't extrapolate from the past. People have changed—both would-be leaders and potential followers. People today respond to different qualities in leaders than they did a generation ago. Take corporations in the 1970s. Most managers were white men who were raised in families with one male wage earner, the father. Today there are fewer of these families than those headed by a single woman; in the current typical family, both parents are wage earners.[4] Although many top leaders have come from traditional families, most people now entering the workforce have not. Presumably, their parents both worked and shared authority in the family, and this will be even more likely for their children. As we'll discuss in Chapter 3, it appears that many people raised in nontraditional families feel stronger ties to sibling figures than to parental-type bosses.

Furthermore, women now hold key leadership roles, and that makes a big difference in workplace psychology. Instead of hierarchies of men following father figures, would-be leaders face a diverse group of followers who may project any number of images—mother, sibling, friend—onto them.

During the past few years, whenever I've met groups of managers, mostly in their late 30s or early 40s, in workshops on leadership in the United States and Western Europe, I've asked for a show of hands from those born into families with a single male wage earner. It's usually a majority. Then I ask how many now live in this type of traditional family. It's usually a small minority, mirroring the historic shift in the role of women and the makeup of families.

Because people are less likely to idealize leaders as father substitutes and they're more critical of parental figures in general, leaders can't lead in ways that worked in the past, especially in the advanced industrial democracies. Yes, fear or pervasive anxiety may, in psychoanalytic terms, regress people for a while so that they project a protective parental image onto a leader who exploits their fear. This is what Freud called transference. It causes us to idealize a leader and ignore his or her faults, and it dulls our own critical faculties. But once that protective image cracks, the new social character asserts itself and we become skeptical about all leaders. This is particularly dangerous in our present time of disruptive change, when we desperately need leaders to inspire diverse groups of people to pull together for the common good.

Our goal with this book is to will help readers understand why people follow different leaders in different times and circumstances, including the present time, and it will show how the leaders who are needed in a given context must engage the social character of followers. We will also explain why people sometimes follow the wrong leaders. After illuminating the dynamic nature of the leader-follower relationship, it will provide a useful typology of the different kinds of leaders we now need, how they can engage followers, and how they need to develop themselves. But first, here's a brief account of how I came to the views of leadership and followership presented in this book.

## STUDIES OF FOLLOWERS AND LEADERS

Over the past 40 years as an anthropologist, psychoanalyst, and then a consultant and teacher to business, government, military, educational, healthcare, and union leaders in North America, Europe, Asia, Africa, and Latin America, I've interviewed a global spectrum of people at work: peasant farmers, entrepreneurs, workers in factories and offices, professionals, civil servants, military and foreign service officers, elected and appointed national and local officials, bank managers; and corporate managers, executives, and CEOs. Actually, I began to study leaders as an undergraduate at Harvard in the 1950s, interviewing political and academic leaders for The Crimson, the daily student newspaper. After receiving a doctorate in 1960, I joined the social psychoanalyst Erich Fromm in Mexico to train as a psychoanalyst in the Mexican Institute of Psychoanalysis he led and to study a village where entrepreneurs were beginning to change the culture and institutions that formed the social character.[5]

After returning to the United States in 1968, with a grant from Harvard I led a study of managers in high-tech companies and initiated projects to improve the quality of working life at Harman International Industries and AT&T. Because of these projects I was hired to consult to companies, unions, and government agencies. Through these studies and my consulting work I was able to observe that the attitudes and values in industrial societies—the social character—were changing, mirroring the historic transformations of work and family that had started in the 1960s and are still playing out today.

What most causes the social character to change is the dominant mode of production in a culture, the way of working in the most competitive and dynamic businesses. The people with the skills, emotional attitudes, and strong values that fit this dominant mode of work are the ones who do well, become models for others, and influence how the next generation is raised. Parents and schools strive to prepare children to become like the people who are making it in the world of work. And the successful innovators, the entrepreneurs who create the new modes of work, lead efforts to change education to develop the next generation for the new workplace. This was the case more than a century ago as innovators like Andrew Carnegie, John D. Rockefeller, and Henry Ford financed foundations to influence education. And it's happening again with the next wave of innovators like Bill Gates, Eli Broad, Michael Dell, Oprah Winfrey, Mark Zuckerberg and others.[6]

In this way, we might say that social character changes by a process of *social selection*, which is comparable to natural selection. But whereas in natural selection certain traits determine biological reproduction—that is, which offspring survive—in social selection, the traits of the most successful people are reproduced in the educational and work practices that shape the social character.[7] Social selection is far faster than natural selection. Leaders who understand this are better prepared to make the best of changing practices

## FARMING-CRAFT SOCIAL CHARACTER

To understand the changing social character, consider the differences among traditional peasant farmers, workers in the industrial bureaucracies, and the technical-professional knowledge workers of today. In Mexico, the social character of the most prosperous villagers that Erich Fromm and I studied was adapted to work that had changed little for centuries in villages throughout the world. The successful farmers were just like their parents and ancestors: self-sufficient, rooted in the land they farmed, hardworking, cautious, and conservative, with a strong sense of dignity based on independence and self-reliance. Respectful, they expected to be respected by others. Used to the repetitive tasks of the seasons, they were patient as nature took its time to make their plantings grow, but also fatalistic and emotionally prepared for unpredictable calamities— droughts, disease, and shifts in market prices. Often cheated by middlemen and politicians, they trusted only family members. A close-knit family with paternal authority reinforced by a patriarchal Catholicism made for a strong economic unit that provided security for the old as well as the young.[8] Village decisions were typically made by consensus among the heads of families, mostly men but also some women.

These people were suspicious of all leaders, believing that they were out to use them for their personal gain. Leaders were followed only in times of crisis, as during the Mexican Revolution of 1910-1920 when villagers in the state of Morelos hired Emiliano Zapata to protect their lands from being grabbed by owners of large sugar-planting haciendas in collusion with the federal government. Some of the farmers I interviewed, however, did follow entrepreneurs who seduced them with visions of riches they'd earn if they'd sell their land to build weekend houses for wealthy people from Mexico City and transform their village into a tourist attraction. These entrepreneurs also persuaded villagers to invest in schooling, roads, and electricity to support changes that connected their village more closely to the modern world.

Reading studies of peasants in other parts of the world and working with George M. Foster, the University of California at Berkeley expert on peasant life, I learned that the social character of these *campesinos* was typical for peasants in Latin America, India, China, and Eastern Europe. And the villagers' behavior conformed to what appears to be a general law about why free people want to follow a leader who pulls them out of their comfort zone. They will do so if they feel they need the leader to rid them of threats and oppression, or to help them get rich—in other words, conscious self-interest.

## INDUSTRIAL-BUREAUCRATIC SOCIAL CHARACTER

Back in the United States in the 1970s, the success of a project I led to improve productivity and the quality of working life at Harman Industries propelled me to study organizations at the heart of the industrial world, among them Volvo and AT&T's Bell System, which included Western Electric and the regional telephone operating companies, giants that were then at their height of power and importance. These were prototypical bureaucracies, with uniform roles structured in a pyramidal hierarchy.

In chapters 3 and 4, the personality of bureaucratic managers is described as inner-directed, obsessive, and father-oriented, with values of loyalty, stability, and expert knowledge. But the only leaders that workers at AT&T and other industrial bureaucracies wanted to follow were not the bureaucrats who managed with carrots and sticks, but those exceptional managers who allowed them to experiment with how they performed their work, listened to their ideas, and coached them. The heads of these companies did not usually place such people in leadership positions, however; they promoted people who were most like themselves.

Nonetheless, it was in a Harman factory in rural Tennessee where I learned that people did not always conform to popular academic theories of motivation.[9] Many workers there were farmers and homemakers who took factory jobs only to supplement their uncertain income. The prevailing theories taught in business schools predicted that workers like these would be on a low level of Abraham Maslow's needs hierarchy and be motivated solely by money. Other academics like Frederick Herzberg disagreed and argued that almost all factory workers would be motivated by more challenging work.

Yes, challenge did motivate some workers, especially those with a bureaucratic social character who sought a career in the company and wanted to show off and also improve their skills. But many rural workers with a farming-craft social character were most motivated by the prospect of going home early to do what they considered their real work on the farm or running a household: cooking and cleaning, preserving fruits, making clothes, raising children and animals. This was more important to them than earning more money at the factory. And when they were given the opportunity to have a say in designing their jobs, with the promise that they could share the time saved and leave work early, the workers doubled their productivity. One group of women on an assembly line actually rejected the offer of more challenging work: Since the work had become automatic, they indulged in chatting about friends and family while at their tasks. More challenge would force them to concentrate on work rather than on each other.

Another, more positive exception I saw in the late 1980s was at a Toyota factory in Nagoya, Japan, where the workers promoted to foreman roles were natural leaders who already had followers because they helped others and created group harmony. This was one example of Toyota's extraordinary ability to combine social intelligence with technical excellence.

It's not that the academics were all wrong. Rather, they formed their theories within one context, one type of workplace with one type of social character, and then they overgeneralized. We will see in Chapter 2 that this is still the case for popular academic theories of motivation and leadership that neglect the psychology of followers.

## KNOWLEDGE WORK AND A NEW SOCIAL CHARACTER

In the budding information age of the mid-1970s, my study of managers at HP, IBM, Intel, Xerox, Bell Laboratories, Schlumberger, the Jet Propulsion Laboratory, and Texas Instruments revealed an emerging mode of production involving teams of knowledge workers creating new technology.[10] Companies needed high-energy project leaders to fire up the engineers who had been raised in a slower-moving bureaucratic world.

I called the most effective leaders gamesmen because they treated their work like a game they were driven to win. They began to break up the bureaucratic hierarchies with a spirit of competition. The obsessive, craftsman-like engineers followed them because they stirred up excitement and heady feelings of being part of a winning team.

At that time, computer programmers operated at the fringes of technology companies like IBM and HP, whose main products were hardware. Managers and engineers saw programmers as oddballs, nerds who worked strange hours and dressed like adolescents. But the software revolution of the 1980s and 1990s transformed some of these social character mutants into charismatic visionary leaders like Bill Gates, Steve Jobs, and Larry Ellison who formed cultlike organizations around revolutionary products.[11] Employees followed them because they promised riches and a role in a great adventure that would change the way people lived and worked.

In this period, the mode of production evolved, as did the experience of growing up. In the 1980s, for the first time, I met people with the new social character in knowledge work, in fields like telecommunications, finance, healthcare, consulting, entertainment, professional services, and government. Surveys that my colleagues and I conducted among managers and professionals showed that the number of people with the new social character was growing.

Unlike the bureaucratic social character, the *interactive* social character is focused less on status and autonomy, and more on teamwork and self-development.[12] The strengths of *Interactives* lie in their independence, readiness for change, and quick ability to connect with others and work in a self-managed team. Many of them, especially those who have grown up with social networking Internet sites, feel at home in the global economy. As long as the rules are clear and the purpose of their work is meaningful, they'll play the game of work, take responsibility for their decisions, and keep learning to stay sharp and marketable. But they don't want to follow autocratic, insensitive bosses who don't listen.

Their weaknesses, like those of all social characters, are the obverse of their strengths. Not expecting loyalty from organizations, they aren't committed to a company, even though they'll commit to a meaningful project. Comfortable with technology and the Internet, they find it easy to escape to alternative worlds, second lives, and assumed identities. Quick to Google the answers, they overweigh superficial knowledge. Although the bureaucratic social character could be annoyingly stubborn and self-righteous, the Interactive can be inauthentically ingratiating and self-marketing.

This psychological shift changes the relation of leaders to followers. For the interactive social character, bonds of affiliation are often stronger with colleagues than with bosses. Unlike bureaucratic employees of large companies a generation ago, the interactive social character does not idealize the boss and questions the very need for a leader. These people won't be led by father figures, but only by role models who engage them as colleagues in meaningful corporate projects, ideally creating a collaborative community.[13] If they are led toward goals they find meaningful by leaders who understand them, only then will organizations be able to meet the challenges of our time.

## WHAT KINDS OF LEADERS ARE NEEDED NOW?

I've seen at first hand and by reading history that the kind of leaders needed always depends on the context—the challenges of the time and the social character of the people who are being led. Here's an example. Right after I wrote *The Leader*, Carnegie Samuel Calian, then president of Pittsburgh Theological Seminary, invited me to participate in a discussion on the book with academics and business executives. He also asked me to talk at morning chapel on my favorite leader in the Bible. I chose Moses for two reasons, one trivial and the other profound.

The trivial reason is that Moses is the only biblical leader with a management consultant—his father-in-law Jethro, who warns him that he'll exhaust himself by trying to judge all the many disputes among his people. He's counseled to delegate to lieutenants whose judgment he trusts and only deal with the tough cases that can't be resolved by one of them. Of course, that's still standard good advice for someone managing many people.

The profound reason is that Moses took people who were slaves in Egypt and afraid of freedom and not only liberated them, but also taught them how to be free. Once in the desert, the people who had followed Moses to escape from the back-breaking work of building the pyramids complained: "We don't know where our next meal is coming from. Why have you brought us here? We were better off in Egypt. At least we knew we'd have food to eat." Talmudic rabbis believed that Moses took two generations, 40 years, to transform these ex-slaves into a free, self-reliant people. He needed time to teach them the law and burn it into their psyches, to turn the fear of Pharaoh into the fear of God, to prepare them for freedom.

Social character changes much more slowly than changes in the social environment. But Moses was not just forging a new social character—he also gave his followers the norms and processes to sustain a free and just society, and the hope that they could be God's chosen people if they lived according to His commandments.

Moses not only led slaves to freedom physically; he transformed a slave mentality. He not only took people to a new place; he took them to a new state of mind. He transformed their social character. Moses was the leader the people needed, not only to become free in body, but also in spirit.

## IT'S NOT ALWAYS SOMEONE LIKE MOSES WHO LEADS

People sometimes want the wrong leaders. Another biblical example comes from the Book of Samuel, a righteous judge leading the Israelites. Because they had been defeated by the Philistines and were afraid, the people wanted a warrior-king to protect them. Samuel warned that a king would enlist their sons as soldiers and grab their daughters to serve him as cooks and bakers; he would take their fields and tax them. Samuel predicted the people would regret their decision, but they'd be stuck with it. They would cry out, but the Lord wouldn't hear them. And so it happened.

Most Americans grow up believing that, notwithstanding a setback here and there, things will always turn out well in the end. Isn't that our history? But there's nothing inevitable about progress and, like the Israelites who wanted a king, people don't always get the leaders they need. Inept, grandiose, or corrupt populist leaders hastened the fall of the great civilizations of Athens and Rome. In the last few years we've seen that people don't always get the leaders they need in corporations, either.

Skillful bureaucrats continue to move up the ranks of business and government to become poor leaders or petty dictators. Rakesh Khurana has shown brilliantly how corporate boards have recruited media stars who, after giving a short-lived boost to the share price, ultimately weaken their company.[14] Even the most innovative entrepreneurs, such as Henry Ford, can become puffed up by success and then lead their companies toward disaster. More recently, great companies like Westinghouse, AT&T, Arthur Anderson, and HP have been led astray by inept leaders.

Why do people follow bad leaders? Sometimes they have no choice. A Mao, Stalin, Castro, or Saddam Hussein sweeps to power in a revolution against corrupt and inept leaders. People are forced to follow. And sometimes people flock to demagogues, populists like Juan Perón, Hugo Chavéz, or Huey Long, who make big promises they can't keep. Sometimes people follow bad leaders because they're frightened or hopeless and believe the leaders' promises of protection and a better future. In his book *Escape from Freedom*, Fromm analyzed Hitler's appeal to the German people.[15] According to Fromm, Hitler's first followers were small shopkeepers and low-level functionaries who shared a social character that was extremely patriotic, hardworking, parsimonious, stubborn, and moralistic. But their sense of self, their pride as successful people, had been crushed. They were humiliated by defeat in World War I, the loss of their father figure, Kaiser Wilhelm, and melting away of their hard-earned savings in the heat of postwar inflation. Also, these traditional and moralistic people were disgusted by what they considered licentiousness in the art and behavior in the Weimar Republic of the 1920s. Angry and seeking a champion, they were drawn to Hitler.

Data obtained from questionnaires filled out by German workers and employees in 1930 led Fromm to conclude that Hitler's original supporters had authoritarian personalities; they admired strong leaders and identified with them, and they were contemptuous of weakness, including their own. Hitler appealed to both their resentment and ambition. He offered power to the powerless, revenge against those who had humiliated Germany, and, tapping into historic anti-Semitism, he blamed the Jews for the cultural decadence. He promised a return to greatness for the "racially pure" Germans.

Once Hitler had taken over, other Germans who did not fully support his destructive vision followed the crowd to share in the spoils. With his early successes and their growing prosperity, Germans began to idealize Hitler. And many of those who did not agree with the Nazis were silenced by fear of the Gestapo, whose spies seemed to be everywhere. The regime tolerated no criticism, and the journalists and labor leaders who resisted Hitler risked being sent to concentration camps and even executed for treason. On the basis of his study, Fromm predicted that although only 10 percent of Germans were fervent Nazi supporters, no more than 15 percent had a strong enough democratic social character to resist Hitler. The majority, 75 percent, would follow as long as Hitler held power.[16]

## WHAT'S AT STAKE

In today's new context, in which understanding people becomes essential for both leaders and followers, unless leaders understand the broad spectrum of personalities in this global economy, they won't create the collaboration needed for economic innovation, political-military security, and environmental protection. And unless each of us understands would-be leaders, we risk being seduced by demagogues who won't improve the world and may even make things worse. We can't afford that. Let's be clear: It's not always easy to see behind the mask a clever leader wears, especially in an age of media manipulation and manufactured identities. To avoid being seduced by these populists, our grasp of personality—our Personality Intelligence—needs a lot of improvement. To recognize the person giving the spiel, and to be better able to predict how would-be leaders will act when in power, we need to understand their personalities. Correspondingly, would-be leaders with a better understanding of social character will be better able to gain willing followers.

In the bureaucratic world, trust in the leader resulted from an idealization that was rooted in unconscious father transference. (We'll describe these dynamics in Chapter 3.) Although such unconscious attachments never fully disappear, in the new context, organizational leaders are willingly, even enthusiastically, followed because they are good role models who articulate meaningful purpose and values, are transparent in their communications, encourage dialogue and truth-telling, and treat people as colleagues and collaborators rather than as subordinates. This kind of openness often scares executives because they think they'll risk losing control. But in my experience such openness enables them to gain rational authority and willing followers.[17]

Beyond this, people trust a leader who responds with heart as well as intellect. The leaders we need will develop their Personality Intelligence, which, as we'll see in Chapter 5 and Chapter 9, combines head and heart: knowledge of personality with direct experience of people's emotions. This is what the Bible tells us that King Solomon asked of God: a heart that listens, wisdom and courage, knowledge of what is right, and the willingness to act on it.

CHAPTER 2

# Revising Leadership Thinking

LEADERS HAVE BEEN DESCRIBED throughout history in every way imaginable—as dictators, demagogues, commanders, bosses, benefactors, guardians, coaches, pastors, and trailblazers. But what's been missing is a definition of a leader that covers all these descriptions. And that is, *A leader is someone people follow.* We can expand this definition to state that people follow leaders within a particular context, since being a leader isn't a personal trait, like introversion. Rather, it's a *relationship in a context* that exists only as long as people follow the leader.

Missing from the stacks of writings about leadership I've been burrowing through is a theory that fits the cultural context of our time. That's because the kind of leadership needed for past eras doesn't fit the age of knowledge work; it doesn't consider differences in modes of production and the leadership that they require. In the craft mode of production, effective leaders are master craftsmen with apprentices who want to become just like their masters. In the industrial mode of production, they are managers who design roles and processes, set tasks, and evaluate performance within hierarchical bureaucracies. The most effective are the paternalistic leaders who forge emotional bonds of trust so that employees with a bureaucratic social character want to follow them. The knowledge mode of production is different: The workers typically know more about their work than their managers. Here the challenge of leadership is to create collaboration among diverse specialists with interactive social characters whose strongest emotional ties are with their colleagues, not their bosses.

We are knowledge workers, and we'd bet that most of you who are reading this are, too—in fields like research, healthcare, education, engineering, law, software, finance, sales and marketing, consulting, government, publishing, the media, entertainment, architecture, and design. Or you may be a student, preparing to enter one of these fields.

Think of a leader you wanted to follow at work. Why did you want to follow that leader? Because the leader was passionate? Because the leader had strong beliefs? Because the leader had integrity? Yes, these are all good qualities in a leader. But, we probably can think of individuals in leadership roles who have had some or all of these qualities and, yet, we didn't want to follow them. Why not? Most likely, because we didn't believe they were taking us to a good place.

Yet, CEOs often cite passion, belief, and integrity when they make speeches about what it takes to be an effective leader.[1] They aren't lying, but they are avoiding the hard reality that a lot of their employees only follow them because they have to, not because they want to. Of course, people feel better following a person with integrity who seems convinced about a goal or strategy. Even if they don't want to follow a leader, they may be more *willing* to follow an upbeat and seemingly honest person. And they may feel energized, at least temporarily, by a boss's optimism and enthusiasm. No one wants to follow someone who is unsure, halfhearted, or an untrustworthy flip-flopper.

These qualities cited by CEOs belong to the bureaucratic-industrial age, in which the model of effective leadership is the good father, and leaders bind their followers by stimulating unconscious transferential ties. But for knowledge workers with an interactive social character who are skeptical of father figures, these ties do not bind. Knowledge workers want to collaborate with a leader who makes their lives more meaningful, and that calls for more than the stellar personal qualities cited by the CEOs.

The need for meaning sets us apart from other primates, and it's always made an impact on motivation. But what's meaningful to one person may be less, or not at all, meaningful to another person. And what's meaningful to both at one time might not be meaningful at another time. For example, people working at repetitive jobs in defense factories during World War II were highly motivated to do what they were told because they felt they were helping to win the war. The same job in peacetime might have felt just plain monotonous.

Many workers I interviewed in the 1970s didn't expect to find meaning in their work beyond getting a regular paycheck, being able to support a family, and being respected for their effort. In some companies at the time, like AT&T, however, employees felt pride and found meaning in being part of a great company that provided valuable services. Yet, even then frontline workers were not enthusiastic about their bosses. And while grudging followership might have been OK in low-level manufacturing and service jobs (although even that's debatable), it won't get great results from knowledge workers whose attitude toward a leader makes a huge difference. That's because they can decide how much of themselves they want to put into their work. Unlike workers performing formatted factory work, knowledge workers can decide whether to just follow or to actively collaborate. So what makes knowledge workers want to follow and collaborate with a leader?

Much of the time those of us in knowledge work don't need a leader; we work as independent professionals or collaborate with colleagues. But when we do join a project, we tend to assume some of the same attitudes I had when I collaborated with Erich Fromm on the village study. I was highly motivated because the project was meaningful, I was learning a lot, and Fromm listened to my ideas and sometimes accepted them. That's essentially the finding from Thomas H. Davenport's studies: "Knowledge workers don't want to work toward a goal because someone else has set it, but rather because they believe that it's right."[2]

In an article on Genentech for *Fortune*, Betsy Morris quoted knowledge workers who said they had joined the company not for the rich stock options, free cappuccino, parties, or other great benefits, but because they could do meaningful work. They were continually learning and on the cutting edge of finding cures for different types of cancer. They enthusiastically followed Art Levinson, their CEO, not just because he was passionate and had integrity and strong beliefs, although he had all those qualities, but because he championed science and focused on "significant unmet needs" in the fields of oncology, immunology, and tissue growth and repair.[3] Clearly, Genetech's workers were Levinson's collaborators, not just his followers.

Although we need a new theory for the age of knowledge work, this doesn't mean we can't learn from past thinking about leadership. There are useful nuggets of wisdom about leadership in the Old Testament and New Testament; ancient Chinese thinking, especially Lao Tzu and Confucius; the writings of Machiavelli and Shakespeare; and histories of great leaders like George Washington, Abraham

Lincoln, Franklin D. Roosevelt, Winston Churchill, Nelson Mandela, and exceptional military and business leaders. Some present-day advice for leaders is also useful: communicating well and often, listening to people and seeing things from their point of view, giving people proper recognition and recognizing their strengths, accepting responsibility for mistakes, and so on. Some of this advice, like walking the talk and self-control, fits as well in our time as it did when Confucius gave it 2,500 years ago. But much of what contemporary gurus have written can be misleading if it isn't understood in a historical context.

## FROM TAYLOR TO MAYO

A great deal of what has been published and taught under the banner of leadership studies during the 20th and 21st centuries turns out to be theories about how to motivate workers in an industrial bureaucracy. We'll see that these theories may fit bureaucracies and the bureaucratic personality at least in part, but not the emerging diverse types of organizations, roles, and followers in the knowledge workplace. What follows is a brief and highly selective review of theories set in their historical context.

Let's go back to the beginning of the 20th century, when Frederick Winslow Taylor propounded the theory of "scientific management" to make industrial bureaucracies into smoothly running machines. Observing workers shoveling iron ore at Bethlehem Steel, Taylor found that they used a variety of methods. Some workers had long shovels, some short ones. Some bent their knees, others bent their backs. Some lifted five pounds of ore at a time, others up to 15 pounds. By studying these different approaches and timing the tasks, Taylor discovered what he claimed was the one best way to shovel ore to increase productivity and minimize backaches. According to Taylorism, the industrial engineer should design jobs, and workers should follow instructions—no deviations from the script. By doing tasks Taylor's way, the one best way, both company and worker would benefit, particularly if the worker shared in productivity gains.

What motivated workers to do such monotonous work? Unless there was a war effort, the sole motivation lay in keeping a job and getting paid, having to, not necessarily wanting to, follow a leader who might be a dictatorial foreman who made sure the workers stayed on task.

Although many auto and steel workers at the beginning of the 20th century were immigrants from eastern and southern Europe who hardly spoke English, or farmers migrating north who were glad to get a steady wage, eager to please the boss, and satisfied to be told the one best way to work, their children in the 1920s were more educated, less malleable, and more responsive to union organizers. These workers learned how to fool the industrial engineers by slowing their pace when the job was timed and ostracizing "rate busters," those who worked too fast when the engineers were timing them.[4]

To go beyond Taylor and mold workers into better followers, a new theory of leadership was needed. Starting in 1924, a famous series of studies, led by Elton Mayo and Fritz Roethlisberger of the Harvard Business School, was carried out at the Western Electric Hawthorne factory in Chicago. A stated purpose of the studies was to counteract unions by helping managers gain worker loyalty and increase productivity— to make managers more effective leaders.[5] Two main findings on how to lead workers emerged from these studies. One was widely adopted, while the other was misinterpreted and generally ignored for some 30 years because it didn't fit the prevailing context.

The first finding was that workers were motivated not only by money, but also by a caring boss. Mayo, a psychologist and anthropologist, believed that first-line supervisors should get human relations training. The idea, which was subsequently taught in business schools and corporate training courses, was that workers would be motivated to do monotonous jobs if they had a boss who listened to their problems with empathy. In other words, you didn't have to change the Tayloristic theory of one best way. You just had to change the boss's attitudes toward workers. (The term "emotional intelligence" had yet to be coined.)

Managers widely accepted this idea. In 1978, when I asked Jim Olson, then vice chairman of AT&T, why he thought company surveys showed that workers were unhappy, he repeated Mayo's teachings: First-line supervisors didn't know how to listen and talk to their people. Olson ignored the fact that AT&T managers had been trying human relations techniques for some 30 years and this hadn't solved the problem.[6]

The idea that a supervisor should be a kind of psychotherapist was linked in the minds of AT&T managers with their belief in the "Hawthorne Effect," an oversimplified interpretation of the study's findings. They often cited this effect to explain a sudden rise in productivity. Their reasoning held that if you pay attention to workers and experiment with different working conditions, productivity will go up. It hardly matters what you do: You can change their routines or even something as simple as the lighting in the room, and workers will work harder. Managers at AT&T and many other companies have explained to me that the Hawthorne Effect means that any new workplace experiment will result in short-lived productivity gains that last only until the novelty wears off.

But both these conclusions were misleading. The workers who were studied at Hawthorne—five women who were assembling relays—told the researchers that, yes, the supervisor made a difference, but not because he was empathic, acting as a sort of psychotherapist. Richard Gillespie, who studied research notes that were left out of the book, found the following comment about the supervisor: "It was he who injected a spirit of play in the group by his comic antics, encouraging them to call everyone by his first name, to take strangers into their facetious conversations, to 'ride' supervisors and fellow operators alike."[7] This isn't psychotherapy, and it's a lot more than paying attention to the workers. It's adding a bit of play to otherwise boring tasks. It's making work fun.

There is also a factor, which neither Mayo nor Gillespie and Rothlisberger mention, that explains why both the therapeutic and playful managers succeeded in motivating the workers: an unconscious transference to a manager who's idealized, even loved, because he's experienced as a good parent.

However, there was another factor that differentiated the therapeutic manager from the playful leader: Productivity increased even more because workers were allowed to decide among themselves how best to do the job. Pay incentives were also a big motivator; productivity rose when workers were paid for the number of pieces they produced. But to admit the efficacy of participation and pay incentives would have undermined the prevailing Tayloristic belief that industrial engineers, rather than workers, could always determine the best way to do a job. And it would have ruined Mayo's theory that it was just the caring manager that made the difference.

It took more than 30 years for management training to begin to shake off the message that Taylorism plus a caring boss, a combination of hard and soft management, was the best formula for effective industrial-bureaucratic leadership.

## THEORY X AND THEORY Y

The human relations approach did not prevent unions from organizing between 600,000 and 700,000 of the 1 million employees of AT&T. How did that happen? Executives like Jim Olson believed that managers had simply failed to develop human relations skills. But workers told me they needed a union to protect them from the rigid rules set by the Tayloristic industrial engineers who didn't understand their resentment at being treated like parts of a machine. Telephone operators even needed a union to demand the right to take a bathroom break, and the first union victory at the Hawthorne plant was getting doors put on the men's room stalls.

Some managers began to question the combination of Taylor and Mayo. They latched onto new theories, especially Douglas McGregor's Theory Y, that was based in part on Abraham Maslow's hierarchy of human needs.[8] Like so much psychological theorizing, Theory Y is also poorly understood by many managers. But that's partly because McGregor failed to put his theory into historical context, leaving it incomplete and misleading.

In brief, Theory Y recognizes that Taylorism turns off workers, and that the addition of human relations techniques doesn't motivate them. This is because they're still being treated as though they'd be passive or resistant to change without management control and paternalistic direction; they're still powerless to make changes in their work, even when they see ways to improve it. McGregor sees Taylorism as fitting Theory X: that people need to be forced to work. Building on Maslow's hierarchy of needs, McGregor writes that Theory X misses the fact that when people satisfy their lower-level needs for sustenance, employment, and security, what emerges are higher-level ego needs for self-esteem, status, and recognition, and beyond that, for self-fulfillment through creative expression. According to McGregor, employees who feel relatively secure become disengaged because their work doesn't let them satisfy their higher needs.

Some managers mistakenly think that Theory Y is soft management, another type of human relations. Not at all. McGregor, a psychologist at MIT, was in touch with new management initiatives in technology companies and service industries. He recognized that if jobs requiring initiative or teamwork—what we now call knowledge work—are designed according to Tayloristic methods, workers will be frustrated and productivity will stagnate. For example, salespeople or telemarketing operators should be empowered (a term not used until the 1980s) to explain products and prices to customers and to deviate from their scripts in doing so, if necessary. Employees should be allowed to use their brains, and even to participate in determining how they do their job.

The importance of context was often ignored by managers. They didn't realize that Taylorism didn't fit changing business needs And Maslow, who lacked McGregor's knowledge of business, saw Theory Y only as a way of motivating employees who had higher-order needs, not of managing in a new way to meet the demands of these jobs. He believed that lower-level people would just take advantage of Theory Y, which he and others misread as soft management. Maslow wrote, "There are many places in the world [he gave Mexico as one example] where only authoritarian management, cracking the whip over fearful people, can work ... Frequently it turns out that the profoundly authoritative person has to be broken a little before he can assimilate kindness and generosity."[9] Having worked with Mexican villagers, I find Maslow's view just plain wrong. It isn't based on any research, or even personal experience. This aside, he misses an essential point of McGregor's theory—that knowledge and service jobs call for leadership that empowers workers, not necessarily leadership that treats them with kindness and generosity.

## THE MANAGER AS EDUCATOR

Maslow and McGregor missed the point that preparing workers for more complex tasks without identifying one best way of doing things was not a matter of boosting them up a needs hierarchy, but of teaching them to develop new skills and preparing them to take more responsibility. Gratifying needs for recognition and status is always a good idea. But more important, to motivate workers to want to follow them, managers had to become teachers and coaches.

I first saw an example of this in the early 1970s. On his own, a foreman in the Harman auto parts factory in Bolivar, Tennessee began to teach machine operators to share some of his management tasks, like job assignment, inspection, and simple maintenance. During his experiment, which raised productivity, a company vice president cited Maslow to explain why he was skeptical of this initiative. After questioning whether the workers would be responsible enough to take on these tasks, he warned the foreman that he would lose control by being too soft. He said, "Aren't you afraid to lose your authority, if everyone can do your job?" The foreman thought about it and said, "Since I started giving it away, I never had so much authority."[10] The workers wanted to follow him because he was teaching them new skills and he trusted them to take more responsibility, and not simply because he was caring.

By the late 1970s, a number of companies like AT&T, Volvo, Procter & Gamble, and the Cummins Engine Company were forging ahead of what was being taught in business schools, training managers to be coaches so that employees would gain new skills, not new needs. At the Volvo marine engine plant at Vara, Sweden, all the assemblers were coached to work in teams without a supervisor, sharing the management tasks among themselves.[11]

In the 1980s, total quality management (TQM)—sometimes called Six Sigma because the goal was an infinitesimal number of product defects six standard deviations from the original mean number of defects—finally left Taylorism in the dustbin of history. As preached by W. Edwards Deming, first in Japan and then in the United States when Deming was in his 80s, TQM made workers internal consumers in a production process, empowered to reject any defective product handed to them rather than adding value to it and passing it on. The role of management was not to give directions, but to design good processes, coach workers, and resolve system problems that caused defects.

But Deming's view of good leadership was more than that. In one of the many conversations I had with him when he was in his 90s, I asked what he considered most important in his work with the Japanese after World War II. He emphasized a context in which the Japanese needed inspirational leadership. "They had lost the war, their products were viewed as inferior, they were depressed," he said. "I made them feel they could be the best in the world." Japanese as well as American managers wanted to follow Deming because, with TQM, he infused new meaning into their work, giving them the conviction that they could surpass themselves and become world-class producers, achieving what they had not thought possible.

But despite his genius, Deming's thinking remained in the context of the Industrial Age. In our conversations, he brushed aside my attempts to point out that his concept of TQM didn't fit the knowledge workplace. To be sure, TQM is the ultimate method for making products that exactly suit the specs. That's essential if the parts have to fit together, as in a car. But what if there are no specs? What if the worker faced with a customer problem can't refer to a formatted process or solution?

A dramatic example of the limitation of TQM is the history of Florida Power & Light (FP&L), which in 1989 won the prestigious Japanese Deming Prize for its quality program. FP&L set up a business to teach TQM to other companies, but its service costs began rising alarmingly, and a few years later a new CEO stopped the whole TQM program. I found out why from an official of the International Brotherhood of Electrical Workers (IBEW) that represented the service technicians. The techs were handed instructions for the exact processes to follow in restoring service after an electrical outage. But in Florida, problems varied and called for different solutions. Based on their individual experiences, the techs had figured out how to deal with problems in urban areas like Miami and rural locations with thick vegetation, along beachfronts, and so on. They had notebooks filled with instructions for doing their work most efficiently and effectively. When told to go by the TQM book, they left their notebooks in their lockers, and the result was less efficient, more costly work.

In knowledge work, productivity doesn't depend only on good processes and getting workers to follow rules, although they may still be important. Even more important, however, is leadership that creates a common sense of purpose and a collaborative environment based on shared values and operating principles. Once leadership has created a collaborative culture, exactly how knowledge workers do their job can sometimes be left up to them.

In the 1990s, there was a rise in knowledge work and a change in worker attitudes. The greater the competence required from a knowledge worker, the more likely that a basic principle of both craft and industrial work no longer held—namely, that the boss knew the job better than the worker. Scott Adams's *Dilbert* cartoons make us laugh at the inept manager of engineers, but the cartoons don't answer the question of how to lead knowledge workers.

And this is not just a matter of leading professionals, as I learned from the union representative at FP&L and directly at an AT&T business service center where a young service technician named Penny controlled a multimillion-dollar corporate account. She was highly motivated by her relationship with the customer, who wanted to do business with her and her alone. Despite their attempts to connect with the customer, neither the account executive nor Penny's manager were invited to customer meetings. I asked Penny whether she had the skills to satisfy the customer's needs. She answered that she got other technicians to help. For example, she was good at solving voice problems, but she needed help from her friend Annie on data problems. So what was her boss's role? He should keep her informed about business strategy, products, and pricing. He needed to be a teacher. Then, Penny would want to collaborate, not because he was a human relations expert, but because he would be teaching her things she had to know to do the job. He would be adding value for her so she could add value for her customer. He would be treating her as a collaborator, not as a follower.

McGregor and Maslow wrote their theories at the very start of the revolution in organization and work resulting from advances in information and communication technology. As we write this, knowledge work has come to dominate the fields of healthcare, software, and telecommunication, and much of industrial work/design, engineering, marketing/sales, and financial services. While Penny was a special case at AT&T because she was empowered by the customer, ever more knowledge workers are empowered by their expertise. To be effective, organizations have to modify, even break down, traditional bureaucratic hierarchies into collaborative heterarchies where leadership shifts according to which person has the relevant knowledge.

While at the University of Toronto in 2004 Anabel Quan-Haase and Barry Wellman studied an information services company with two departments, programming and marketing. In the programming department, the programmers had more specialized knowledge than their managers. Quan-Haase and Wellman wrote that "the type of work done by these high-tech employees has reached such complexity that the boss often cannot give much input for dealing with a technical problem. Such circumstances preclude direct hierarchical-bureaucratic supervision. Management needs to trust and rely on their employees to provide them with the necessary information to make decisions because they are dependent on their expertise."[12] Similarly, in software companies like Google and Facebook it's not a matter of getting workers to cooperate. Individual workers have to collaborate to do their jobs.

In the marketing department that Quan-Haase and Wellman described, the individuals who work directly with customers were managed in a more traditional hierarchy because such a system proved more effective. To do their jobs, employees didn't need to collaborate so much with coworkers, but they did need coaching from their managers.

By viewing the personalities of leaders and followers through the lens of a needs hierarchy, leadership theorists missed what was happening in the workplace. This is not to say that Maslow and his followers were all wrong. It does make sense to think of lower versus higher, more developed needs. But as we'll try to show in Chapter 4, these needs should be viewed in the context of social character. The farmers working in a rural factory had a need to leave work early, not because they were on a low level of the needs hierarchy, but because they wanted more time for their independent farming. And the women working on the assembly line who preferred socializing to taking on more complex tasks didn't lack creative needs. They just satisfied them at home, by cooking, weaving, and caring for their families.

I've wondered why Maslow has appealed so strongly to both tough managers and soft liberals. The answer I've come to is that his theory seems to justify the prejudices of both groups. First of all, part of the theory has a simple and seemingly practical face value. Of course, hungry people think of little else other than food. Proponents of economic development can use Maslow to make the compelling argument that starving people won't be productive; if you don't satisfy their basic needs, there will be no economic development.

Furthermore, Maslow's view of human nature—that all people have the potential to be creative if their basic needs are met—has its roots in the humanistic philosophical tradition going back to Aristotle's Nicomachean Ethics. His view gives hope that the most downtrodden people can someday build a productive society.

As for the hard-nosed managers using Maslow's theory, they argue that lower-level workers need to be controlled. Because these workers are interested only in making money, there's no point in fussing with more difficult participative management. I heard this argument from a manager in New Delhi in the mid-1980s. He said he'd just become CEO and had tried to engage the workers in Theory Y–type management, but they'd resisted and he believed Maslow's theory explained why. He invited me to a meeting with worker representatives so that I could see for myself.

At the meeting, I asked the CEO to describe his idea of employee participation. He did, and I then asked the union leader for his response. "We are not interested," he said. I asked him why not. "Because we want more money," he answered. "You see," said the CEO, "they are low on the needs hierarchy, so they don't need to participate."

I had a hunch and asked the worker, "Have you always felt like this?" "No," he said. "Before this CEO arrived, we did have a scheme to participate, but we were promised a share in the productivity gains. We improved productivity, but we didn't get the money we were promised, so why should we trust management now?" The CEO might have found this out if he hadn't coded information according to the needs hierarchy.

Has Maslow's theory ever been tested? Edward E. Lawler III, a leading expert on motivation at the Marshall School of Business at the University of Southern California, reports there is "very little evidence to support the view that a hierarchy exists above the security level."[13] That means that once people have enough to eat, you can't predict what will be most meaningful to them by referring to the hierarchy of needs. Even without enough to eat, many people have found meaning and purpose as powerful motivators to survive horrible conditions, as did Viktor Frankl, an Austrian psychologist in a Nazi concentration camp.[14]

I've interviewed hundreds of workers at all levels of companies and administered surveys asking about values to thousands more. Rather than fitting into a single hierarchy, all the needs or values cited by Maslow are shared by all people, along with other needs that he doesn't include, such as the need for play, dignity or respect, and meaning.[15] Each need or instinctual tendency has its own developmental hierarchy. For example, Jean Piaget, the great Swiss psychologist, described how the need to play develops from infancy to adolescence.[16] Piaget and Lawrence Kohlberg, a Harvard psychologist, described a hierarchy that's missing from both Maslow and McGregor, namely, levels of moral reasoning.

Piaget described how children grow out of egocentrism and authoritarian reasoning only when they start to cooperate with other children and learn to see things from another's point of view. Kohlberg's lowest level is unquestioned obedience to authority. At the next level, people conform to a limited view of what is good for their family or organization. At higher levels, they decide what will benefit others beyond the immediate group.[17]

As knowledge-work organizations become more complex, they require communication among workers and trust that people are acting according to higher-level moral values. This is not just a question of the worker's personality. Leadership makes the difference in the moral level of an organization, whether people are ruled by fear and expected to obey without question or whether they are trusted to do what is best for the organization and its stakeholders, even if this means criticizing the boss. The recent history of corporate corruption has eroded trust in corporate leaders. But creating moral organizations is not only a matter of having leaders who stay out of jail. Autocratic leaders reinforce egocentrism that blocks open communication and keeps people from caring about the common good. Everyone tries to please the boss they fear. The boss's actions are not questioned. And other workers become rivals, not collaborative colleagues.

Although the theories of Maslow and McGregor had the value of getting leaders to think beyond Taylorism, they were too flawed to provide a guide for the age of knowledge work. They failed to understand context, both the changing nature of work and the changing social character.

## LEARNING FROM MACHIAVELLI ABOUT PRINCES AND CEOS

So far, we've focused on organizational leadership below the very top. In thinking about why people follow a CEO, theorists often refer to Machiavelli to justify harsh management. But even though Machiavelli has much to teach us, his lessons are poorly understood because they aren't seen in context.

What can we learn from Machiavelli? If we're not put off by his cynicism, his praise of immoral leaders who succeeded by cruelty, lies, and betrayals; or his amoral advice, we can find bits of wisdom. Adolf Hitler, Joseph Stalin, and Saddam Hussein, among other despots, used *The Prince* as a guidebook. But Machiavelli is more than a guru for monsters. In a course taught by Leo Strauss, a Machiavelli scholar, at the University of Chicago, I learned that Machiavelli describes not only how a leader gets results in different contexts, but also what kind of a leadership personality succeeds with different types of followers.

*The Prince* was written in a time of continual war.[18] As he reviews the history of his time, Machiavelli concludes that princes need to learn not only the art of war, but also how to get people to follow. Most of these followers, he explains, are frightened and disorganized. Therefore, Machiavelli advises princes to be ruthless, to make themselves feared rather than loved, because they can control fear. He cautions that unless you're a prince who is totally in charge and already feared, gaining love by being benevolent is always an uncertain venture. That's because your followers will be loyal only as long as they have to follow you out of fear or want to follow you out of greed. Machiavelli writes: "A prudent lord, therefore, cannot observe faith, nor should he . . . And if all men were good, this teaching would not be good, but because they are wicked and do not observe faith with you, you also do not have to observe it with them."[19]

We should view all this is in the context of 16th-century Italy, a time when war and betrayal were the norm. But when Machiavelli looks back at ancient Rome, he tells a story about two generals who led a different breed of followers. One, Valerius Corvinus, was kind and considerate. He treated his men who, like him, were Roman citizens, as equals. The other, Manlius Torquatus, was harsh and a stickler for the rules—so much so that he had his son publicly beheaded for corruption. Who was more effective? Both were, says Machiavelli, because they were true to their natures, consistent, and virtuous, so the troops knew what to expect from them. The troops could trust them.[20]

Notably, Machiavelli appears interested only in the effectiveness of the generals—their results. Their troops were willing to follow, in contrast to other generals' troops, who deserted or rebelled. Did the troops want to follow these generals? Machiavelli doesn't tell us. Maybe he assumes that the troops would naturally want to follow successful generals for the booty and glory they'd share. What he doesn't consider is that these troops, especially those following Valerius Corvinus, might have projected strong father transferences onto their generals. Machiavelli concludes, "It does not matter much in what way a general behaves, provided his efficiency be so great that it favors the way he behaves, whether it be this way or that."[21] Every personality has defects and dangers, he notes, but they can be corrected by outstanding virtue, at least enough so that they don't hinder the leader's effectiveness.

And yet, Machiavelli notes that depending on the challenges of the times, a leader's personality does make a difference. He writes in *The Prince* that when there is a great deal of turmoil and uncertainty, an impetuous person is more likely to succeed, while in times of relative peace, a cautious, patient person will have the advantage.[22]

Can't people change their behavior to fit the moment? That would be the view of some modern proponents of situational management. Machiavelli doesn't think so, because he observes that people can't and don't deviate from their natures. Of course, we can learn new techniques, but how we apply them is always flavored by our personality; and when it comes to the almost instinctual way we approach big decisions, our nature (personality) largely determines how we'll act.

Machiavelli's observations illustrate the difference between situational management and contextual leadership as described in this book. Some management writers contend that personality doesn't matter, that leaders can tailor style to fit any situation. Obviously, this is true to some degree. Almost all leaders can be commanding or consultative. Any leader can learn when to be close to and when to increase distance from the troops. But as Heraclitus wrote 2,500 years ago, character is man's fate. There are limits to behavioral plasticity, and when a leader is stressed, personality prevails. A CEO put it neatly when I asked his view of situational leadership: "Most of my interactions are taking place in chaos. I can't stop and think about what my style should be with different people. My style is my personality." Given this, certain leadership personalities are better suited to certain contexts; however, leaders who use their personality as an excuse for unproductive actions will fail to develop. Those who learn to recognize changes in contexts and situations can also learn to act differently and more effectively without compromising their values.

Does this mean that organizations must change leaders every time the context changes? Sometimes, like when an entrepreneurial startup like Yahoo! under Jerry Yang becomes a large company a different kind of leader is needed. Leaders do need to regularly assess themselves against current threats and opportunities. When new skills are called for, leaders need to be open to developing themselves or partnering with others who can complement their skills. Otherwise, the organization may need to change leaders.

## APPLYING MACHIAVELLI

Leaders still look to Machiavelli for lessons on leadership, but they often take away misleading advice because they read him in only one context, the chaotic state of wars and revolutions in 16th-century Italy.[23] Regrettably, Machiavelli's advice to the prince, to appear humane and compassionate while grabbing power through lies and betrayals, can still get results, especially when disorganized and frightened people want security and protection, even at the price of their liberty. There are all too many Machiavellian leaders in organizations, sociopaths able to charm their way into power.[24]

But even more benign bosses provoke fear. When I give workshops on leadership to midlevel managers and executives from large companies and government agencies, sometimes I ask them to estimate *how much fear* of the boss exists in their organizations, using a scale of 1 (little or no fear) to 4 (high level of fear). Generally, the mean estimate is 2.5 to 3.0. When I ask what they think the level should be, the result is almost invariably about 2. What comes out in our discussions is that most managers don't trust people to want to follow. They think that without some fear of the boss, the people in their organizations would not always follow. But beyond this, people will always, to some degree, fear a boss who evaluates them and has the power to reward, punish, and fire them. The only subordinates who feel no fear at all are those who don't need the job and those who are sure they are needed.

If we apply Machiavelli's methodology of analyzing leadership effectiveness to our time, I don't see that we've advanced very much from his thinking. Take the most popular business leadership book of recent years, Jim Collins's *Good to Great*. Like Machiavelli, Collins describes the personality of effective business leaders and gives advice to modern-day commercial princes. Collins's great leaders are described as "disciplined, rigorous, dogged, determined, diligent, precise, fastidious, systematic, methodical, workmanlike, demanding, consistent, focused, accountable, and responsible."[25] They are also described as "humble" and "self-effacing."[26]

To a large extent, these leaders are like Machiavelli's cautious and patient type, as opposed to the impetuous risk takers. But unlike Machiavelli, Collins does not take the intellectual step of describing the context of his findings. Almost all of Collins's CEOs ran retail or commodity businesses, where they succeeded in reviving a mature company by streamlining processes, cutting costs, and getting rid of people who didn't add value. None of these businesses have produced innovative products, unless you include marketing innovations like Gillette's Mach3 razor blades. Collins misses the point that Machiavelli astutely observed: In times of rapid change, as in our time, risk-taking and self-promoting rather than self-effacing CEOs—larger-than-life figures like Bill Gates, Larry Ellison, Jeff Bezos, Elon Musk, Mark Zuckerberg, Larry Page, and Sergey Brin—are the ones who exploit new technologies and, with their products, change the way we work and live.

Instead of seeing different personality types in context, as did Machiavelli, Collins's hierarchy of leadership qualities expresses a bureaucratic mindset that inhibits contextual thinking about leadership. At the bottom of his hierarchy is the capable employee. Then comes the competent manager, followed by the charismatic but egoistic visionary. At the top of the hierarchy sits the self-effacing great executive who puts the good of the organization above his own needs. (There are no women in *Good to Great* because only male CEOs happened to fit the researchers' criteria of exceptional financial results.)

The two types at the top of Collins's hierarchy fit two personality types I've written about, the exacting obsessive and the visionary productive narcissist.[27] These two types correlate to the analytic-autonomizing (Green) and assertive-directing (Red) types from the Strength Deployment Inventory (SDI) described in Chapter 6. They provide a classic contrast that I've found pops up in many different cultural contexts. Narcissists like Napoleon and Hitler in politics and Henry Ford and John D. Rockefeller in business boldly grab hold of power in tumultuous times but often overreach themselves, while the obsessives carefully build sustainable institutions in more stable times. *Good to Great* was published right when the narcissistically led dot-com bubble burst and grandiose CEOs like Jean-Marie Messier of Vivendi and Bernie Ebbers of WorldCom crashed. Naturally, the disciplined self-effacing obsessives, with their steady results, seemed not only safe but also appealing. The *Good to Great* companies did not continue to outperform the market, however. Some, such as Circuit City and Fannie Mae, performed terribly.

History aside, what Collins misses is that at the top of organizations today, it's become essential to select managers whose personality fits the role they play, who want to do what they need to do for success; and the right candidate doesn't always fit Collins's model of greatness. In his book *Winning,* Jack Welch, a great business leader who was not at all humble and self-effacing, showed his acute awareness of personality types when he described how he picked people for leadership jobs. For a commodity product business he chose a leader who was "in his element with people who sweated the nitty gritty details talking about ways to squeeze efficiencies out of every process. He was a master of discipline." This is the obsessive type that Collins spotlights. In contrast, the head of an innovative risky business required a visionary, a person who "hated the nuts and bolts of management... But he sure did have the guts and vision to place the big bets."²⁸ He probably also had a big ego that gave him the confidence to take these risks.

Like Welch, the best professional football coaches have learned which personalities best fit which roles. For example, the best offensive linemen typically are conservatives who uphold authority and protect the quarterback, while the best defensive linebackers are rebels who take pleasure in smashing the quarterback—they challenge rules and regulations and are harder for coaches to control.²⁹ Because personality can make the crucial difference among players with similar skills, these coaches need enough Personality Intelligence to understand followers and collaborators.

Some coaches and managers, however, have become aware of the fact that the attitudes of followers have changed, and that the kind of leadership that was effective in the past no longer gets results. This is not only because the challenges at work have changed, but also because the social character of followers is not the same as it was a generation ago.

In the early 1970s, when I studied leaders and followers in high-tech companies like IBM, Hewlett-Packard, Intel, and Texas Instruments, most of the craftsmanlike engineers had an obsessive bureaucratic social character. Within the hierarchy, they valued their autonomy. They liked to work at their own pace, and it was hard to get them to communicate and to cooperate among themselves, as well as to inform management about the status of their work. Some were entrepreneurial, but this usually meant that they'd try to sell an idea without any evidence that people would buy the product. This mindset at AT&T Bell Labs led engineers to try (unsuccessfully) to sell picture-phones while rejecting cellular telephones.

In my book *The Gamesman*, I described a manager in his early 30s at one of these companies, who seemed to be a prototype for the kind of antibureaucratic leader needed for companies to innovate and succeed in a time of increasing competition.³⁰ In retrospect, this manager seems like a warmer, less self-promoting version of Jack Welch. He eventually reached the top of his company, but rejected the CEO job.

I'd given him the pseudonym Jack Wakefield, but the business press subsequently discovered he was Dick Hackborn of HP.³¹ Hackborn saw early on that to get results, he had to light a fire under the obsessive engineers, threaten that their slow pace would doom their product, but excite them with the promise of glittering success. He was also a teacher and coach, educating the engineers about the business, the competition, and corporate strategy, loosening them up in a playful way to create teamwork and collaboration.

Hackborn, like Welch, saw himself not as growing people up a hierarchy of needs but as developing them to fit the company's needs. Both Welch and Hackborn spent much of their time with their people, answering their questions, responding to their arguments—all while projecting a vision of success.

Although both Welch and, less so, Hackborn provoked some fear in their followers—because it was clear they wouldn't tolerate anyone who didn't get with the program and perform—for the most part, people were persuaded to follow Hackborn and collaborate with each other. Once they wanted to follow, they could be trusted with considerable authority to make decisions on their own.

Hackborn had the foresight to realize a generation ago that the new knowledge workers, a term he found by reading Peter Drucker, would no longer accept paternalistic control, and that a leader had to create loyalty not to himself, but to a winning team and a shared purpose.

Leaders can still learn from the way Hackborn and Welch engaged their followers. In the 40 years since I wrote about Hackborn, however, the social character of followers has been changing. There are fewer obsessive, uncooperative, bureaucratic types. The emerging interactive social character is naturally more collaborative, but as Hackborn predicted, less responsive to paternalistic control, and with stronger sibling ties (as we'll describe in the next chapter). At one high-tech company, the MITRE Corporation, members of project teams are free to work whatever hours they want at home or at the workplace. The CEO told me he doesn't worry about performance, because team members won't stand for anyone who isn't getting results.[32] The manager needs to be a leader who communicates purpose as the collaborators manage themselves.

The best professional football coaches have reflected on the shift in players' attitudes. The tough-talking paternalistic coaches of the past like Vince Lombardi, who'd berate and shame his players when they lost, would alienate many of today's players. Coaches like Joe Gibbs, formerly of the Washington Redskins; Bill Belichick of the New England Patriots; Andy Reid, who used to coach the Philadelphia Eagles and now coaches the Kansas City Chiefs; and Lovie Smith, formerly of the Chicago Bears and Tampa Bay Buccaneers and currently head football coach at the University of Illinois model an attitude of collaboration and shared responsibility in the manner of older brothers rather than fathers. If there are mistakes, they work together with players to understand and remedy them.

After a Redskins loss in the fall of 2005, the quarterback, Mark Brunell, said of Gibbs, "He's always positive. He expects us to work. He's not asking us to do anything he's not committed to doing himself. The best thing about Coach Gibbs is that we're all in this together. And that's the way it should be."[33] To avoid making his criticisms of players seem personal, Lovie Smith uses processes like objective grading systems for game behavior, with consequences for loafing or missing tackles.[34] The players consider this system to be fair, In contrast, Tiki Barber, a Pro Bowl running back and the New York Giants' all-time leading rusher, blamed his team's postseason losses on his coach's autocratic style. "I think he has to start listening to the players a little bit and come our way—their way—a little bit."[35]

After some losing seasons, Sasho Cirovski, coach of the University of Maryland soccer team, hit on a way to identify winning leadership for Interactives. Using a survey with such questions as "Who do you rely upon when your team needs unity and motivation?" he identified the team's natural leader and made him captain. In other words, he dropped any attempt to use father transference to inspire his team and, instead, engineered unity with a trusted sibling figure, who incidentally wasn't even one of the best players. But with an interactive leader, Maryland went on to a national championship in 2006.[36]

Some readers of this book will immediately identify with the interactive social character while others will find it harder to do so. This is because we are in a period of transition in which bureaucratic and interactive social characters coexist. In the next two chapters, we'll compare them, with a focus on the kind of leader each wants to follow and the personal dynamics that explain why leader-follower relationships are not always as they seem.

CHAPTER 3

# Why We Follow

*The Power of Transference*

I GOT INTO A CONVERSATION with George Raymond (not his real name) on a flight to London on my way to teach a workshop at Oxford University on coaching leaders. At the time, George was a 34-year-old leader of a technical team in a large media company. He told me his boss was a bureaucrat who didn't listen to good ideas, even when they'd save money. The boss wanted to be admired and told that his ideas were great, but George just saw the boss as an obstacle, even as an evil.

George described his own team as a collaborative community where information flowed easily, where he led within the group, not above it. Both George's parents, he told me, were professionals, and his closest ties were with his friends and brothers. He loved playing video games, particularly MMORPGs (massively multiplayer online role-playing games) in which he created international teams and made quick decisions on his own. At work, however, George's boss would tell him he'd better play by the company rules, or else. George said he was ready to quit if he could find a job with a company that respects what he can do.

A few months after our conversation, George e-mailed to tell me he'd joined another company where he's a lot freer, and he gets along well with a boss who is more of a colleague. There will be many more people like George who follow a bureaucratic boss only as long as they have to.

Let's be clear about the importance of leadership in a world of individualistic knowledge workers. Leaders are needed not only to drive results, but also to adapt and change organizations and to build bridges and networks to connect people who are diverse in skills, outlook, and identity. In any business, good leadership may be the most essential competitive advantage a company can have. Furthermore, without exceptional leadership, we won't solve our national problems: new sources of clean energy, quality education, and quality healthcare for everyone. It's not surprising, then, that management scholars focus relentlessly on the attributes of successful leaders.

But in the effort to grasp and master the skills of great leaders, we tend to lose sight of the fact that there are multiple parts to the leadership equation. For leaders to lead, they need not only exceptional talent, but also the ability to attract followers who get short shrift in the management literature, where they are described largely in terms of the leaders' qualities. In other words, they're seen as merely responding to the leaders' charisma, passion, integrity, or caring attitude. What most analysts seem to ignore is that followers have their own motives and identity, and that they can be as powerfully driven to follow as leaders are to lead.

==Followers' motivations fall into two categories: conscious and unconscious.== The conscious ones are well known. They have to do with hopes of gaining money, status, power, new skills, or entry into a meaningful enterprise by following a great leader—and fears of missing out if they don't. What can be even more powerful are the unconscious, sometimes irrational motivations that lie outside awareness and, therefore, beyond a person's ability to control them. In part, these motivations are rooted in emotional attitudes formed early in life, but they largely arise from the strong unconscious images and emotions that we tend to project onto our relationships with people who have power over us.

## THE POWER OF TRANSFERENCE

At the end of the 20th century, historic changes in family life and the workplace formed an interactive social character that began to shove aside the bureaucratic personality. Nonetheless, the bureaucratic experience has deeply engraved a powerful model of leadership in our thinking, buttressed by the various schools of psychology. Even Freudian psychoanalysis, with its emphasis on the father transference, reflects the typical attitude of the bureaucratic personality in organizations—the idealizing of paternalistic bosses. In this context, sibling transferences are viewed as rivalrous, like the Biblical stories of Cain and Abel competing for God's favor, or Jacob outmaneuvering his brother Esau to gain Isaac's blessing. For the interactive personality, in contrast, sibling transferences can strengthen a band of brothers and sisters allied against an irrational boss. It's time, therefore, that we focus on the psychology of followership that fits the new context.[1]

Sigmund Freud, the founder of psychoanalysis, was the first person to provide some explanation of how a follower's unconscious motivations work. He explained how different characteristics like super-neatness, obstinacy, and stinginess fit together in what he called the anal character.[2] This insight into character formation is the foundation of psychoanalytic understanding of personality. Freud also discovered a process that explains a lot about why people want to follow leaders.

After practicing psychoanalysis for a number of years, Freud was puzzled to find that his patients—who were, in a sense, his followers—kept falling in love with him. Although most of his patients were women, the same thing happened with his male patients. It is a great tribute to Freud that he realized that his patients' idealization of him couldn't be traced to his own personal qualities. Instead, he concluded, people were relating to him as if he were some important person from their past—usually a parent. In undergoing therapy—or in falling in love, for that matter—people were transferring experiences and emotions from past relationships onto the present. Freud thought the phenomenon was universal. He wrote, "There is no love that does not reproduce infantile stereotypes"— which, for him, explained why so many of us choose spouses like our parents.[3]

Freud called this *transference*, and it was one of his most important discoveries. Indeed, for Freud, patients were ready to end therapy when they understood and mastered their transference and no longer idealized the therapist. And even today, identifying and dissolving transferences are the principal goals of psychoanalysis.

As important as the concept of transference is, it remains little understood outside clinical psychoanalysis. This is unfortunate, because transference is not just a missing link in theories of leadership. It also explains a lot about the everyday behavior of organizations.

Typically, transference is the emotional glue that binds people to a leader and makes them want to follow, even when they are unclear about where the leader is taking them. Employees in the grip of positive transference see their leaders as better than they really are—smarter, nicer, more charismatic. They tend to give their leaders the benefit of the doubt and take on more risk at their request than they otherwise would. And as long as the leaders' actual capabilities and characteristics are not too different from their followers' idealization of them—and the leaders don't start to believe in the glorified image that their followers' have of them—this can work very well.

The transference dynamic is most likely to get out of control during periods of organizational stress. In such situations, followers tend to be dominated by irrational feelings—in particular, the need for praise and protection given by all-powerful parental figures. At the same time, leaders are preoccupied with handling the crisis at hand and, as a consequence, are probably less alert to the likelihood that their followers are just acting out childhood fears. This is what happened to a vice president of AT&T I was coaching in the mid-1980s, during the breakup of the Bell System. While he was focusing on strategy, his followers felt frustrated that he was not dealing with their anxiety and reassuring them. Even though he was charting a promising new course for his division, employees complained that he wasn't leading them.

Another example of how transference is triggered by doubt and stress is the way people feel better just by going to see a doctor, even before the doctor has done anything for them. In large measure, this phenomenon can be explained by patients' trust, which transfers the childhood experience of being cared for by parents when sick. This type of transference makes it extremely hard for scientists to evaluate certain medications, such as mood-altering drugs. Clinical studies show, for example, that up to 30 percent of people respond as well to placebos—again, trust—as they do to antidepressants. People who volunteer for a study in the hope of finding a cure for their ailment may be especially receptive to the placebo effect.

Transference comes in many guises and is blind to both age and gender. Therefore, leaders must be careful to avoid stereotyping. A male leader, for example, should never assume that he is a father figure or a brother figure to a follower, just as a female leader shouldn't assume she's being seen as a mother or a sister. Psychoanalysis has shown that someone can have a paternal transference with a woman in authority and a maternal transference with a man.

Clearly, positive transferences are closely linked to productivity. Suppose an employee believes that her boss will care about her in a parental way. To ensure that this happens, she will make superhuman efforts to please her leader. As long as she perceives that these transferred expectations are being met, she will continue to work hard. Will this benefit the organization as a whole? Yes—she'll want to follow the leader, and this will be fine as long as doing so is just a matter of following directions. But she's also less likely to think for herself, and this may limit her potential for the kind of creativity needed in a knowledge company.

Transferences can be negative as well as positive. Commenting on my article on transference in the *Harvard Business Review*, Stephen Schneider wrote to me about his experience consulting to a company with a highly effective COO "unusually committed to her work" and to her boss, the CEO. When, following an acquisition, the CEO became less available for her, the COO, who had been so eager to please, suddenly became distant and aggressive. Schneider found that on a rational level, the COO was clear about her role and content with her status. Unconsciously, however, she was angry that the relationship with the CEO was no longer the same. The COO had idealized her boss when he had time to nurture her, for he represented all she had never experienced from a distant father. When he turned away to work in the acquisition, the boss became the "bad father" of her childhood, and all her resentment from the past was projected onto him.[4]

Another big risk in transference comes from the fact that it's a two-way street. Just as followers project their past experiences onto their leaders, leaders respond by projecting their past experiences back onto the followers. Freud called this phenomenon *countertransference* and saw it as one of the most serious obstacles to resolving patients' psychological issues. The danger was that a psychoanalyst would respond to a patient's transferential protestations of love by accepting that love as real. As a result, the analyst might assume the role of a protective parent, furthering the patient's dependency. Or, the analysis might end in a love affair rather than a cure. Countertransference is at least as big a problem for business leaders as for it is psychotherapists.

In his novel *Disclosure*, Michael Crichton describes how a ruthless and dishonest woman was promoted above a more qualified man because she reminded the CEO of a favorite daughter who'd been killed in an auto accident. The CEO did not see the employee as she was, but responded to her as though she were his beloved daughter. In the real world, a boss often will favor a subordinate who shows filial admiration.

Although strong transferences to a parental figure can hold an organization together, once the leader leaves, rivalries can fracture an organization. That's what happened with Freud's group and with various psychoanalytic organizations founded by charismatic leaders. As long as the competitive, ambitious analysts had to please the parental leader, they cooperated with each other and sheathed the knives of sharp criticism. Once the parental founder died or left the scene, different training analysts, with their own transferential follower-students, let go of their aggressive inhibitions; the result was the splintering into different schools.[5] Of course, the same thing can happen in family firms after the founding parent leaves the scene, but this relationship of children to a parent isn't transference. It's the real thing.

## CHANGING TRANSFERENCES

The images we project from childhood are shaped by the family cultures we grew up with. It is particularly important to recognize, therefore, that today more people have family experiences that differ—sometimes quite radically—from what was long considered the norm. For an increasing number of people, the significant person from the past is not a parent, but a sibling or a close childhood friend.

As we'll discuss later, the shift from parental to sibling transferences can fit organizational needs for boundary-crossing project teams and networks. At a meeting I attended in 2004, a consultant to Boeing reported that when managers there sought a leader for a software team that required a lot of collaboration among members, they joked about finding someone who was the fifth child in a family of nine siblings, someone who was used to mediating among brothers and sisters. In other words, the job called for a different kind of leadership than the traditional hierarchical boss would provide. Sibling leaders are used to facilitating problem-solving and building consensus. They invite collaboration and criticism more than parental leaders do. As we noted in Chapter 2, they are part of the team, not above it.

Another factor complicating relationships at work is that people can have multiple transferential relationships in an organization. It seems very likely to me that at GE, many employees not only had such relationships with their immediate bosses, but also transferred childhood feelings onto Jack Welch when he was CEO, even though they had never met him. In cases of multiple transferences, both the immediate boss and the CEO might unconsciously be seen as father figures. When this happens, however, the employee usually experiences the transferences differently. Typically the employee will relate to the immediate boss from the perspective of a child who is 5 or even older, but view the CEO from the perspective of an infant or toddler as an earlier father figure, someone who is more protective and all-knowing.

What is making it harder for would-be leaders is that transferences no longer necessarily work in their favor. In other words, people no longer want to follow leaders because of a positive transference. That's because the changing structure of families—more single-parent homes, dual working parents, and kids growing up with less respect for authority—combined with changes in companies has begun to shape work environments in which people value traditional leadership less. The paternalistic model of leadership that flourished in the large monopolistic firms I worked with from the 1970s to the turn of the century has been frayed beyond recognition. Employees can no longer count on lifetime employment; even promised pensions may be lost as great companies flounder and others downsize or restructure. Furthermore, like my fellow traveler George Raymond mentioned earlier, knowledge workers often know more about their jobs than does the boss.

In light of these developments, the role of the leader has to change from all-knowing parental figure who is followed because of unconscious transference to someone who clearly adds value for followers. Otherwise, the transference can be negative—the boss experienced as an interfering, witless, or inept parent. When I was lecturing about the first edition of this book at Google headquarters in 2007, interactive employees expressed this kind of criticism of managers that they claimed did not add value for them.

On the one hand, a positive transference can be a facilitator of followership and, therefore, a source of strength for leaders. On the other hand, it can be a real threat to leaders because it distorts objectivity. This is why, as we'll see, the kind of leaders we need will try to understand transference and will work hard to help executive team members see one another as they really are. The future of an organization may depend in significant measure on this ability. It's worth taking a moment, therefore, to examine the most common types of transference. In doing so, we'll more clearly understand the changing social character and how people with the emerging social character can be led. In Chapter 6, we'll show how a personality assessment, such as the Strength Deployment Inventory, can make it easier for people to see each other at a core, motivational level and to give them a common language for describing what they see.

## THE MOTHER TRANSFERENCE

There are still many people in the workplace who were raised in traditional families, have a bureaucratic social character, and make traditional transferences to parent-like bosses. Increasingly, however, they are most likely encountering a more diverse spectrum of bosses who are vastly different from their parents and come in all genders, races, and nationalities. And that can lead to transferential misunderstanding and false assumptions.

For example, Lydia Thomas, former CEO of Mitretek (now Noblis) in Virginia told me that employees often expected her to be maternal,. How did she respond? She told them: "I'm not your mother, but maybe, just maybe, I can be your friend."[6] Maternal transference differs from paternal transference in that it usually draws on an earlier childhood relationship. Unlike the father, who is often perceived as distant and detached, and whose approval is dependent on performance, the mother is often seen as both an authority figure and a giver of unconditional love. She is the protective parent who gives us life and showers us with support, but she is also the first person who says no. It's the mother who weans us and, for the most part, who toilet trains us. Later it is she who separates herself from us to go back to work or to attend to other children. Not surprisingly, she is represented by both the fairy godmother and the evil stepmother in children's stories. She is both deity and witch, and this deep divide in our psyches can play itself out to dramatic effect in business situations. One has only to look at the public's extreme reactions of love and hate toward Margaret Thatcher, Hillary Clinton, or Angela Merkel to realize that women leaders stir up some of the most conflicted feelings in our unconscious.

Followers may have a hard time dealing with strong women precisely because they stimulate in subordinates the feelings of awe and fear that the mother once did. Children depend on the help and support of the all-powerful mother. They also want her to be happy and proud of them, and they feel deep guilt if they cause her suffering—a dynamic that some mothers use to control their kids. In my clinical work, I have found that sometimes an unconscious fear that the mother will cut off her life-giving nurturance lies beneath the guilt.

A negative aspect of maternal transferences in the workplace is that they can generate greater expectations of empathy and tenderness from bosses than can realistically be met. Similarly, these maternal expectations can contribute to perceptions that a strong female leader is overly demanding, controlling, or bitchy. Followers whose frames of reference were formed in households with a strong man and compliant woman may unconsciously assume that a strong female has usurped the man's power and could damage the family.

A colleague of mine saw an example of a maternal transference to a male leader when he coached the 40-year-old vice president of a home-building company, who'd been told in no uncertain terms by the male president that he had handed in a bad proposal. The VP complained that the president should have shown more emotional intelligence in rejecting the proposal. When the president dismissed this complaint as "psychobabble," the VP grew irate. As my colleague immediately realized, the VP was projecting an inappropriate maternal transference onto his boss (maternal transferences can be made onto male or female authority figures). When the company president didn't respond as the VP wanted, the VP reacted like a rejected child.

Positive maternal transferences, however, can give people a powerful sense of support. Think of Ronald Reagan, whose wife, Nancy, was like a protective tigress during and after his presidency. He even called her "Mommy" at times. Whereas his father had been a failed shoe salesman, Reagan's strong mother nurtured the self-confidence that contributed to his success. And yet, even positive maternal transferences can have bad effects. A close friend of mine taught for 18 years in a private school where most teachers had a maternal transference with the headmistress, who created a family-like culture. The teachers loved their boss and felt cared for and protected by her, but the warm feelings they had were not a good measure of her ability to perform. As she neared retirement, the school was losing money, and it became clear that the headmistress had done little to evaluate and develop the teachers or to help them deal with discipline problems. Although her successor was less comforting and more demanding, he succeeded in raising money from wealthy parents, improved teachers' salaries, and established rules that were followed.

## THE FATHER TRANSFERENCE

The father transference was a powerful glue in an age when male managers who had been brought up in traditional father-led families looked up to male bosses in bureaucratic hierarchies. This dynamic was nicely illustrated for me by a top executive who told me his dream of walking into the powerful CEO's office and looking down in horror to see that he was wearing short pants. When I asked what he thought the dream meant, he said, "That's the way I felt when my father was about to scold me for something I did wrong."

Most male CEOs in traditional organizations have consciously or unconsciously encouraged paternal transferences. They tend to show themselves in paternalistic settings—presiding over large meetings or smiling on a video feed where the message is invariably reassuring, upbeat, hopeful. Even when times are bad, these leaders assure their followers that the downturn is temporary. The message is always the same: "Trust me to steer you through these troubled waters." CEOs who claim that their success is based on their integrity or their concern for their people, rather than on good business thinking, indicate that consciously or unconsciously they are counting on the power of transference.

Some company leaders go to great lengths to promote practices that strengthen paternal transference, although they wouldn't describe them that way. In the early 1970s, when I worked with managers at IBM, they told me that the company had a strict rule against teams and against shared decision-making. The rule had come directly from Thomas Watson Sr., the firm's legendary CEO, and it had the effect of forging a direct link between employees and their bosses. Whether he was aware of it or not, Watson was sanctioning paternal transference at IBM. It was further reinforced by the company's paternalistic commitment of lifetime employment for well- performing employees.

I saw similar dynamics at work when I was a consultant to the executive team of AT&T Communications during the 1980s. Most of the vice presidents there were uncritically worshipful of their business-unit presidents and the several CEOs who were making disastrous strategy moves—giving up cellular telephony, for instance, and losing billions in an effort to compete in computers. Instead of encouraging healthy debate about the future of the company, bosses expected—and rewarded—transferential veneration.

One vice president stuck out because he didn't comply with this company culture. Although his division produced the best results within the long-distance business unit, the executive team didn't appreciate him—not only because his realistic attitude toward his business unit's president implicitly criticized the other vice presidents' transferential overvaluation of the leader, but also because he was an unconventional manager for AT&T at that time. Unlike the others, he delegated responsibility, didn't need to take credit for his division's success, and initiated new businesses. Ultimately, he took early retirement, frustrated by his failure to push his ideas through the bureaucracy.

From a social character point of view, this vice president was a mutant who didn't fit the bureaucratic world. In the new context of a collaborative knowledge workplace, his behavior would have been better appreciated.

In my coaching practice, I've helped a number of executives whose careers have floundered because of their father transferences. A brilliant technical manager in his 30s had reached a level right below the top in two companies before being fired.[7] In each case, he idealized a boss who seemed to treat him like a favored son. But when the boss didn't support his innovative ideas, he rebelled, tried to bypass the boss, and was reined in and fired. Once he understood and overcame his need to attach himself to a father figure, his career took off.

## THE SIBLING TRANSFERENCE

The father transference has been shown to be powerful enough to lead people to idealize their political leaders and ignore their faults. U.S. presidents like Franklin D. Roosevelt and Ronald Reagan, for instance, stimulated intense father transferences in their followers. This type of transference, however, has yielded to another kind of transference with subsequent presidents.

Sibling transference made its debut in national politics with the first baby boomer U.S. president, Bill Clinton. People didn't relate to Clinton as a father—the kind of transference you might have expected with the nation's commander in chief—but, rather, as an admired older brother or "buddy" (as Clinton named his dog). Although he had his supporters, Clinton was never really expected to be a model of good behavior. Unlike Lyndon Johnson, who saw Americans' positive attitude toward him flip when their paternal-transferential expectations were shattered by his inability to end the Vietnam War, Clinton remained popular despite his womanizing because he was perceived by much of the public as a naughty brother.

The growing power of sibling transference is a growing phenomenon. I could find only one reference where Freud writes about a sibling transference, and that was based on a woman's experience of a ridiculing brother.[8] But Freud's patients came from traditional patriarchal families in which sibling rivals competed for paternal approval. He had no experience with interactive families in which it's just as likely that parents compete for the affection of their kids—who themselves are more concerned with being popular with other kids.[9]

At work, the sibling or peer transference can be to someone who is like a helpful older sister or to peers who are like childhood friends who banded together in defiance of authority. Unlike parental transferences, which make people feel small and idealize authority, sibling transferences forge bonds of affection that allow for critical ribbing as well as mutual aid. Perhaps the huge popularity of J. K. Rowling's *Harry Potter* books among this interactive generation owes something to the fact that Harry's parents are dead, his foster parents are abusive to him, and his closest relationships are with sibling-like friends, Hermione and Ron.

Transferential feelings about George W. Bush changed over time. Before 9/11, his popularity was low and, like Clinton, he was seen as a brother or buddy figure, the kind of guy you'd feel comfortable hanging out with. His strong leadership response to the 9/11 national trauma triggered infantile paternal transferential feelings in many Americans, the kind of transference toward a protective leader provoked by pervasive anxiety about what might happen next. The Bush team reinforced these feelings politically by emphasizing continued threats by terrorists, ratcheting up the color-coded terror alert at key points in the 2004 reelection campaign, and contrasting the image of a resolute Bush, the nation's protector, to that of his opponent, John Kerry, whom they tagged as an unreliable flip-flopper on the invasion of Iraq. Of course, positive transferences can turn negative: The image of protector, forged in the anxiety after 9/11, was shattered by the Iraq fiasco and the federal government's inept response to Hurricane Katrina.[10]

The relationship of Americans to Barack Obama has been more complex. When he ran for the presidency in 2007, he encouraged people to project their hopes for positive change and political collaboration on to him. This was not transference, but more like a belief in a magic helper. Because of Obama's mixed racial background, most Americans did not identify with him or see him as a father figure or brother. Once in the White House, his enemies emphasized his otherness, claiming that he was born in his father's homeland of Kenya and that he had a colonial anti-American attitude. He managed to maintain overwhelming support, however, from African-Americans who could both identify with him and transfer their positive fraternal feelings onto him.

In 2016, Donald Trump persuaded many Americans, particularly those left behind by globalization, innovation, and social change, that he was the strong champion or magic helper that could win back their jobs and pride. He may have stimulated different kinds of transferences in the people who voted for him. Like Bill Clinton, he may have provoked sibling transferences that cast him as the rebellious, yet successful brother who gets what he wants by breaking the rules. Trump also may have stimulated parental transferences in other followers: a strong mother figure saying that everything would be great again, or a decisive father figure who says he can get rid of the people who are causing them problems. In contrast, Hillary Clinton seemed to provoke love-hate transferential feelings, especially in younger women who had mixed feelings about their mothers and men who were resentful about powerful women

## DEALING WITH TRANSFERENCES

If all relationships are colored by transference, how can you as a leader ever know if your followers' relationships with you are real? The short answer is that you can't. Even the closest relationships combine objective reality with images and emotions carried over from the past, and there will never be any way around that. People's motivations for following don't have to be totally grounded in reality. What's more, there are ways of managing transferences that not only reduce the potential for negative transferences, but also actually increase the likelihood of positive ones.

A key way that leaders can influence their followers' positive and negative transferences is to become aware of their own transferences. The classic path to self-knowledge is introspection—the approach favored in psychology. The trouble with introspection, however, is that it can paralyze a leader, especially one with a strong obsessive bent. Endless self-analysis will prevent a leader from making the quick decisions every CEO must make. Consequently, many of the most effective leaders rely on an outsider to provide an incisive reality check. The "consultant" can be a member of the family: Bill Gates, for instance, routinely uses his wife as a sounding board. Or, the advisor can be a longtime friend or associate: British tycoon Lord James Hanson relied heavily on his U.S.-based business partner, Sir Gordon White. Increasingly, leaders also work with executive coaches to get an outside perspective on what's going on and to check their views of subordinates. I've played this role with a number of leaders.

To manage followers' transferences, as well as their own, leaders might start by raising the level of awareness in the team, bringing the unconscious into awareness—which is what Freud is all about. This effort is especially important when various staff members view a leader through different transferential lenses. In such a situation, a leader can deal with his followers' multiple transferences by showing himself as he actually is, thereby demystifying his professional relationships. But to do this, he needs to have a lot of self-confidence. With some executive teams, I've used the Strength Deployment Inventory (presented in Chapter 6) or other techniques described in my books *Narcissistic Leaders, Transforming Healthcare Leadership* and *Strategic Intelligence*.[11] When executives share their personality types and discuss how their personalities explain their behavior, this knowledge dilutes transferential projections.

But don't count on these steps to eliminate such projections. So long as they're unconscious, transferences remain strong. What's worse, the positive transference of the follower is likely to become negative before it disappears, as we've seen with public attitudes toward U.S. presidents.

Since subordinates will almost never lose all fear of a leader with power over them, childlike transferences—positive and negative—won't totally disappear. But increased candor and knowledge between leaders and followers can turn a leader from a projection of hopes and fears into a flesh-and-blood role model that collaborators can emulate. Furthermore, the more people know each other, the harder it is to project, and the more obviously unreal the projections will be.

Leaders will never be able to completely control their followers' unconscious motivations. Transference is too deeply ingrained in human nature for that. And no leader can fully understand all followers and collaborators. Yet, if the organization is to be protected from itself, followers' projections and motivations must be identified, channeled, and managed. This challenge is especially urgent for today's organizations, in which an increasing diversity of people requires us all to move away from stereotyping and really understand differences in personality and ways of thinking and learning.

In this chapter, I've described how a powerful unconscious process, the father transference, was the glue that tied followers to leaders in bureaucratic organizations. Leadership was relatively easy because leaders didn't have to understand a diverse bunch of followers. But as family dynamics and the mode of production have changed, leaders can no longer count on paternal transferences. Furthermore, as organizations become global, leaders are faced with a diversity of identities, cultural values, and personalities. To gain followers and collaborators, would-be leaders would be wise to understand their attitudes regarding work and leadership. In Chapter 4, we'll describe the changing social character—the psychological frame that organizes all the other elements of personality so that people are motivated to do what they need to do to succeed in a particular socioeconomic context. Then, in Chapter 5, we'll address the challenge of what we should know to understand people in the global knowledge workplace.

CHAPTER 4

# From Bureaucratic Followers to Interactive Collaborators

IMAGINE THAT YOU'RE a 50-year-old male executive, brought up in a traditional family, now leading knowledge workers in a global company. You think back to how you rose up the ranks by helping your boss to succeed—and how he, in turn, had showed you the ropes and stuck out his neck to tout you for upper management. You now have some subordinates who want this kind of relationship, but you're not sure they're the best of the bunch. You're impressed by some of the younger men and women who are more entrepreneurial—they don't wait for you to give them objectives; they tell you what needs to be done. But while these go-getters work hard and well together, they don't seem committed to the company; you don't feel the kind of warm tie you felt with your boss. You're not sure they'd be good leaders. To bring out the best in both the bureaucratic and interactive subordinates, you need to understand your motivation and theirs. A significant part of that motivation is social character.

We invite you to imagine yourself as each of these four types: the traditional bureaucratic executive, the bureaucratic subordinate, the interactive leader, and the interactive subordinate. As a leader you'll have to understand the strengths and weaknesses of each type of subordinate in order to bring out the best in both.

Social character is an elusive concept, because like individual personality, it entails both conscious and unconscious aspects of human psychology. We may be conscious of the values that give our lives meaning, our talents, and our identity or sense of self. The unconscious aspects may have to do with emotionally charged attitudes, motivational value systems, or experiences from childhood that have shaped how we relate to others and what most drives us at school and work—what makes us want to do what we need to do to prosper in a particular social context.

The concept of social character may be confused with the more simplistic concept of generational differences. It's easy to sort people into groups based on their birth years and assume that they share a set of characteristics; everyone has heard about the differences between Baby Boomers, Generation X, and Millennial—and everyone knows somebody who doesn't fit the stereotype of their generation. While some events, such as world crises or significant changes in technology, can affect people of about the same age in similar ways, there are many other variables at play. The slow transition from a predominantly bureaucratic social character to a predominantly interactive social character is like a changing tide—and each generation is like a set of waves. The waves are easier to notice, but the tide is a subtler, though more substantial change. When you understand the forces that shape social character, you'll be better able to understand why the generational stereotypes don't always hold up.

In well-functioning people, the conscious and unconscious attitudes and values are, for the most part, connected. The total personality is in tune with the social character, and the social character fits a person's social role. For example, a key element of the bureaucratic social character is the hardworking, obsessive, personality that has internalized a dominant father figure from early childhood. People with this social character will consciously value order and expertise and will want to follow managers who are like good fathers—demanding but caring mentors. While they may be aware that they value a fatherlike leader, they're also likely to be unaware that they're projecting an infantile image onto a manager who may not be very caring. Furthermore, in making that projection, they're making themselves dependent on this manager, ascribing a level of knowledge and understanding to the manager that he or she may not have and undervaluing their own competence.

For people with an interactive social character, the significant person from the past they project onto a leader is often not a parent, but a sibling or a close childhood friend who might have brought them into a team or musical group, or initiated them into a new activity. These ties may be weaker than traditional parental transferences, but for Interactives raised in the new context, parental images are not the dominating father or nurturing mother. The parental image is a more complex figure who sometimes was caring, but couldn't always be counted on to be there when needed.

Furthermore, a defining aspect of the interactive social character is the ability to easily take on new identities. That makes some of these people argue that they can't be described in terms of a social character stereotype; they just adapt, whatever the situation. But Interactives are not always conscious of how they adapt to different situations. The need to design oneself according to what sells on the personality market differentiates the interactive social character from the social characters of the past.

Compare the interactive social character to that of the Mexican *campesinos* Erich Fromm and I studied. Their social character wasn't adapted to the industrial world that was fast overtaking them. They were farmers and, with the exception of the hacienda peons who had been liberated by the Mexican Revolution of 1910-1920, their way of life was the same as that of their parents, grandparents, and great-grandparents. Their social character had not changed from that of their long-ago ancestors. Their identity or sense of self was rooted in family and place.

Although the villagers liked to think of themselves as unique individuals and even had a saying for it—"*Yo soy yo y no me parece a nadie*" (I am myself and I'm not like anyone else)—they had the social character shared with free peasants around the world described in Chapter 1: cautious, independent, frugal patient, fatalistic, dignified, respectful, and egalitarian but suspicious of anyone outside the family.

There were, however, two sets of villagers who did not share this social character. One was made up of the families of the landless hacienda peons. They had been so damaged by their virtual enslavement that they didn't believe they could ever succeed as independent farmers. Even when given land, their passive, fearful, and submissive social character—a survival strategy in the hacienda where independence provoked beatings or worse—made them vulnerable to exploitive entrepreneurial bosses. These bosses were the second exception, productive narcissists who in less turbulent times seem out of sync with society, but who are the first to exploit new opportunities whenever there are dramatic changes in the mode of production.[1]

Free peasants throughout the world share a social character. In their attitude toward work and relationships, they more closely resemble each other than the city people in their own countries. And if we look back at the United States in the 19th century, the large majority of American families, not including native Americans and slaves, also made their living from farming as independent land owners (more than 75 percent as late as 1870). They expressed some of the attitudes of free, liberty-loving peasants throughout the world, but there were important differences. As the French political scientist and historian Alexis de Tocqueville observed during his tour of America in the 1830s, many American farmers combined business with agriculture. They wanted to get rich, and a number of them were speculators, risk takers. Since most had fled oppressive European societies, they were more daring and less fatalistic than peasants whose families had been rooted to the same ground for centuries. Also, as Tocqueville noted, unlike Europeans (and most peasants throughout the world), Americans were educated for public affairs, and encouraged to participate in a democracy.[2]

In contrast to the Mexican peasants, who were kept in check by a semi-feudal society until the revolution of 1910, many of the Americans who left their farms for the cities flourished in the late 19th century, taking advantage of the new technologies in transportation (railroads and cars), metals (steel), energy (oil), and communications (telegraph and telephone). Part of their social character had already been shaped by the pioneers who ventured westward and forged trails that later become stagecoach routes and railroads. Their experience of dealing with the highly bureaucratic railroads has even left a permanent mark on the language of business. Expressions like jumping the tracks, derailing, getting back on track, having a full head of steam, being railroaded, or seeing the light at the end of the tunnel are still used.

## THE BUREAUCRATIC PERSONALITY

The outcome of these entrepreneurial ventures of the late 19th century were great companies, such as the railroads, that were organized into bureaucracies with functional departments and specialized roles, regulated and controlled by rules and, increasingly, by professional managers. As Peter Drucker, the outstanding interpreter of management, wrote, bureaucratic management deals with the integration of people into a common venture; therefore, what managers do in Germany, in the United Kingdom, in Japan, or in Brazil is exactly the same, even though how they do it may be somewhat different.[3] And one thing they were doing was shaping the bureaucratic social character.

By the start of the 20th century, many American families were raising their sons not to be independent farmers, but to be managers or government employees in bureaucracies. Daughters were raised to support their future husbands' careers, which meant not only taking care of home and children, but also joining clubs and socializing with the wives of men who could help their husbands' careers.

Bureaucracies and bureaucrats had been around for a long time. Since the days of ancient Mesopotamia, Egypt, and China, bureaucrats had served emperors, pharaohs, and kings. They'd been tax collectors, scribes, clerics, or clerks in the court, customs house, or archives. Czar Nicholas I supposedly said, "Not I, but ten thousand clerks rule Russia." As far back as we can see, large organizations have been run by bureaucrats.

And bureaucrats have long had a bad reputation, spread by novelists and social scientists, as well as politicians. Nineteenth-century novelists pictured bureaucrats as dry, narrow, and heartless. In *Little Dorrit*, Charles Dickens describes Tite Barnacle, who runs the Circumlocution Office with the mission of making sure that nothing ever happens for the first time. Writes Dickens, "He wound and wound folds of tape and paper round the neck of the country. His wristbands and collar were oppressive, his voice and manner were oppressive."[4] In Herman Melville's short story *Bartleby, the Scrivener: A Story of Wall-Street* (1853), the title character, an American bureaucrat, becomes like a robot whose only vestige of humanity is to resist all orders, saying, "I would prefer not to."

Melville described the American stereotype of the bureaucrat. Even before the rise of big business and big government, Americans were especially opposed to bureaucracies and bureaucrats, and the stereotype of a bureaucrat still distorts popular perceptions of dedicated public servants and industrious managers. The negative attitude goes back to America's Calvinist founders, rebels against all forms of state and church authority—any institution that imposed intermediaries between citizens and elected representatives, between individuals and their God. The ideal for American Protestants was voluntary service to create community. When the new national government was formed in 1789, there was a small public service, with most jobs in finance, record keeping, and the copying of official documents. But liberty-loving Americans, who feared the kind of controlling bureaucracy that served George III, agreed that if they had to have one, they wanted a bureaucracy that served the people in a society of equals. And to a degree, they succeeded. In 1830, Tocqueville was impressed with the egalitarian behavior of American public servants.[5]

That view of the bureaucrat as egalitarian public servant changed in the post–Civil War period. The bribe-taking customs official, land agent, and Indian agent soiled the relatively clean image of the American public servant. Reforms, beginning with a merit system instituted by the Pendleton Civil Service Reform Act of 1883, somewhat improved the bureaucratic image, and new functions of science and technology increased the prestige of federal employees as the public recognized the civil servant's productive role in agriculture, public health, and education. But the negative stereotype persisted, even though bureaucracies in both government and business have been essential in organizing experts to create and protect our fabulously rich society.

Many social scientists, as well as fiction writers, have reinforced the negative image of the bureaucrat. Although the German sociologist Max Weber defined bureaucracy as a more just alternative to arbitrary rule and a spoils system, he also wrote that the iron cage of bureaucracy had clamped shut on the free spirit of the Enlightenment. He called bureaucrats "specialists without spirit, sensualists without heart," adding, "This nullity imagines that it has attained a level of civilization never before achieved."[6]

Other social scientists elaborated on Weber's stereotype of bureaucrats. The philosopher and educator John Dewey wrote about their "occupational psychosis," an extreme version of the economist and sociologist Thorstein Veblen's concept of "trained incapacity"—the loss of ability to reason or think creatively that results from following rigid rules. The sociologist Daniel Warnotte agreed and described bureaucrats as becoming intellectually and emotionally damaged by their roles, suffering "professional deformation."[7] Erich Fromm put it in psychoanalytic idiom, writing, "Roughly equivalent to the sadomasochistic character, in a social rather than a political sense, is the *bureaucratic character*. In the bureaucratic system every person controls the one below him and is controlled by the one above. Both sadistic and masochistic impulses can be fulfilled in such a system. Those below, the bureaucratic character will hold in contempt, those above he will admire and fear."[8]

Although the sociologist Robert Merton was less harsh in his judgment of the bureaucratic personality, he emphasized that bureaucratic structure reinforces a pecking order.[9] A psychologist might add that this structure formalizes the hierarchical motivational patterns found in all primates. Merton notes that bureaucracy, power, and privilege belong to the role, not the person, and rules can protect people lower down in the system from arbitrary authority.[10]

Merton also affirms that although the bureaucratic personality tends to be precise, reliable, efficient, and prudent, bureaucrats are or become timid and conservative, resisting change. This begs the interesting question of whether certain personalities are attracted to bureaucratic roles or whether the role shapes their personality. Perhaps it's a mixture of both, but the forging of the bureaucratic personality begins in the traditional family, long before entry into a bureaucracy, and some people develop a personality with strong needs for clarity, precision, and unambiguous authority that fits smoothly into bureaucratic structures.

It's notable that neither the novelists nor social scientists who stereotyped the bureaucratic personality ever studied these people systematically. Of course, some observers, like Franz Kafka, worked in bureaucracies, but most have been individualists who naturally resent bureaucrats who make them conform to rules and regulations in universities and companies.

Having worked as a consultant in government and industrial bureaucracies in 36 countries and interviewed hundreds of managers and employees in the process, I've found variations of the bureaucratic personality. As Drucker stated, managers, almost all of whom share a bureaucratic social character, have done the same kind of thing and have fit in more or less the same kinds of structures everywhere. However, as Drucker continued, they may play the role somewhat differently, because of variations in personality type and cultures.[11] Once you view bureaucrats from inside bureaucracies rather than from afar, you will see that although they fit Merton's stereotype in some essential ways—particularly, most find meaning in being respected as experts—there are variations in their intrinsic motivations at work. Some bureaucrats want to help or educate people; others want to defend the public; most take their greatest satisfaction in just doing their job well.[12]

AT&T managers and technicians before the breakup of the Bell System are notable examples of public-spirited bureaucrats. In the late 1970s, what most gave their work meaning was service to the public. And even though their roles and rules came to be defined in an increasingly rigid way over time, whenever there was a disaster—hurricane, blizzard, or flood—they ignored the rules and worked together day and night until they had restored telephone service. When people were in need, the hierarchical system was suddenly transformed into a heterarchy where the person with the relevant competence took the lead and others were quick to follow.

Even bureaucratic Americans never lose their love of liberty, and they always try to maximize their autonomy at work.[13] Note the popularity of Drucker's management by objectives (MBO) or the cartoonish version, The *One Minute Manager*, the pipe-smoking daddy figure who sits back after giving terse one-minute instructions or feedback and lets subordinate managers do their jobs their own way as long as they reach the agreed-on objectives.[14] But this approach no longer works in the increasingly interactive workplace, where autonomy can get in the way of the collaboration needed to achieve results.

The description of the bureaucratic personality by the novelists and sociologists was a caricature, an extreme example of the type, verging on psychopathology. It would be like describing the interactive personality in terms of Woody Allen's Zelig, a human chameleon, a plastic person without a center who shapes himself to fit whatever sells. Sure, there's truth to this description, but it's the extreme case. As we'll see, the positive potential of the interactive social character supports a more collaborative community in the workplace.

## FROM BUREAUCRATIC TO INTERACTIVE SOCIAL CHARACTER

By caricaturing the bureaucrat, looking with disdain at the conformity and self-importance of the organization man, the critics were distancing themselves from this social character, perhaps even projecting away aspects of themselves that clashed with the ideal of a free, independent people. (Table 4-1 displays the values associated with the bureaucratic and interactive characters.) Who of us in modern industrial society has escaped a socialization process in schools and workplaces where we've had to play a role in a bureaucracy, to think and act as bureaucrats?

**TABLE 4-1**

## Bureaucratic and Interactive Characters

|  | Bureaucratic | Interactive |
|---|---|---|
| **Ideals** | • Stability<br>• Hierarchy/autonomy<br>• Producing Excellence | • Continual Improvement<br>• Networks/Independence<br>• Free Agency<br>• Creating Value |
| **Social Character** | • Inner Directed<br>• Identification with parental authority<br>• Precise, methodical, obsessive | • Other directed<br>• Identification with peers, siblings<br>• Experimental, innovative marketing |
| **Socioeconomic base** | • Market controlling bureaucracies<br>• Slow-changing technology<br>• National Markets<br>• Employment security<br>• Traditional family | • Entrepreneurial companies<br>• Internet<br>• New technologies<br>• Global markets<br>• Employment uncertainty<br>• Diverse family structures |

[15] To some extent, all middle-class Americans growing up in the age of the manufacturing mode of production, and especially those who were raised in traditional families, were shaped to fit bureaucratic roles. Yet, unlike some of the Asians I've interviewed who are content to submit to paternal leaders, many of the Americans I've talked to feel conflicted about their submission to bureaucratic bosses, even though this conflict may not be entirely conscious.

I learned about this attitude when studying managers in high-tech companies. In 1969, I received a grant from the Harvard Program on Technology and Society to study the people creating new technology—how their personalities influenced their effectiveness and the products they built and how their work, in turn, shaped the further development of their personalities, especially their values. To get the grant, I had to gain entry into companies and permission to interview managers, scientists, and engineers. At that time, I was spending the year as a fellow at the Center for Advanced Study in the Behavioral Sciences at Stanford. While there, I met a first-level manager of a large high-tech company who liked the idea of the study, but was too low in the hierarchy to invite me in. He then introduced me to his manager, who also liked the idea of the study and said he was too low in the hierarchy to invite me in. But he connected me with the human resources vice president, who said that although my project was interesting, only a group vice president could invite me in. He introduced me to one who he thought might be open to the idea.

The group vice president listened as I described how I'd do the study, and I offered to share the results with him. Then he said, "I've never met a psychoanalyst before. Tell me something about myself that I don't know, and I'll let you come in and do your study." I said, "I'm not a mind reader, but I can tell you something about yourself you may not know if you're willing to take a Rorschach test, to describe what you see in a set of ten inkblots." He agreed and took the test.

I had spent many years learning to use the Rorschach as both a diagnostic tool and a research instrument for interpreting emotional attitudes and cognitive style. During our first meeting, the vice president said nothing about himself; his only comments were telling me what he saw in the inkblots. What I interpreted from his responses was deep anger at having to submit to higher-ups and a passionate drive to be free—in other words, inner rebellion against his bureaucratic situation. When I told him my analysis, he said, "OK, you're in." Obviously, I didn't tell him something that he didn't "know," or else he would not have been so quick to accept my analysis. Rather, I was affirming feelings that he had never talked about, maybe never even admitted to himself. He decided to let me in because he felt known and thought that he could learn from me about the people he managed and maybe his bosses as well.

*The Gamesman*, the book that resulted from my study of 250 managers in ten technology companies, was based on interviews lasting from three hours to, in a few cases, more than 20 hours. In it, I described a variation of the bureaucratic personality then rising to leadership positions in these innovative and fast-paced companies.[16] I wrote that the new type—unlike the security-seeking bureaucratic type described by William H. Whyte, Jr., in *The Organization Man*—was excited by the chance to cut deals and gamble.[17] Although the gamesman wasn't a visionary who created new industries, he was skilled at organizing teams and found his greatest satisfaction at work in winning. As the executive who invited me in put it, "Our main ability is that we know how to win at this game of business."[18]

The gamesman became a model for managers in fast-paced competitive companies. Like Jack Welch, who explicitly described business as a game and compared his role to a manager of a professional baseball team, executives in large bureaucratic companies tried to put a new face on their bureaucratic image.[19] After the breakup of the Bell System in 1984, AT&T's motto of universal service was replaced by the goal of winning. But the attempt by AT&T executives to look like the high tech managers in Silicon Valley aided by legions of PR advisers, didn't make them any less bureaucratic in their behavior. The real gamesmen in the Silicon Valley companies that tried to partner with AT&T gave up in frustration with the bureaucrats who over-analyzed everything and then made some disastrous decisions that eventually brought the company close to ruin.[20]

In the 1980s, I interviewed men and women at work who fit neither the classic bureaucratic type nor the gamesman variation.[21] These people had an instinctual dislike for bureaucracy and bureaucratic bosses. They saw themselves as businessmen and businesswomen, not bureaucrats. They were attracted to work where they were clearly adding value for customers and also developing their own business competence. Unlike the bureaucratic types who sought *autonomy* within the organization, these interactive types strove to maintain *independence* from the company by constantly sharpening their marketable skills.

Unlike the bureaucratic social characters who want a good father-like boss who gives them objectives, leaves them alone to achieve these objectives, and then evaluates them, Interactives typically work in teams where everyone is expected to push each other to get results.

People with the interactive social character fit naturally into projects and teams, but only if they are treated as equals and have a say in how things are done. Unlike bureaucrats who focus on meeting objectives set by the boss, Interactives think business: Who are my customers, and how can I add measurable value for them? Bosses who don't help to get the job done are just roadblocks or worse.

Like any social character, Interactives have both strengths and weaknesses that make them hard to lead. In *Got Game: How the Gamer Generation Is Reshaping Business Forever*, John C. Beck and Mitchell Wade report on attitudes regarding work and leadership among business professionals who've grown up with video games. That cohort included more than 80 percent of people age 35 and under in 2004; presumably a larger percentage of people in that age group is now working in the businesses surveyed by the authors.[22] The gamer attitudes the authors describe fit closely with my own observations of the interactive social character:

- They find meaning at work in adding value for customers.

- They want their rewards based on measurable results, not on position or evaluations by bosses.

- They're so confident of their skills that they believe they don't have to work as hard as other people. They think highly of themselves and are quick to label themselves as "experts."

- They see business like a video game in which they can always find a way to win, and they're optimistic that they'll succeed. Failure is just a learning experience.[23]

- They see leaders as useless, even "evil" because they smother innovation. Even in MMORPGs (massively multiplayer online role-playing games), everyone can take a turn at leading "The game generation believes in skill, they don't believe in following orders."[24]

- They shift roles and identities easily, depending on what's required in the game. And they agree with this statement: "The best way to handle people is to tell them what they want to hear." According to Beck and Wade, "It's almost as if they see life as a game, and themselves as skillful players. A strong majority of the game generation agrees with the statement, 'I can control the way I come across to people, depending on the impression I wish to make.'"[25] This is similar to what Erich Fromm described as the marketing personality, and what the psychologist Elias Porter identified as the flexible-cohering (hub) personality.

For Interactives, parents served as enablers and cheerleaders. At work, Interactives want continual feedback from bosses; they want to know how they're doing. But since they don't identify with father figures and distrust parental-type relationships at work, seeing them as stifling independence, they resist the kind of mentoring enjoyed by the bureaucrats. An interactive banking executive told me she didn't want her boss as a mentor or coach, because she didn't want him to know any more than he already did about her doubts or weaknesses. She wanted to be able to hire a coach she could fire if she didn't get the help she wanted. Interactives accept help only from people who collaborate with them and do not emphasize their power, position, or authority."[26] Also, let's not forget that many Interactives can mentor their elders, particularly when it comes to technology.

Interactive attitudes are spreading throughout the industrialized world. In the 1970s, when I met with a group of bureaucratic Volvo managers in Sweden, they defined themselves in terms of the company. The company determined their roles and goals, and they didn't question the company's values. They served the company loyally; they were proud to be Volvo men. In contrast, I recently spoke with young Swedish entrepreneurs, both men and women, who demand that companies implement values they share. Otherwise, they're not interested in working for them. The identity of interactive individuals remains separate from the company unless the company becomes an expression of them and their values, with a purpose that is meaningful to them.

The interactive social character has been formed in a world in which we must adapt to constant change, and we can't count on stable institutions to take care of us. Corporate promises have evaporated with corporate mergers and bankruptcies. People succeed and prosper by staying in competitive condition, physically as well as mentally, and by building their own support networks at work and in personal relationships.

Despite insecurity at home and at work, the interactive social character has grown up in a richer and more abundant society than has ever existed. Interactive individuals want to enjoy life wherever they are. They want excitement, fun, and adventure even when they're competing, as shown in TV shows like *The Bachelor* and *Survivor*. But as mentioned in Chapter 1, the psychopathology of the interactive social character is the obverse of its strengths; the interactive person can be emotionally detached, unwilling to commit, superficial, disloyal, and centerless. Indeed, fans of *The Bachelor* can readily recount stunning examples of superficiality and "failure to commit."

When they lead productively, Interactives are likely to focus on collaboration, teamwork, and building connections. The Morning Star Company, a tomato-processer that the *Harvard Business Review* called "the world's most creatively managed company," uses a radical approach to self-management without structural authority.[27] Workplaces and workspaces are incorporating more open spaces, more flexible settings, and fewer of the cubicle-farms that are so characteristic of the bureaucratic office. Many questions remain about how Interactives will perform in leadership roles when they take charge of large bureaucratic organizations—or when their entrepreneurial ventures stabilize and require some bureaucratic processes. Perhaps Interactives will be more willing to partner with or hire professional managers so they can focus on the work they prefer—like Larry Page and Sergey Brin, the cofounders of Google, did.

After I wrote this, interactive entrepreneurs created two fabulously successful interactive companies, Uber and Airbnb. Their founders, Garret Camp and Travis Kalanick of Uber and Brian Cheske and Joe Gebbia of Airbnb all were brought up in dual-career families. They developed their businesses interactively, partnering with IT experts and getting advice from venture capitalists. Their business purpose has not been to change the world but to add value for people who are interacting for the purposes of transportation and hospitality. They have been willing to challenge bureaucracies and regulations. But like Page and Brin, they are not interested in leading people. For them, an organization is like a game where everyone has a role. But organizations need productive leadership as shown by the mess at Uber that led to Kalanick's resignation. We need interactive leaders, and we need to understand how to develop them.

CHAPTER 5

# Developing Personality Intelligence

WHY HAS IT BECOME ESSENTIAL for leaders to understand the people they lead? Why do leaders need to develop their Personality Intelligence? We believe the answer has to do with the new context of the leader-follower relationship. When the dominant mode of production in a society shifts, such as from manufacturing to the creation of knowledge, the tools used to create value also change. In manufacturing, hand and machine tools are applied to raw materials to create value. In knowledge work, ideas and information are tested against each other, and people need to interact with others to gain access to ideas and information. Consequently, people with better relationships will have access to more useful information, and stand a better chance of creating valuable knowledge.

## THE LEADER-FOLLOWER RELATIONSHIP

Leadership is a relationship in a context. We have found it useful to think about this relationship in terms of four categories, which are based on the interaction between the motivations of the leader and those who are led (see Figure 5-1).

A leader may be motivated by a desire for the common good or by a drive for personal power. Of course, motives may be mixed, and leaders who hunger for personal power over others generally cloak their motives in promises and visions of the common good. But events usually reveal which motive is dominant, especially when they conflict.

**FIGURE 5-1**

## Motives of the Leader and the Led

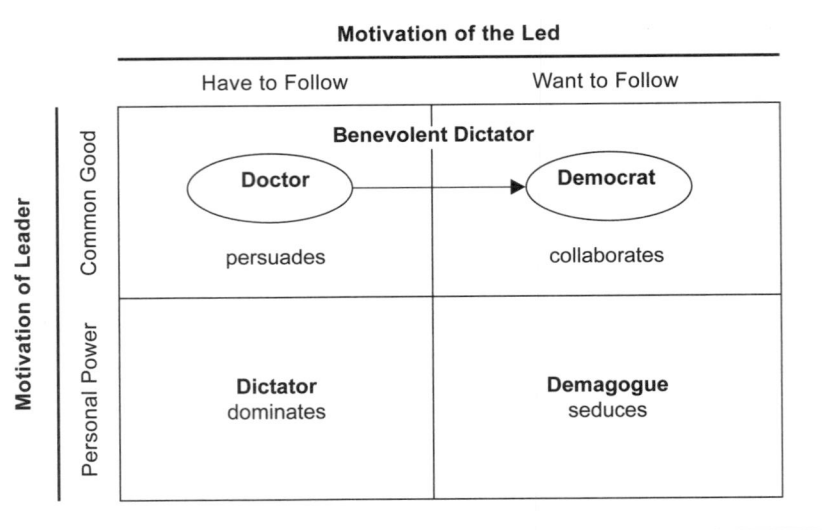

|  | **Motivation of the Led** | |
|---|---|---|
|  | Have to Follow | Want to Follow |
| **Common Good** | Doctor — persuades | Democrat — collaborates |
| **Personal Power** | Dictator dominates | Demagogue seduces |

(Motivation of Leader on vertical axis; Benevolent Dictator spans from Doctor to Democrat across the top.)

In turn, people follow either because they want to or because they have to follow the leader. These dichotomies give us four possibilities:

- People want to follow a power-driven leader.
- People feel they have to follow a dictator.
- A leader who is working for the common good has resistant followers
- People want to follow a leader who is trying to achieve a common good.

Let's focus on each of the four alternatives. When people want to follow a leader who's out for personal power, they get a seductive demagogue like Napoleon, who appeared at first to be a liberator but ultimately devastated France with his compulsive drive for conquest. Hitler is another example. He gained power with a promise of German glory, but he murdered Jews and others who did not fit his Aryan ideal or who opposed him. When faced with defeat, he ordered Albert Speer to destroy the country to punish all the German people for failing him. Leaders of terrorist organizations seduce followers by demonizing opponents and promising to reward suicide or death-in-action with otherworldly bliss. In a less drastic way, people can be taken in by political or organizational leaders who trigger transferential idealization and promise to protect them, but who prove to be just out for themselves. Contrast these power-driven leaders with George Washington, who, like the Roman leader Cincinnatus, could have stayed in power, but gave it up to return to his farm.

When people feel they *have* to follow a power-driven leader, they end up being oppressed by a dictator whom they obey out of fear. He could be a Machiavellian prince, a Saddam Hussein, or a Stalin. On a smaller scale, these dictators might be bureaucratic or even psychopathic bosses. Who among us hasn't had to suffer a dictator at school or work?

When a leader who wants the common good has unwilling or lukewarm subordinates who feel they have to follow but do so with resistance we find an interesting variety of leadership possibilities. Consider a company that needs to change—to adapt to new markets, face competition, improve results, innovate—but has employees who resist change. One way to deal with this is by engineering change without ever relating directly to the followers. Well-meaning managers avoid the challenge of leadership by designing new structures, a slimmed-down workforce, and new processes, as well as incentives that force change, as Mark Hurd did at NCR and then at HP. Or they may act more like diplomats by arranging mergers or selling off parts of the company, like Richard Parsons at Time Warner or Howard Stringer at Sony.

A hands-on leader of resistant followers could be a benevolent despot who forces change with both positive and negative incentives, rewarding those who change and threatening to fire those who won't budge. The despot may even trigger a positive infantile transference in bureaucratic followers, and if he produces great results, the resisters may even become willing followers. In some contexts, like in the traditional Chinese culture of Singapore—Lee Kwan Yew was an example of this type of leader—a protective benevolent despot is welcomed.

But in the new context of knowledge work and Interactives, the leader of a resistant workforce is better advised to be more like a kind of doctor who educates and persuades patients to change behavior in their own self-interest; who makes it clear that unless patients follow a new diet and start to exercise, the doctor will stop treating them; and who explains fully the reasons for change, answers all questions, and responds to all doubts. The goal of the doctor is to transform patients into collaborators who manage their own conditions, to move from being a doctor to becoming a "democrat".

In the process of moving from doctor to democrat, the goal of the leader is to become more interactive to collaborate with the people who share the same view of the common good. To become a democratic leader, the doctor-leader must communicate and practice a leadership philosophy and institute learning processes. This may be the only way to fully engage the new generation of professionals in a common purpose.

Ideally, the leaders we need will be democratic in the sense that they'll have the full support of their follower-collaborators. But to get democratic leaders, we'll need many skillful doctors who have no illusions about what it takes to become democratic, And in the context of different national cultures in the global economy and knowledge workplace, they'll have to understand potential collaborators by developing their Personality Intelligence.

This kind of understanding was not so important in the early 1970s, when I was hired by B.O. Evans, the innovative president of IBM's Systems Development Division, to teach six of IBM's highest-potential managers to understand themselves and others. Known for his unique skill in getting difficult people to work together, Evans hoped that I could teach these managers to do what he did intuitively. I tried to teach the group in a seminar, but the managers asked me to meet with them individually instead. That was because they didn't want to expose themselves to people they saw as rivals. They knew that at some point in the future they might possibly manage or report to one of the others, meaning that they would either be giving or receiving commands. But they foresaw no need to collaborate with each other.

Evans and a few other executives who were interested in understanding people were ahead of their time. In the age of industrial bureaucracies and national companies, understanding people wasn't essential. To lead the bureaucratic social character, managers were trained to present themselves as paternal and reassuring, to communicate clearly, and to recognize and reward good behavior. And they didn't need training to understand people they thought were just like themselves. In choosing successors, executives typically tapped clones. They were all men. At AT&T they wore suits size 42 long; at Ford, CEOs were shorter, just like Henry Ford and his descendants.

Many companies remain stuck in a bureaucratic mind-set. But in the late 1980s and early 1990s, some leaders of knowledge companies, especially those in the global arena, decided that to create collaboration they needed to understand the diverse mix of people in their organizations. The drive to create this understanding started with executive teams, especially in global companies.

At the end of the 1980s, I was hired by Göran Lindahl, then the hard-charging head of Transmission and Distribution for ABB, the global energy giant, which had just been formed by a merger between Asea, a Swedish company, and Brown Boveri, a Swiss company. There were also large departments in Germany and the United States. Lindahl was concerned because managers from these four countries were complaining about each other, and there was a lack of collaboration. What was causing the anger and distrust? Lindahl asked me to find out. As described later in this chapter, the reasons had to do with national variations in the social character, which when understood and discussed by the top managers from these countries, improved trust and collaboration.

In the 1990s and the beginning of the 21st century, the corporate leaders who hired me wanted help in understanding themselves, team members, and candidates for top jobs. At first, I used the Myers-Briggs test, an easy nonthreatening way to reveal differences in the way people think (extrovert versus introvert, sensing versus intuitive, feeling versus thinking, perceiving versus judging).[1] When members of executive teams wanted to understand each other even more, I developed a questionnaire that elicits the different personality types based on psychoanalytic theory discussed later in this chapter. Team members shared their profiles and discussed how understanding each other could improve communication and collaboration.[2]

What had changed to increase interest in understanding people? Why did the concept of emotional intelligence suddenly become so popular? The answer, I believe, is that in the advanced knowledge workplace, knowledge workers are being forced to collaborate, and that's a lot easier to do if they understand each other.

The term collaboration has a shady past. During World War II, it meant helping the enemy; a collaborator was a traitor. But now the term has reverted in association to its Latin root, *collaborare*, working together.

According to an IBM global survey of 500 CEOs, collaboration has become the major challenge of the knowledge workplace.[3] Consider the different kinds of collaboration that knowledge leaders need to create: across departments for concurrent engineering and to produce technical solutions for business customers; among projects within departments where designers have to interact to develop complex software; between and among companies and governments; and all kinds of collaboration across cultures.[4]

To facilitate collaboration, some companies are trying to shake up bureaucracies with a strong dose of interactive medicine. To move the IBM culture, which was firmly rooted in clear lines of command and individualism, CEO Sam Palmisano organized "jams," online town meetings to get IBMers interacting. The jam on values in 2003 triggered so much criticism of management that some feared a corporate revolution. But by staying the course, Palmisano gained the trust of IBMers when they realized that they wouldn't be punished for their candor.[5] In the 2006 jam on innovation, 70,000 IBM employees and 70 invited partners offered ideas on four topics: transportation, health, the environment, and finance. These ideas were organized into projects. IBMers say the culture has changed. When they need help, they can call on experts in other areas who respond. Collaboration is reinforced with "thanks awards," symbolic recognition in the form of shirts, umbrellas, backpacks, and the like embossed with the company logo. Any employee can give six of these "thanks" a year.

Interactive jams, even global virtual teams, don't require that people know each other. In fact, there's some evidence that people in virtual global product development teams brainstorm better when they don't see or know each other.[6] The reason may be that when participants are unseen and anonymous, the flow of ideas isn't blocked by quizzical or disapproving looks. But you can't escape into anonymity or assume another identity when you're working closely with others face-to-face.

No amount of jam or any other online interactive activity teaches you to understand the people you need to work with. That requires a different kind of learning. Emotional intelligence—especially the ability to sense how people are feeling---is part of Personality Intelligence. But understanding and predicting how others will behave in key roles requires knowledge of their motivational values and personal philosophy.

What does it mean to know another person? Ideally, it means describing the person behind the *persona*, the mask of self-presentation, much in the way a good novelist or playwright does. Few people have that valuable skill. For most of us, even recognizing the persona is a step ahead of assuming that others are motivated just like we are.

You will better understand people in the knowledge workplace if you learn to focus on four conceptual variables that will strengthen your Personality Intelligence. They are:

- Social character: how we are like people brought up in the same culture
- Personality types: variations of the social character—motivational value systems
- Identity: how we are defined and define ourselves—our personality philosophy
- Intellectual skills and talents: especially type of intelligence.

These concepts are windows on the self—the person—including values, emotional attitudes, characteristic ways of working and relating to others, the identity we give to ourselves, and our ways of acquiring, retaining, and transforming information. Of course, we can't see these aspects of our brains and personality directly, but we can observe patterns of behavior and interpret them in terms of personality type and social character. These concepts are useful only when they equip us to predict and understand motives, attitudes, and behaviors. We may be aware of our sense of identity and, to some extent, our values. But like transferential attitudes, part of personality may not be conscious to us, even though a trained observer can see it in action. Yet we can develop our Personality Intelligence to become more alert to patterns of behavior, and that starts with making use of these concepts.

## SOCIAL CHARACTER DIFFERENCES—HOW THOSE OF US FROM DIFFERENT CULTURES ARE NOT ALIKE

Once you are aware of the descriptions of the various social characters—peasant, bureaucratic, and interactive—it's relatively easy to differentiate among them. As the experience of ABB showed, however, cultural variations of social character are not so obvious, and they can cause misunderstandings in a global company.

To understand these differences and the reasons why they caused conflict at ABB, I asked ABB managers from Sweden, Switzerland, Germany, and the United States to tell me about how they worked together, their relationships with customers, how they made decisions, and how they compared themselves to managers in the other countries. It turned out that while they all had the same formal organizations, each national company had different informal organizations and decision-making practices reflecting cultural variations of the bureaucratic social character. These differences caused misunderstandings and also negative stereotyping. For example, the Germans saw the Swedes as lacking integrity and concern for quality, and the Swedes viewed the Germans as contentious and autocratic.

In fact, the Swedes believed in consensus, and to make sure everyone was singing from the same hymnal, they held frequent off-site meetings. Managers got to know each other well and even called each other "brother," so they were less likely to disagree with each other. Sometimes spouses and children joined these gatherings, tightening the bonds.

The Germans saw all this sociability as a dangerous form of seduction that undermined objectivity and integrity. According to their reasoning, if you socialized outside work, you'd be less likely to shoot down faulty arguments; you'd want to please each other. German managers valued objectivity above sociability, and they maintained very formal relations, using the formal sie form of address with each other even after years of working together. The Swedes, on the other hand, used the intimate du as soon as they met.

While the Swedes avoided conflict and kept quiet even if not fully convinced that the boss was right, the Germans valued tough, sometimes contentious debate, as long as it was based on facts and not on position in the hierarchy. But once the German *meister*—always a respected technical expert—made a decision, everyone marched in step. For the Germans, this was not autocratic, but both reasonable and effective.

The Swedes' avoidance of conflict sometimes led them to make decisions bureaucratically, based on hierarchical position rather than on an open clash of fact-based views. Although they appeared more autocratic, the Germans were arguably the more democratic decision makers, for the *meister*'s decision was transparent and based on clear business logic and all available information.

The Swedish and German approaches to product development also differed, owing to their economic histories. Since much of their business was export—going to Middle Eastern, Latin American, and Southeast Asian countries where the products had to withstand the heat and be easy to repair by local people—the Swedes were used to producing robust, easy-to-service electrical-energy products that could withstand rough climates. Furthermore, since the Swedish engineers knew a lot more about the products than their customers did, they decided what the customer needed. They joked that if the customer is king in the industrialized world, the King is the customer in some of the Middle Eastern countries they served.

The Germans produced more complex products for domestic use, and their customers were typically electrical engineers with advanced degrees who knew as much as they did about the products. Since they were producing for a highly developed industrial infrastructure rather than for developing countries, the keys to success were zero outages and continual quality improvement, a strong German value.

No wonder the Swedes and Germans misunderstood each other. They found common ground, however, in their distrust of the Swiss, complaining that they often reneged on agreements. Furthermore, Swiss costs were out of control. It turned out that one of the reasons that Swiss managers sometimes asked to change an agreement stemmed from the fact that they all were in the army reserve, and a subordinate at work might be a superior at the military camp. It was considered best to get agreement from everyone to avoid making powerful enemies. But sometimes after one manager had made an agreement, another disagreed with it, which meant the issue would have to be reconsidered. As for costs, the Swiss were used to customizing expensive energy solutions for different cantons. As with Swiss banks and hotels, Swiss quality at ABB proved expensive.

The Americans were different from the others. They had factories that mass-produced products for very competitive markets. Their margins were thin, and they focused on cost control. Organized in traditional industrial bureaucratic hierarchies with much less job security than the Europeans, the Americans were politically astute about which leader they needed to follow. And in this Swedish-controlled company, they did not make waves. They were not going to be anybody's problem.

By describing and discussing these differences, ABB managers cleared up a lot of distrust and miscommunication. They clarified how decisions should be made, and they encouraged more of the German style of open debate, which moved them toward an interactive style of collaboration.

European managers, especially those at the top who have a bureaucratic social character, continue to struggle with cultural differences. A Financial Times survey of 200 CEOs in France, Germany, and the United Kingdom found that German managers, just like the ones at ABB, supported constructive conflict. French CEOs boasted of making decisions without having to listen to subordinate views.[7] This is in the tradition of the graduates of France's grandes écoles, especially the École Nationale d'Administration, who move between the public and private sectors with an attitude of superiority and entitlement. French CEOs who run family firms never have to answer to outside directors.

Even if French CEOs wanted to be more collaborative, they'd have a hard time getting subordinates to play along. One of my students at the executive program run by the Säid Business School at Oxford University and HEC Paris moved from IBM, where he led a collaborative team, to become CEO of a French company. Even though he asked his direct reports to call him by his first name, they insisted on addressing him as "*Monsieur le président.*"

The U.K. CEOs cited in the survey claimed they liked to be challenged. In my experience in the United Kingdom, however, the openness of British managers to new ideas depends on how secure they feel. Certainly, unlike the French, they don't want to look like autocrats; and the British enjoy making fun of puffed-up leaders.

Lindahl later sent me to nine Asian countries to find out how local managers and expatriates viewed strategy, organization, and one another.[8] Besides asking about these factors, I asked two other questions: "What is your view of a good manager?" and "What is your view of a good father?" The answers were always related—a good manager was similar to a good father. But there was a sharp divide between the responses of Westerners and those of many Asians.

The Westerners, Americans and Scandinavians in particular, viewed good fathers and good managers as people who were helpful when needed but who generally granted their followers autonomy. By contrast, the Asians— especially the ethnic Chinese in Taiwan, Singapore, and Indonesia—wanted a father-manager who protected them and taught them: a benevolent despot. In return, they would give the leader complete loyalty and obedience. Not surprisingly, these Asians also experienced Western leaders as bad parents who woefully neglected their children. However, young managers from Beijing, where the Cultural Revolution had broken traditional family patterns, responded more like Interactives. They described the ideal leader as a good basketball coach who put people into the right roles, promoted teamwork, and knew how to adapt strategy to changing competition.[9]

Differences between the West and much of the East are further amplified by the decline of parental authority in the United States and Western Europe. Managers from many Asian and Eastern European companies come from traditional families and, thus, tend to develop paternal transferences. Therefore, they often find it difficult to interact with American organizations that increasingly are motivated by maternal and sibling transferences. And Westerners often fail to appreciate Asian and East European organizations' need for leaders who reward loyalty with paternal support.

Global managers face a huge challenge in leading people that they don't see—people who operate in different time zones, may speak little or none of their language, and have different cultural values. The Interactives—who from age 10 or 11 have been in touch with global correspondents—will, I believe, be a lot more comfortable with global management. Furthermore, global business, the Internet, and video games are creating common values at work and are shaping the interactive social character. At a seminar on changing organizations that I attended, one interactive software expert remarked that leaders should forget about trying to deal with different personal values and, instead, get everyone to sign on to a common purpose and organizational values. That's good advice.

Meanwhile, researchers try to provide global managers with guidebooks on cultural differences. The pioneer in this field is Geert Hofstede, who in the 1970s surveyed IBM employees in 64 countries. While Hofstede reported suggestive differences on four (later increased to five) dimensions, he advised, "to understand management in a country, one should have both knowledge of and empathy with the entire local scene." Hofstede cites history and novels to describe the context of the dimensions he used, a good practice.[10]

When I consulted in Finland to Nokia, Cultor, and Ahlstrom, I was advised to read *The Unknown Soldier*, a novel by Väinö Linna about the Continuation War between Finland and the Soviet Union, told from the viewpoint of Finnish soldiers. One of the Finnish officers in the book is distant and arrogant, hated by the soldiers who only grudgingly follow him. Another is modest and brave, lives just like the troops, leads them into battle, and is unquestionably followed. This is the ideal for a Finnish CEO—to be a role model, not a father figure. But there are problems when an admired leader is followed without question and followers don't disagree with the boss, even when they think he's wrong.

Hofstede recognizes the limitations of findings based on responses to surveys. On their own, they lack context, and none of the studies I've seen takes account of social character differences among subcultures within countries. Furthermore, a statistically significant correlation may explain only a small percentage of the variance in the responses to survey questions. (These studies report product-moment correlations that, when squared, show the percentage of the variance explained. For example, a correlation of 0.5 may be highly significant, meaning it could occur by chance alone less than once in 100 samples or more, but only accounts for 25 percent of the variance, leaving 75 percent unaccounted for). If this seems too academic, we can just say that these correlations are suggestive about cultural differences but leave much unexplained. And it bears repeating that correlations don't prove causality.

## PERSONALITY TYPES—HOW WE ARE LIKE MANY OTHERS

Social character is the part of learned personality shared by people in a culture or social class. To understand the people you work with and determine which roles they'll best fit, you'll have to focus on individual motivational value systems that are variations of the social character.

Companies typically seek employees who demonstrate behavioral strengths, positive patterns of behavior. The Gallup organization offers a useful inventory of strengths that combine elements of genetic and learned traits and talents.[11] But these behavioral traits—like "achiever," "command," creating "harmony," "woo" (win others over), or being "strategic"— can be performed in different ways with different motivations. For example, achievers can be obsessive perfectionists aiming to be the best at their game, like Roger Federer, or driven to change the world with their products and create a new game, like Steve Jobs. A skillful wooer may be caring, seductive, or inspirational. Although it's good to focus on strengths, we increase our Personality Intelligence by understanding the underlying motivational value systems driving those strengths.

There is little agreement among psychologists about how best to describe individual personality. Each psychological theory views personality from a somewhat different angle. That's understandable, since we are dealing with interpretations of complex behavior patterns, emotional attitudes, and experience. Psychologists do agree, however, on five genetically influenced personality traits that can be observed from infancy on. These traits of temperament, called the Big Five, are:

- Openness to experience, curiosity, interest in variety versus sameness
- Agreeableness versus suspiciousness

- Emotional stability or resilience versus emotional instability or neuroticism
- Conscientiousness, self-discipline, and sticking with a task versus being easily distracted
- Extraversion versus introversion[12]

Although these five factors show strong correlations in almost all personality research, they do not explain motivation or describe practical personality types.[13]

Another approach to personality, based on Carl Jung's theories, describes "archetypes" that leaders can take on, such as "wise king," "magician," "nurturer," or "warrior."[14] (Franklin Delano Roosevelt, for instance, thought of himself at different times as a magician, a warrior, and a quarterback.) Some of these archetypes are similar to roles in games like *World of Warcraft*, so popular with Interactives. These roles appeal more or less to the different personality types observed by Sigmund Freud and Erich Fromm that I describe in my book on narcissistic leaders. I'll briefly review the four types here.[15] Freud named them *erotic, obsessive,* and *narcissistic,* and Fromm added *marketing*. I have renamed them according to their positive qualities as *caring, exacting, visionary,* and *adaptive*. Elias Porter renamed them according to positive qualities in term of colors: *blue* (altruistic-nurturing), green (analytic-autonomizing), *red* (assertive–directing), and *the hub*, a mixture of colors termed flexible-cohering. Keep in mind that no one is a pure type, but while we are all mixes, one type usually dominates a personality. Also, each type has positive or productive potentials, as well as negative or unproductive potentials that can result in personality disorders. Each type can be either good or bad.[16]

The productive, caring blue (which Freud called erotic) type is a helper: cooperative, idealistic, communicative—the kind of person who stimulates love and supports others. The unproductive ones are dependent, needy for love, and gossipy. They tend to avoid conflict and to exaggerate their emotional reactions. Freud writes that erotics "are dominated by the fear of loss of love and are therefore especially dependent on others who may withhold their love from them."[17] Professionals of this type are likely to be found in healthcare, education, and the arts. I've also found them in staff roles in companies, where they often attach themselves as helpers to top executives. We have also found them in leadership roles in the military where their helpful attitude gains collaboration.

The productive, exacting green (which Freud called obsessive) type is inner-directed with a strong sense of responsibility and high standards, conscientious, and reliable. The unproductive ones are nit-picking, over-controlling, stubborn, and stingy, demonstrating the elements of what Freud termed the anal character. Productive exacting people can be effective in leadership roles in the professions and industry, especially when the challenge is efficiency or cost cutting, but less so when there is a need for innovation. When they also have some blue caring characteristics, they have the motivation of good physicians and coaches.

Freud drew a distinction between narcissism, the drive for survival that we all have, and the narcissistic personality. Without a dose of narcissism we wouldn't value ourselves any more than anyone else. Although any personality type can have an excess of narcissism in the form of egoism or hubris, with success the narcissistic personality is more vulnerable than other types to getting puffed up. That's because narcissists care less than the other types about what others think of them. They answer mainly to their own internal ideal self. Fromm called this type exploitative, and Porter called it assertive-directing (red), but both are based on Freud's narcissistic personality type.

Freud describes the narcissistic personality as "independent and not open to intimidation. The ego has a large amount of aggressiveness at its disposal, which also manifests itself in a readiness for activity . . . People belonging to this type impress others as being 'personalities', they are especially suited to act as a support for others, to take on the role of leaders and to give a fresh stimulus to cultural development or to damage the established state of affairs."[18]

Narcissists, and Freud saw himself as one, have not internalized parental models. Lacking a strong superego that programs a moral code, they are free to write their own. The gifted and productive ones are visionaries: innovators, independent thinkers who want to project their vision onto the world and are the type best able to inspire followers with their passionate conviction.

Unproductive narcissistic traits are arrogance, grandiosity, not listening to others, paranoid sensitivity to threats, extreme competitiveness, and unbridled ambition and aggressiveness. These traits have undermined narcissistic leaders—witness those who have gone from great success to disaster, like Napoleon and Hitler.

When Freud observed personalities in the early 20th century, obsessives were the dominant type, the model for character development. This was because their personality type fit hand in glove with the social character formed in the era of craft and bureaucratic-industrial production. But as the mode of production and its cultural frame shifted to service and knowledge work, a new personality type was formed by the new conditions. Fromm termed this chameleon-like type the marketing personality. It is the dominant personality type of the interactive social character.

The productive adaptive hub (flexible-cohering) type combines independence with interactivity. Flexible to the point of being protean, these individuals are decisive when adapting to changing situations. Negative traits include: lack of a center, insincerity, disloyalty, and superficiality. Like narcissists, they lack a strong superego because they don't identify strongly with parental figures, but their moral code is continually programmed and reprogrammed by groups they consider essential for their success. The effectiveness of a leader with a marketing personality depends greatly on the quality of the leader's close colleagues, since hub adaptives tend to form their views interactively, shaping them to what they think leads to success.

Why do we suggest using these psychoanalytic types rather than simpler behavioral types? There are two reasons. First, although behavioral typologies like introvert versus extrovert describe observable traits, these are inborn elements of temperament, not motivational values. And behavioral patterns like the Gallup strengths discussed earlier don't predict how or why these strengths will be expressed. Although the psychoanalytic types may be influenced by inborn personality traits, they are mainly formed in the socialization process. Each type expresses a particular constellation of universal human needs or emotionally energized values: motivational systems shaped in the stages of development described in Chapter 7. The genius of Freud included the ability to think systemically, to connect dynamic behavioral traits with types of motivational value systems. Each psychological type describes the interaction of universal motivational patterns—fight-flight, attachment, play-mastery, pleasure-pain, exploration— but each type shuffles these differently, with one or another element dominant. Furthermore, Freud worked at describing how these types develop in childhood. Although some of his descriptions are partial or unconvincing, they open up an area for further research of the sort reported in the Fromm-Maccoby study of the Mexican village.

Clearly, personality types should be viewed through the lens of social character. For example, the green obsessive personality takes on a different form in the peasant, craftsman, bureaucratic, and interactive social character frames. The cautious and frugal farmer, the precise and hierarchical professional, and the expert and precise interactive knowledge worker all share obsessive values of mastery, autonomy, and hard work. All have tendencies to be over-controlling, compulsively clean, and frugal. But they use different tools and master different modes of production with different roles, rules, and relationships. They have internalized different cultural values. The hub marketing personality isn't found in traditional peasant villages where identities are firmly rooted in family and place. It was formed in the post-industrial culture, where all types take on its elements of flexibility and interactivity. Given this relationship between individual personality and social character, the social character might also be called the cultural personality, a macro personality that both frames and colors all the micro personality types within a culture.

The second reason I suggest using these psychoanalytic types is that I've observed them in my clinical work as a psychoanalyst and in supervising other therapists. The types were useful both in my research on Mexican villagers and my study of corporate managers. Furthermore, in applying the questionnaire based on these types in leadership workshops, my students, colleagues, and I have been able to understand and predict styles of leadership. Not surprisingly, we've found that high-tech entrepreneurs who take the big risks are red narcissistic visionaries, the executives who squeeze efficiencies out of every process in production companies are green exacting-obsessives, and professionals who customize their services and sell their personalities are often hub adaptive types.[19] Furthermore, these types are consistent with the observations of such diverse analysts as Machiavelli and Jack Welch about fitting personalities to leadership roles.

When I've used valid and reliable personality assessments, such the Strength Deployment Inventory (presented in Chapter 6) with executive teams, the result has been a more open conversation. For example, the vice presidents of one executive team complained that the CFO didn't respond to their queries. The CFO's questionnaire showed that he was a blue caring helper, but his interest in helping was directed solely to the CEO, who he saw as a father figure. As a result of a discussion about this, which brought to light an attitude that the CFO had not been aware of, stronger links were forged between the CFO and the vice presidents. Furthermore, the CFO came to understand why he'd so often felt insufficiently appreciated by his boss: The CFO had been unconsciously experiencing his boss as an uncaring father he was desperately trying to please.

In these conversations about personality, team members have become more interactive, I asked Tony Barclay, then CEO of DAI, a global development consultancy, what impact sharing the results of the personality assessment had made on his team. He said, "We began to talk to each other in a different way and ultimately to be more direct with each other. It saved time." Barclay added that the process of discovery also sensitized executives to differences in cognitive style. "Some people respond to new proposals right away. Others need time to digest them," he explained. "If you respect that and don't judge it as stubbornness, you sometimes get better results by waiting a while until they come back with their views."[20]

## IDENTITIES—HOW WE ARE DEFINED AND DEFINE OURSELVES

We'd like to think that we alone define ourselves and that we decide how others see us. But from an early age, others define us as well, by how we look and where we're from. Later, talents and achievements are added to how we are seen. As we grow older, we start to define ourselves. Our cultures influence how we shape our identities. In the pre-industrial era, people identified with family above all, and then with place and religion. Recent developments in Iraq and Syria have shown that when there is a breakdown of law and order, people revert to family, tribal, and religious identities as their only refuge in the midst of civil war.

In the United States, like in other countries, people take national identity as a given. They are Americans, and feel a sense of identity with other Americans when they meet them abroad. This feeling can be even stronger if they are from the same area or went to the same school. But American identity is younger than that of other nations with a longer history. After the Revolutionary War, many in the former British colonies only reluctantly accepted the new American identity, and the Southerners fighting the Civil War in the early 1860s were ready to discard it. But just as U.S. national identity was threatened by the Civil War, so World War I and World War II strengthened it, when most Americans shared a powerful purpose.

Despite the creation of the European Union (EU), some citizens of the member nations resist a common identity. In some European countries—for example, Italy with its north-south differences, Spain with its separatist Basques and Catalans, regional identities still compete strongly with national identity. And in the U.K. after Brexit, people in Scotland and Northern Ireland debate about remaining a part of Great Britain.

During the bureaucratic-industrial age, people started to identify with the companies, unions, and professional associations that gave them a sense of security and status. Asked to describe themselves, managers of major companies would invariably mention the company (for example, "I'm an IBMer"). To be sure, family, place, and religion remained part of their identity, and identifications were sometimes expanded to include membership in fraternities, service organizations, schools, and colleges, especially those that added to the person's sense of importance.

Compared with the interactive social character whose sense of identity can be protean, the bureaucratic social character is strongly attached to an identity. Rather than identifying with a company, Interactives identify with a project, mission, sport, or consumer group. They practice shaping their identity to get them a job or get a date on the Internet. Identities can even be malleable or serve multiple purposes; for instance, a tweep can mean a Twitter employee, a person who sends tweets, or a person who follows another Twitter member.

The identities of the bureaucratic social character are essentially individualistic and vertical, like military ranks, buttressed by identification with parents or other authority figures. Interactive identities are more fluid and horizontal, moving among and between identifications with siblings and peers, often combining meaning with self-interest, cultural identification with political agenda.

In this new age of diverse identities at work, we risk confusing cultural-social character differences with identity interest groups. Kwame Anthony Appiah, a philosopher, points out that identity groups can include people from very different cultures with a variety of individual values. He argues, "the diversity that preoccupies us is really a matter not so much of cultures as of identities."[21]

But identities differ according to how deeply they are rooted in our personalities, and a characteristic of Interactives is their ability to tailor their identity for different settings. Sometimes people choose to belong to an identity group at work, like unions and professional societies, mainly because the group promises to gain privileges for them. People may choose to identify themselves with ethnic groups like Hispanics, a name that corresponds to no particular country and that covers people who don't even come from the same culture or even necessarily speak

Spanish. In terms of social character, a Mexican villager may be more like a Serbian or Indian villager than like a professional from Mexico City or Havana. But people with a family background from a Latin American country can choose whether or not to take on a Hispanic identity in the United States, especially if that gives them some advantage.[22]

By satisfying the demands of identity groups, leaders don't necessarily gain willing followers. But if these identities are not respected, leaders will be less willingly followed, and possibly resisted. In a democratic society, we enjoy the right to have multiple loyalties, based on multiple identifications, while in an autocratic society, and in some companies that are autocratically led, those in power are threatened by loyalties to any group other than the regime.

Keep in mind that group identities can be extremely powerful when attached to deep human needs for respect and support from people we can trust to care about us. Identities can be powerful motivators because they provide meaning for our lives. This is especially true when we feel that an identity determines our friends and enemies. When an identity gives us a feeling of security and pride, any attack on identity is a blow to self-esteem, even a threat to survival. Clashes between religious, racial, and tribal identities continue to ignite bloody conflicts, especially in those societies that have not developed institutions that provide security and strengthen trust. Understanding people must take account of their group identity

Effective leaders create group identities for organizations and teams. Of course, this is easier if the team is winning or the company is admired. Then people are proud to be identified with the organization. But leaders will be better able to create successful teams and organizations if they communicate an organizational philosophy, a purpose and set of values that inspire and engage people. The leaders we need will not only produce products and services that improve lives. They will also develop collaborative learning organizations rather than rigid bureaucracies.

Our identity or sense of self changes as we grow up and grapple with the psychosocial challenges of developing relationships at school, work, play, and home. In the process of shaping our identity, we are developing our philosophy of life, the purpose and values that direct our energy and give meaning to our behavior, forming our personality. The most developed personalities are given meaning by a consciously developed philosophy that defines us and creates a basis for others to trust us.

## INTELLECTUAL SKILLS—HOW WE THINK

In traditional bureaucracies, not much attention was paid to styles of thinking. Some people were considered brighter than others, quicker at solving puzzles and citing facts, with their analytic intelligence measured via IQ tests. Recruiters judged job applicants' intelligence mainly on the basis of their grades. In the knowledge workplace, analytic intelligence is still necessary, but not sufficient on its own. Effective leaders also have different types of intelligence, such as creative intelligence, including systems thinking; practical intelligence; and Personality Intelligence. To place people in roles where they will be most effective, particularly in knowledge work, a leader needs to know their talents, intellectual qualities and motivational value system. In this book we focus on understanding the motivational value systems of leaders and followers. We recognize, however, that to fully understand people, intellectual qualities and talents are also important.

To understand the people we want to follow us or collaborate with us concepts like identity, social character, and personality are valuable cognitive tools. But even though they can sensitize us about people's values and patterns of relatedness we can't really know other people or experience them directly unless we are also fully present with them, listening with our hearts. Otherwise, even when people smile and nod their heads, we won't know whether their enthusiasm is real or their feelings are really positive; when they cry, we won't know whether they are sad or furious. To understand others, we have to listen actively, using the conceptual framework presented in this chapter as a context to understand what we see, hear, and experience.

Clearly, the diversity of identities and personalities complicates leadership for the knowledge workplace, particularly since leaders can no longer count on the bureaucratic character's paternal transferences. Interactives seem to grasp this and to recognize that the capability to understand differences in culture and personality is essential for effective collaboration in knowledge work.

Leadership development in the age of knowledge work requires continual learning, especially learning about self and others to create collaboration and avoid destructive conflict. Chapter 6 will describe in more detail what it takes to apply Personality Intelligence in the workplace.

CHAPTER 6

# Applying Personality Intelligence

*by Tim Scudder*

THE WORKPLACE IS BECOMING increasingly diverse with global teams, different age groups, a narrowing gender gap, and all other types of diversity that can enrich organizations by including the diverse perspectives shaped by different life experiences. But leading a diverse group is a challenge. And diversity of personality—with our different motives, drives and methods of responding to conflict—can make it even more difficult if we do not have a common language for understanding personality types. Does knowledge of personality make it any easier for leaders? Yes. But leaders need to start with self-awareness, which is the pre-requisite to understanding others. In this chapter, I'll give you some examples of how personality affects strategy, leading teams, and resolving conflict—and how personality intelligence makes leaders more effective in these areas.

Personality is an enduring set of traits that define the character of a person and help to highlight similarities and differences between people.[1] Chapter 5 introduced different elements of personality: social character, personality type, identity, temperament, and intellectual skills. This book focuses on the dynamic patterns of motives and values that become personality types, because these drive behavior in all different contexts and situations.

Freud viewed personality through a lens of motives and drives.[2] His personality types, further developed by Erich Fromm[3], were advanced by Michael Maccoby in a leadership context[4] and Elias Porter, using a whole-life perspective.[5] My own work and research has built on this foundation and focused on integrating the whole person within their social and organizational contexts.[6] The Strength Deployment Inventory (SDI), which is based on Porter's theory of Relationship Awareness, has proven to be extremely useful in helping millions of people create a common language about motives and personality differences.[7]

**TABLE 6-1**

## Comparative Personality Typologies

| Freud | Fromm | Maccoby | Porter | SDI |
|---|---|---|---|---|
| Three normal types, based on psychoanalysis | Four non-productive orientations of adults in society | Four productive types with an emphasis on leadership | Seven productive types | Seven motivational value systems |
| Erotic | Receptive | Caring | Altruistic-Nurturing | Blue (people) |
| Narcissistic | Exploitative | Visionary | Assertive-Directing | Red (performance) |
| Obsessive | Hoarding | Exacting | Analytic-Autonomizing | Green (process) |
|  | Marketing | Adaptive | Flexible-Cohering | Hub (three drives about equal) |
| Recognition of blended types | Recognition of blended types | Combinations of above types, based on dominant and secondary types | Assertive-Nurturing | Red-Blue (two drives about equal) |
|  |  |  | Judicious-Competing | Red-Green (two drives about equal) |
|  |  |  | Cautious-Supporting | Blue-Green (two drives about equal) |
| Personality differences between productive state and conflict state are not described | | | Two states of personality: going well and conflict | Related typology of conflict sequences |

**FIGURE 6-1**

## SDI Triangle

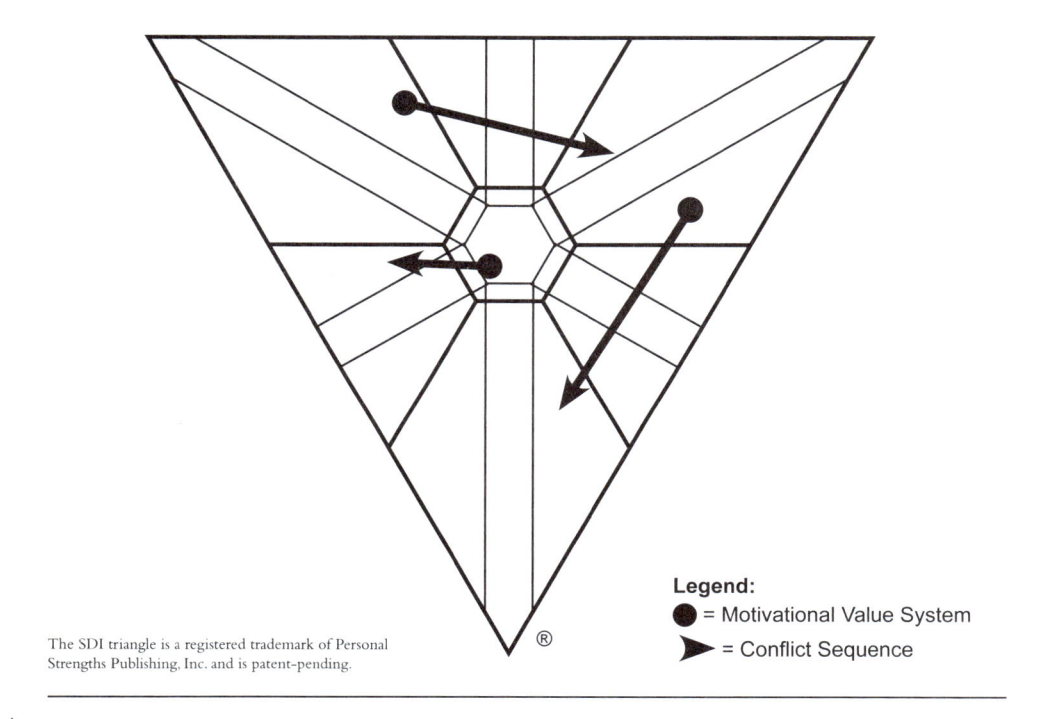

Legend:
● = Motivational Value System
▶ = Conflict Sequence

The SDI triangle is a registered trademark of Personal Strengths Publishing, Inc. and is patent-pending.

The SDI, outlined in Table 1, shows the relative balance of drives (or motivational values in this theory), which we will simplify and make easy to remember with 3 Ps: People, Performance, and Process. To describe a drive to help people, Freud, Fromm, Maccoby, and Porter used the following terms respectively: erotic, receptive, caring, and nurturant. Regarding the performance drive we see the terms: narcissistic, exploitative, narcissistic/visionary, and directive (again respectively). Regarding the process drive: obsessive, hoarding, exacting, and autonomizing.

These three primary drives, when color-coded and juxtaposed on the SDI triangle, make it possible to create pictures of personalities and relationships. Blue=people, Red=performance, and Green=process. Each dot represents the blend of motives when things are going well for a person and each arrowhead represents a sequential activation of motives when a person feels a conflict or threat to their self-worth or dignity. There are seven distinct Motivational Value System (MVS) types on the SDI triangle, and the center (the hexagonal Hub type) is similar to what Fromm described as the marketing orientation and Maccoby described as the adaptive leader.

Now that we have a basic working definition of personality and a common language (a typology), let's take a look at how personality influences organizations, starting with the way personality affects leaders' views of organizational purpose. Then we'll look at personality's affect on leadership team development, accountability, expectations, change and conflict, leadership philosophy, and communication.

## PERSONALITY AND ORGANIZATIONAL PURPOSE

Consider PayPal. In mid 2015, PayPal had recently been spun off from eBay and was an independent organization again. I had the SDI results for all the leaders in the program and asked them to form groups, based on the seven Motivational Value System (MVS) types described by the SDI. In their groups, I asked them to respond to several questions and prompts, including this: "What is the purpose of PayPal?" In other words, why does PayPal exist? What fundamental problem is PayPal trying to solve – or what fundamental opportunity is PayPal trying to seize?

A purpose differs from a mission because a purpose cannot be accomplished, it is a more enduring drive for an organization, such as to prolong life or improve the quality of life, or to be prepared for natural disasters, or to provide liquidity to financial markets, or to preserve natural beauty for future generations. None of these purposes can ever be check-marked as "done"; a clear purpose provides a sustainable reason for an organization's existence. It describes why a business gains and retains customers.

How did these leaders' personalities affect their views of PayPal's purpose? The Green, Analytic-Autonomizing, leaders described the purpose as connecting people to the goods and services they need – a utilitarian purpose that is consistent with the conservative, practical nature of the Green MVS. The Red, Assertive-Directing, leaders described the purpose as being the platform of choice for all financial needs – a more ambitious and high-visibility statement that is consistent with the achievement orientation and competitive nature of the Red MVS. The Blue, Altruistic-Nurturing, leaders described the purpose as enabling safe, secure, and friction-free payments — a purpose that has an element of protecting people and preventing conflicts, which is consistent with the supportive, conflict-averse nature of the Blue MVS. And the Hub, Flexible-Cohering, leaders described the purpose as connecting people with each other through money exchange — a purpose that focuses on including people and is consistent with the interactive nature of the Hub MVS.

Why do these differences matter? In times of change, such as PayPal's new independence from eBay, leaders' personalities may subconsciously influence their assumptions about the purpose of their organization. If the diverse personalities in a leadership team all have different assumptions about the purpose, it will be difficult to get consensus on strategy and tactics. Leaders do not always have an opportunity to shape the purpose of an organization, but they always have the opportunity to consider how the organization's purpose is personally meaningful to them.

PayPal's website states: "We believe that by transforming money, we're powering the potential of people all around the world." People in each MVS group connect to this shared purpose in different ways. In summary: Blues are most likely to connect to PayPal's ability to reduce risk and build trust between people; Reds connect to PayPal's speed, performance, and growth; Greens connect to PayPal's clarity of process and utility; and Hubs connect to PayPal's versatility and ability to build a community. When leaders are aware of the ways people with different MVS types connect to a shared purpose, they can communicate the shared purpose in a way that helps each person connect to their intrinsic motives and values. This connection sparks people's initiative; they've tapped their intrinsic motives, and increased their willingness to do what needs to be done.

## PERSONALITIES AND LEADERSHIP TEAM DYNAMICS

The ideal of the sole leader who knows all the answers is a holdover from the bureaucratic era. In the knowledge/interactive era, leadership teams are the norm. Teams, even more so than individual leaders, need to apply personality intelligence to work effectively together and to become high-performing teams. Classic models of team development, such as Tuckman's forming-storming-norming-performing model,[8] take on new life when individual differences in motives and values are considered.

To see how this plays out, we need a brief overview of this model, because the single, rhyming words for each stage do not carry the full meaning of the concepts. First a caveat, team members can do their jobs in any stage of the model, task accomplishment is not limited to the performing stage.

The *forming* stage is characterized by tentativeness and uncertainty; it's a getting-to-know-you stage and a team reverts to this stage anytime a member is added or removed. The unfortunately named storming stage does not necessarily imply conflict; rather, it is characterized by a free exchange of ideas and testing of assumptions, as in brainstorming. The *norming* stage is where teams clarify and document their shared assumptions create their internal rules, or norms, about how to work together. The performing stage assumes that a team has successfully made it through the norming stage, although many teams never really do. The *performing* stage is characterized by highly motivated, self-directed, and accountable people who enjoy their work and their working relationships. One way to test whether a team has truly reached the performing stage is if they want to work on future projects together.

Given the importance of the performing stage, it's no wonder that organizations spend a lot of energy trying to get teams, especially leadership teams, to this stage. With one team of high-potential leaders at GEI Consultants, a US-based environmental engineering firm, I asked the team members to form groups based on the MVS results of the SDI—then to describe what they would need to be able to move between each of the stages of team development. This idea of moving between stages is a systems thinking concept. Rather than having them describe the static and independent stages, I challenged them to describe the movement and connections between stages. Here are some highlights:

*To Move from Forming to Storming.*

The Blues and Blue-Greens said they needed to understand each other, to feel included and wanted, and to have a sense of each team member's strengths. On the opposite side of the triangle, the Reds and Red-Greens said they needed to know the challenge or problem to be solved – or that they felt pretty comfortable going straight into Storming without much time devoted to the Forming stage. Meanwhile, the Hubs said that they needed to feel comfortable with the group and to have a sense of commitment to the group.

Not surprisingly, many teams never get fully through the forming stage and into the storming stage. When this happens, teams can find themselves playing it safe, not challenging assumptions, and performing below their potential. Personalities can get in the way; if the Blues want to feel included first, while the Reds want to define the goals first, the Blues may find themselves reluctantly going along with the Reds' goals just so they can feel included, but they may not feel fully engaged.

*To Move from Storming to Norming.*

Leaders with MVS dots on the top-half of the SDI triangle (the Blues, Red-Blues, and Reds) all said they wanted some form of brainstorming or idea generation in order the make the transition. However, those with MVS dots on the lower portion of the triangle (with higher scores in the Green, process-oriented motive) wanted additional clarity on roles and decision-making criteria. The Hubs talked about needing to create a shared vision and getting consensus.

This transition, from the Storming phase to the Norming phase, is where teams need to set up the ground-rules for interaction. When some try to get there by establishing criteria for decisions, while others want to just try something and see if it works, it can be difficult to reach consensus. Clarity about what people are looking for in the process improves communication and understanding. Awareness of team members personalities helps the team progress more quickly through these stages.

*To Move from Norming to Performing.*

Leaders with Blue and Blue-Green MVSs talked about the need for support, sharing the workload, and continued communication. But those with Red and Red-Green MVSs said they needed clear work assignments and demonstrable progress in order to feel that the team could truly enter the performing stage.

A benefit of getting into the performing stage, especially in project environments, is that team members typically want to work together on future projects. They also tend to be more committed to the work and hold themselves and each other accountable for outcomes.

## PERSONALITY AND ACCOUNTABILITY

When people talk about accountability, they are usually talking about management skills such as delegating tasks, following up, and creating incentives or consequences. While these techniques may secure compliance, they do not necessarily create accountability. Accountability comes from choices. And when these choices are made in a way that feels consistent with people's core motives, with their personalities, people make commitments and take responsibility for outcomes. They are then more likely to innovate, take risks, and challenge assumptions while they attempt to deliver on commitments. When people make free choices, they feel more accountable for the results of their choices.[9]

The opposite experience helps to clarify the point. Think for a moment about the times when you've done something that you did not feel you freely chose to do, i.e. because you "had to" or when someone else "made you" do something. If it doesn't work out, don't you tend to assign responsibility to the person, constraint, or system that "made you" do it? When we feel that our actions are constrained or dictated, we don't feel accountable for the results of our actions. When we are not involved in the choice about what to do we don't feel liable for the consequences. Conversely, when we feel that we have freely chosen our behavior, we do so with our goals and motives in mind. We're striving for something and we put ourselves into it.

Leaders and managers who are looking for more accountability often increase the amount of control they use with followers. But an over-emphasis on a control-oriented approach tends to generate compliance or defiance, followers ignoring the directives. Either way, an over-controlling approach causes dependence in followers, who can simply wait to be told what to do and how to do it. Followers are then alienated from their sense of choice and do not feel accountable for outcomes if they are just "doing what they're told."

A choice-oriented approach can also be overused. While the intent of a choice-oriented approach is to involve people, to get them to collaborate in the decision-making process, too much latitude can also create an intolerable level of uncertainty for both leaders and followers. Since choice promotes accountability, collaborative choices create a shared sense of accountability, while unbridled choice gets people feeling accountable only for themselves—not for what the organiza-

**FIGURE 6-2**

## Approaches to Accountability

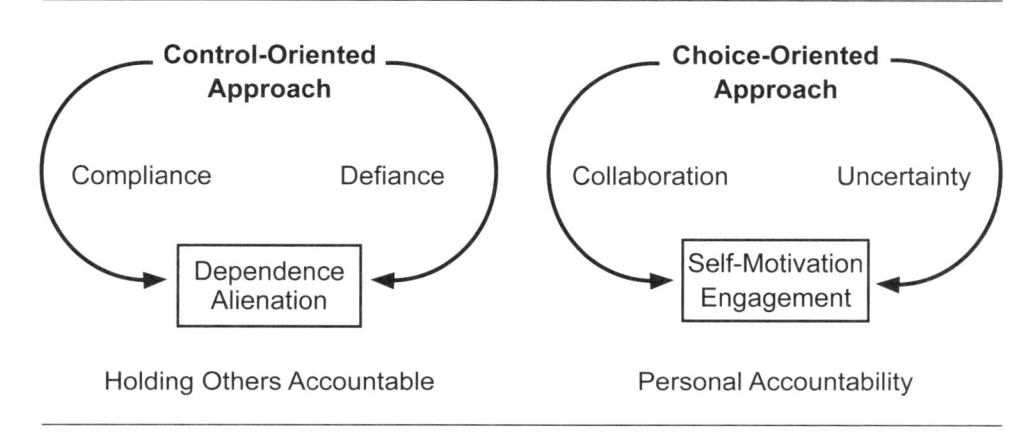

**Control-Oriented Approach**
- Compliance
- Defiance
- → Dependence / Alienation

Holding Others Accountable

**Choice-Oriented Approach**
- Collaboration
- Uncertainty
- → Self-Motivation / Engagement

Personal Accountability

---

tion needs. Another risk with over-reliance on a choice-oriented approach is that leaders may assume followers have the necessary skills and resources, therefore overlooking training needs or other constraints.

One of the most effective techniques for managers and leaders who want to create sustainable accountability is to offer bounded choice. For example, a leader may set a constraint or expectations such as a budget, deadline, or deliverable, but offer some individual choice about how to work within the constraints that are important to the task, project, or organization.

A personal example may help to illustrate the point. My daughter had two dolls of about the same size. One was an expensive gift. The other she bought with some money that I gave her. Technically, both of the dolls were gifts, because she did not earn the money to buy the second doll. However, after I gave her the money (the amount was my decision) she made the decision about which doll to buy. This subtle difference produced a significant difference in the way she cared for these dolls. While we (her parents) had to remind her frequently to put the expensive gift away, she took much better care of the one she bought. In fact the expensive one got damaged due to neglect while the one she bought remained in good condition for as long as she played with dolls.

The intrapersonal dynamics are the same at work – although the choices and responsibilities are considerably more complex. As a leader, once you know what constraints are essential, you can offer your followers choice within those constraints. When followers accept those bounded choices, they make decisions with their own goals and motives in mind and naturally tap into their intrinsic motives.

Different motives can link people in different ways to the same situation or required task. Blue, caring types are more likely to feel a sense of ownership for a situation or task when they see how it will benefit others. Reds take ownership if the goals are challenging or lead to a greater opportunity. Greens take ownership if the situation makes logical sense and there is a clear process or criteria for making decisions. Hubs take ownership if the task will bring people together, secure future flexibility, or create value as uniquely defined by the customer.

## ADJUSTING STRENGTHS IN CONTEXT

A team of leaders at NOAA Fisheries (National Oceanic and Atmospheric Administration) wanted to improve the quality of the workplace, and become a "great place to work." Their purpose is to provide vital services for the US ocean resources and habitat. Practical values include sound science, an ecosystem-based approach to management, and sustainability.

I administered the Strengths Portrait[10] to a group of leaders, and asked a random sample of staff who report to these leaders to complete an expectations edition of the Strengths Portrait. The expectations were to convey the strengths staff need from their leaders in the leader-follower relationship.

Overall, there was a strong positive correlation between the leaders' mainly blue strengths and staff's expectations, which was interpreted as an indication of generally healthy leader-follower relationships. However, there were some significant gaps. Some of these gaps between leaders' strengths and staff expectations caused the leaders to challenge whether expectations were realistic—and other gaps caused them to seek further information to understand the gaps.

To engage leaders in the conversation, I prepared posters, highlighting all significant differences in strength rankings. After I described the differences, I asked people to work in small groups and prepare to present the following:

- What story do these gaps tell?

- What is the meaning of the story?

- What would be the effect if leaders changed the frequency, duration, intensity, or context of these strengths?

Staff said they needed leaders to be more supportive, tolerant, and trusting – and less helpful, loyal, and devoted. While they struggled initially with idea of being more supportive, but less helpful, the message that emerged was insightful: Staff needed leaders who would support them with tools and resources, but not be overly directive about how to do the work. In essence staff were saying that leaders were being too helpful, which could come across as micro-management or give the impression that leaders thought staff were not competent. Staff needed leaders who would give them more autonomy—allow them to be more self-directed and to make their own decisions about how to do their work.

Initially, leaders also struggled with the idea that staff needed them to be less loyal and less devoted. But the meaning of this gap was that staff were saying "Don't work such long hours and send e-mails late at night. Trust us to know what we need to do." They further reflected that over-devotion could appear self-sacrificing, and would make future leadership positions unappealing to some staff—or cause stress or conflict for staff that felt obligated to check e-mail and respond late in the evening.

## PERSONALITY INTELLIGENCE AND CONFLICT

Leadership involves navigating change, sometimes initiating it and sometimes responding to it. Change generates emotions in people, sometimes there are positive responses to needed changes, but sometimes it generates conflict. You can be sure that whatever is changing will in some way be threatening to someone, whether they fear losing something important, or fear the future. The word "conflict" is used to describe a wide range of experiences in the workplace, from simple disagreements to deeply personal struggles. While disagreements, differences of opinions, and contrasting views can be productive and spark innovation, conflict has the potential to turn destructive or to limit effectiveness. Elias Porter was the first to describe and validate the idea of conflict sequences as part of understanding personality. He observed that each person has a tendency to tap into three motives in a somewhat predictable fashion as their focus concentrates. Each conflict sequence is constructed from the nine blocks in Table 6-2, with the caveat that some people do not have a clear sequence and may blend or alternate motives within these stages.

In times of conflict, people feel different and experience their motives in different ways. SDI results shows this difference and describe each person's conflict sequence – the predictable order in which people tend to respond to conflict with attempts to accommodate others, assert themselves, or analyze the situation. When leaders are aware of their own motives in conflict and the motives of others, they are better at anticipating and preventing unnecessary conflicts. And when they understand how motives change in conflict situations they are able to identifying conflict more quickly and accurately so it can be managed and resolved more effectively.[11] Conflict is most effectively managed in stage one (where people see themselves, the problem, and each other). When conflict reaches stage two (where others are not in focus) conflict can become polarizing and lead to shortsighted or self-interested solutions. It has the greatest potential to be destructive in stage three.

**TABLE 6-2**

## Focus and Motives during Three Stages of Conflict

| CONFLICT Stage | FOCUS On | BLUE *Accommodate* | RED *Assert* | GREEN *Analyze* |
| --- | --- | --- | --- | --- |
| 1 | Self, Problem, & Others | Wanting to accommodate others | Wanting to assert oneself | Wanting to analyze the situation |
| 2 | Self & Problem | Wanting to conditionally give in or defer to others | Wanting to prevail against the issue or others | Wanting to disengage from others or clarify the issue |
| 3 | Self | Feeling driven to give up | Feeling driven to fight | Feeling driven to retreat |

Managers and leaders often find themselves mediating conflicts in the workplace; the time spent managing conflict is a significant factor that contributes to overall cost of conflict, which is probably one of the largest preventable costs facing most organizations.[12] Followers may not be able to hear leaders accurately when they are in conflict; they may feel afraid, attacked, excluded, unappreciated, or disregarded. These emotions can act like filters that screen out information and lead to misunderstanding and the ill-informed actions that proceed from these misunderstandings.

At a time when Washington Mutual was experiencing significant growth, their employee-relations department was unable to keep up with the number of problem cases being referred to them by branch managers. Branch managers estimated that they spent close to 40% of their time involved with, or dealing with the effects of, interpersonal conflict. They decided to initiate a conflict management training program for managers that focused on understanding motives during the conflict management process, which Ken Smith and I designed and delivered. They tracked the number of cases being referred from the offices where managers were trained and compared to the baseline and offices where training had not yet been delivered. They found a significant reduction in cases, which means the managers had been able to prevent or manage more of the conflict than they had previously. Since the WaMu system had historical data accessible, the ER leaders were able to assign an average cost to every case—and then document a significant financial return on investment just from the cost savings of fewer cases in the system. Beyond that, managers who applied personality intelligence in their branches experienced higher employee retention than other offices.

A case at a Veterans Administration Healthcare Network facility helps to highlight the cost of conflict and the benefits of its resolution. A team had essentially stopped work and was threatening a formal grievance and possible legal action due to the way they had been treated by their leader. The team agreed to a full-day mediation session where everyone's SDI results would be used to help explore the issue and everyone's motives. By the end of the day, following robust and challenging conversations, the team agreed to rescind the allegations. Additionally, they agreed to let the VA's in-house counsel review the allegations. In-house counsel estimated that the cost to the VA, had the claim gone forward, would have been about $500,000, which is a pretty good return on investment from a one-day training program.

Conflict can also serve to clarify or establish identity. The things we are willing to go into conflict about give clues about our values and beliefs about what is important. Leaders who know their conflict triggers can make them known to followers.

## PERSONALITY INTELLIGENCE AND LEADERSHIP PHILOSOPHY

Every leader has a philosophy, but not every leader takes the time to clarify their philosophy so followers will know how the leader makes decisions and what the leader values. Our personalities influence our philosophies; in fact, one way to think of a developed personality is as a philosophy of life.[13] Our motivational value systems and conflict sequences are given meaning by our philosophies, which affect

**FIGURE 6-3**

## Sample SDI Result

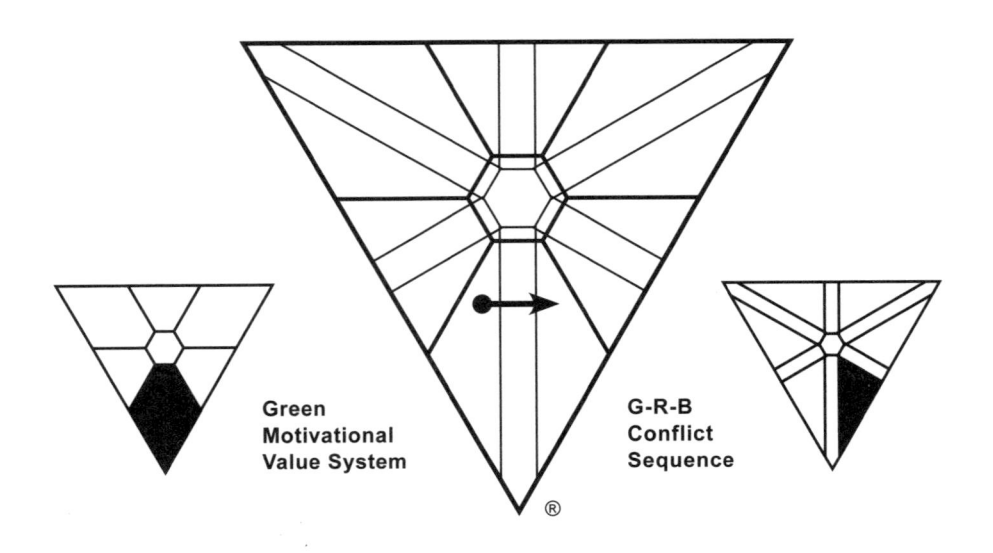

Green Motivational Value System

G-R-B Conflict Sequence

our decisions and actions. They help us to focus on the things that matter to us, and when there is conflict, to protect or defend those things. SDI results can help leaders clarify their philosophies and communicate them consistently. But if leaders do not clarify their philosophies, followers will make up stories about the leaders' philosophies that are based on their perceptions of the leaders.

*Coaching Example*

One leader I coached was concerned about feedback she'd been getting. Many people found her to be intimidating. As she described some of the interactions where she received this feedback, I started to notice a pattern and we looked at her SDI results to see if they would help us sort through her concerns. Her MVS was Green (Analytic-Autonomizing) and her conflict sequence was G–R–B (Green analyzing, followed by strong red assertion, with a blue surrender as a last resort). See figure 6-3.

Here is how I connected her personality to her leadership situations. Note that for ease of reading I've written this like a monologue, but it was really a conversation.

"When things are going well for you in your role, you have a strong concern for process. You want things to be well thought out and to make sense. You prefer situations where things are organized, there is clarity of roles and responsibilities, and you like people to be able to work independently.

"But when some of that process, order, or logic is disregarded or at risk, you are likely to enter your first stage of conflict, which is the green, analytical approach. In this first stage, your motives get even more concentrated on finding a logical explanation or solution. You're looking for information you can use to bring order out what appears chaotic to you. What you really want here is for things to get back on track and to prevent further disruptions. In your first, analytical, stage of conflict you are thinking about the best basis for making a decision and the best method to implement it once the decision is made.

"But this analysis may be done quietly, in fact, the arrowhead is not far from your MVS dot. And when those two points are close together, other people generally have a hard time noticing the change from a going well state into the first stage of conflict. So it's likely that other people don't see much of a difference in you until (or unless) the conflict reaches the second stage.

"In your second stage, your focus is primarily on yourself and your own view of the problem. The second stage is where other people and their concerns get out of focus for you. In second stage red, your assertive and challenging stage, you have all the analysis from your MVS and first stage available to you. The difference is that in second stage you get vocal. It may be that people don't notice all the thought you put into situations and then, when you finally speak up in meetings about the things that are bothering you, you do so with great energy and passion, which probably looks like anger to other people. You use forceful arguments to convey your position, which has already been well prepared and rehearsed in your first stage. When you finally bring all this analysis to the table in your second stage, you are a force to be reckoned with – and you feel that other people are being illogical. In situations where you are in a position of formal authority, your second stage assertion may come across as dictates or directives. The bad news for you is that that's what people see and what they remember. They don't see all the introspection and thought that went into it before hand, because you do that quietly, by yourself.

"Another thing about people with your conflict sequence, Green-Red-Blue, is that they generally do not want to give up. Nobody likes to be pushed to the third stage of conflict. And for you, my guess is that your determination to win in your second stage of red is further fueled by a fear of being pushed into a third stage of conflict, in the Blue, where you would have to surrender. My guess is that you only get to third stage at work in situations where someone else has formal authority over you and that when that happens, you mentally check out, but just go through the motions to comply.

"In summary, if you can't find a way to help other people see your concerns and motives when things are going well and in your first stage of conflict, there's a risk that other people will begin to define you by the way you act in your second stage of conflict. I think that's where the feedback that you're intimidating is coming from."

By the end, she was convinced that she needed to share her SDI results and her leadership philosophy with her team. This does not mean she will stop having conflict. Rather, it's a way to be clear about what is important and to be open about the motives and values that drive her when things are going well and during conflict. The benefit to the team is the ability to see past their own perceptions and assumptions That'll be less likely to be triggered into a wicked-stepmother or fairy-godmother transferences, and more likely to learn what is really driving the actions they were concerned about.

## CME Group Example

Phupinder Gil, the former CEO of CME Group, kicked-off the leadership development programs by sharing his philosophy with the group. At one session I facilitated he opened by reinforcing CME Group's purpose of advancing the global economy and sharing his view of CME Group's context: the regulatory, social, globalization, and internal challenges and opportunities affecting the Chicago Mercantile Exchange, Chicago Board of Trade, NYMEX, and other financial exchanges operated under the CME Group banner. As he discussed the organization's efforts to flatten the organization chart, he emphasized the growing importance of the leader-follower relationship. He challenged the group to always think about what could change, to run scenarios as if there were no constraints, or with more constraints. He said they must always view the organization, their roles, and their relationships as systems, and that when they understand the interconnections, they will become more accountable to others, and others will be more accountable to them.

Gil's self-described strengths as a leader? He gets people to see each other's perspectives, which gets them to know each other's strengths so they can collaborate and get things done. He will listen to anybody, because he is more concerned about what is right than who is right. He's also quite funny. When Gil shares his philosophy it's both inspiring and humanizing. He speaks from the heart, with personality intelligence, and while everyone doesn't always agree with him, they understand what drives him and how he makes decisions.

## Microsoft Example

While consulting with Microsoft, I had the opportunity to observe the moment of transition between the end of Steve Ballmer's tenure as CEO and the beginning of Satya Nadella's time in the role. Bill Gates was also there and the three of them shared the stage. The only three people to have held the CEO role of Microsoft in its 40-year history told the story of the past, present, and future of Microsoft.

It is interesting to think about how each of these leaders' personalities influenced—or will continue to influence—their engagement with the role. While I do not have the SDI results of these three men, they are public enough figures to form a picture of their motivational values. Gates, who I infer has a Red–Green MVS, seems most strongly driven by concerns for both performance and process; his initial vision was based on technical innovation, while Ballmer adapted the innovations to the market. He was most strongly driven by performance, followed by perspective, and sometimes neglected process, which sounds like a Red or Red-Hub MVS, and Nadella seems to me have a Green or Green-Hub MVS; he seems most strongly driven by process and perspective, exacting in his speech and seeming to be acutely aware of context and how to adapt to it. Each leader has held the reins in a different part of the organization's development and faced a different context. Gates' time saw the foundation and explosive growth of the organization. Ballmer's the commoditization of the company's products and services, and Nadella has focused the organization on a shared purpose of empowering people to do more through technology.

Nadella calls himself a learner; that's a key element of his philosophy and it helps him focus on the innovations needed to continue fulfilling the purpose of empowering people with technology. Nadella's learning applies to people and technology. Understanding people is essential not just for good working relationships, but also for products that people want. He asks "Where is this person coming from?... What makes them tick? What are they excited or frustrated by something that is happening, whether it's about computing or beyond computing?"[14]

But personality is more than any one assessment can measure; it is also shaped by chosen beliefs and life experiences. Witness Nadella's well-intentioned response to a woman's question at a conference. She wanted to know what Nadella thought women should do if they were underpaid and afraid to ask for a raise. Nadella replied that they should not ask for a raise, but instead have faith that the system will work – and that good karma will come back. As a Hindu, this was a well-intentioned response, one that was consistent with his philosophy. However, it was not correct in that context and he shortly thereafter apologized and corrected his response for the context – saying that women should ask for raises and should expect equal pay for equal work when compared with men. And what practical value did he cite in his apology? His value of learning from his own mistake. Leaders who have a clear philosophy that is consistent with their personality can rely on their philosophy to navigate change, make difficult decisions, and adjust their approach when they do not get the results they expect.

## COMMUNICATING WITH PERSONALITY INTELLIGENCE

A clear philosophy helps with communication, especially when communicating with large groups. For smaller groups, or for one-to-one interactions, you need to take into account the motives and feelings of the individuals involved.

As you listen to others, try to connect what you are hearing to their motives. Why is this person making a suggestion or a complaint? Understanding motivation doesn't tell you whether or not what you have heard has merit. But it helps you to weigh the communication and to decide what to do about it. Is this a person who always wants to push for quick results even when it is better to take more time? Or is this a caring person who wants to avoid hurting someone at the cost of the organization's best interests? Or is this a cautious person who is never satisfied that there is enough evidence?

Of course, you need to be alert not to be manipulated by self-serving Machiavellian people. But the communications of well-meaning people may be clarified if you know their motivational values. By adding this lens to your perception, you are more likely to see what they really mean—and less likely to make a quick, incorrect judgment. Additionally if you are able to accurately reflect their concerns, they'll be more likely to collaborate with you, and if you decide not to do what they ask or suggest they'll be more likely to understand and accept your decision.

To fully understand others' communication, you also have to experience the feelings expressed. Are these people anxious? Do they need reassurance? Are they angry and not telling you why? How you respond to an idea or a complaint will be informed by understanding both motivation and emotion.

Effective listening and making use of what you hear and understand is greatly enhanced by personality intelligence. This requires both learning about personality and developing a heart that listens, not being distracted by your conflict triggers, or thinking about what's next, but being fully present and open.

In the final chapters, we discuss the question of whether leaders are born or made—and the process of developing the leaders we need with qualities of head and heart. We'll see that personality intelligence is increasingly important for leaders of knowledge workers, because effective interaction is essential to creating and applying knowledge in teams and organizations.

CHAPTER 7

# Developing a Productive Social Character

THE STRENGTH of both an organization and a society depends on people, their productiveness, and the quality of their relationships. In this age of knowledge work, a productive and collaborative workforce requires a productive interactive social character, shaped in families, schools, fields of play, and the workplace. Although childhood development may seem irrelevant to life in the workplace, people in the leadership workshops we've led almost always bring it up in relation to personality differences. They want to know whether their personality is the result of the way they were raised or whether they were born with it. Although people are born with certain traits, their development at work builds on the developmental foundation laid in childhood and youth. Having a framework that describes the way development occurs from childhood through adulthood helps us to understand how the relationship between psychosocial pressures and the choices we make shapes our individual personalities.

Erik H. Erikson's theory of personality formation through eight stages of life provides a framework that allows us to contrast the formation of the bureaucratic social character with that of the interactive social character and to identify the responses to the psychosocial challenges at different stages that result in a successful life.[1] Erikson based his stages on the idea that people had to respond to the

### TABLE 7-1

## Positive life-cycle development: Bureaucratic and Interactive social characters

|  | Bureaucratic | Interactive |
|---|---|---|
| **Basic Trust** | Focused on parents | Focused on parenting network |
| **Autonomy** | Self-directed conformity | Negotiating with parents |
| **Initiative** | Knowing your place, learning the role | Interpersonal competence, teamwork |
| **Industry** | Passing the test | Learning to learn |
| **Identity** | Choosing a career and belief system | Seeking a vocation, finding a center |
| **Intimacy** | Mutual care and focus on male success | Mutual development, building a network together, and focus on male and female success |
| **Generativity** | Parenting, protecting | Coaching, facilitating |
| **Ego Integrity** | Playing the bureaucratic role with dignity and effectiveness, resisting illegitimate commands and corrupting pressures, detachment | Pragmatic development of ideals, living with contradictions and uncertainty without losing hope, staying engaged |

challenges of both their maturing bodies and their culture's expectations of them at different ages. How they met those challenges formed their competencies, values, emotional attitudes, and identity. Table 7-1 compares the positive life-cycle development of bureaucratic and interactive social characters. Table 7-2 lays out the negative outcomes of these developmental stages. The context of the challenges — the social-cultural factors — makes a difference. Context, such as family dynamics, quality of schooling, and incentives at work, influences the challenges and provides incentives for behavior that effectively meets them.

Erikson's theories, that he first published in 1950 and then revised in 1963, were written in a context that has changed almost beyond recognition. His context was that of a culture and typical family that formed the bureaucratic social character. If you were born in the 1980s or 1990s, it's hard to imagine a pre-pill culture where

**TABLE 7-2**

## Typical developmental problems: Bureaucratic and Interactive social characters

|  | Bureaucratic | Interactive |
|---|---|---|
| **Basic trust versus basic mistrust** | Dependency on mother; hot-house environment | Feeling abandoned; detachment |
| **Autonomy versus shame and doubt** | Obsessive conformity | Lack of boundaries; impulsiveness |
| **Initiative versus guilt and anxiety** | Oedipal struggle and over-identification with parents | Anxiety about group acceptance causing over-conformity |
| **Industry versus inferiority** | Loss of self-confidence—poor grades, performance | Overestimation of self as defense against loss of self esteem |
| **Identity versus role confusion** | Compulsive conformity to parental role model or peer group | Self-marketing and lack of a center |
| **Intimacy versus isolation** | Tribalistic relatedness | Superficial coupling |
| **Generativity versus stagnation** | Becomes a narrow role | Nothing to teach |
| **Ego integrity versus despair** | Tostoy's *Death of Ivan Illich*—the lost self | Burnout; anomie |

two-thirds of families were headed by a single wage earner, the father; where few women aspired to leadership roles in business and government, and most of those who did identified with their fathers.[2] At that time, even the most educated women were repeatedly told that their role was to create a warm home culture, a haven from the rough-and-tumble corporate battlefield. That's what Adlai Stevenson, the Democratic presidential candidate, advised the graduating class of Smith, the elite women's college, in 1955. Of course, all that has changed. The 21st-century emphasis at Smith is strengthening the department of engineering so women can gain management jobs in technology companies.

At the present, when both members of a couple are typically in the workforce and there are as many families headed by single women as there were traditional families of the 1950s, it's much harder to describe a typical experience for a child growing up. Clearly, families also differ in wealth and in the opportunities they can offer their children to succeed. Richer parents get involved early on in their children's careers, poorer parents less so. Yet, with universal access to current events through TV and radio, and real-time access via social media and the Internet, children are acutely aware of what they have to do to succeed in a world of fierce competition and global business, where both intellectual and social capabilities for knowledge work are the keys to success.

As we contrast the eight stages of life of bureaucratic and interactive social characters, what it takes to prosper in this new world will become clearer.

Do national cultures make a difference to the psychosocial challenges people face? Although there are cultural and class differences in how children are raised, the common culture of global business is pulling the most educated young people in different countries toward a common interactive social character.

In building on Erikson's framework, we have combined findings from developmental psychology and sociology studies that were made after Erikson's time with our own observations and those of colleagues.[3]

Erikson's eight stages with approximate ages are:

- *Trust versus mistrust*: Birth to age 1

- *Autonomy versus shame and doubt*: Age 1 to 3

- *Initiative versus guilt*: Age 3 to 6

- *Industry versus inferiority*: Age 6 to 12

- *Identity versus role confusion*: Age 12 to 20

- *Intimacy versus isolation*: Age 20 to 40

- *Generativity versus stagnation*: Age 40 to 65

- *Ego integrity versus despair*: Age 65 on

These stages should not be thought of mechanically, as though people were moving through life on a track, stopping at fixed stations to wrestle with psychosocial challenges. Although our success in mastering the challenge of any given stage greatly increases the chances of success at the next level, failure at a particular stage doesn't mean we are forever blocked from developing ourselves. Despite early setbacks, some people, often with help, can recover and find their way back on a productive path.

## BASIC TRUST VERSUS MISTRUST

We're all born with a rudimentary sense of identity, me versus not-me, but in the first few months of life "me" includes mother. Then we begin to recognize ourselves in the mirror and to recognize other babies. In the bureaucratic family, the infant is focused almost exclusively on the mother. An attitude of basic trust and love of life grows from the infant's connection with a loving mother and the expectation that she'll satisfy basic needs. Ideally, the bond between mother and child includes a deep sense of knowing, sensing, and responding to each other.

The typical developmental problems at this stage have to do with overdependency—failure to cut the umbilical cord—sometimes because the mother is so intensely attached to her child. Problems with basic trust also can stem from a cold, frightened, inadequate mother or a rejecting or ambivalent mother who resents the mothering role that keeps her trapped at home.

In the interactive family, mother usually starts out as the main infant caretaker, continuing the physical symbiosis of childbearing. But early on, when she returns to her paid work, others share this role. In the 1960s only 10 percent of women were working three months following the birth of their first child. In the 2000s about half were working when their first child was three months old.[4] More than 60 percent of women with children under age 6 work outside the home.[5] Increasingly, the father also participates in caring for the baby, and babies may also be put in day-care centers or, depending on the family's circumstances, in the care of hired nannies or grandparents.

On the positive side, as infants receive care from others, trust is expanded beyond the mother. On the negative side, children may lack the security of deep maternal attachment. Feeling insecure and abandoned, they may become distrustful, anxious, and self-protectively avoidant. Later in life, these feelings may make it more difficult for them to develop intimate relationships and accept the deep feelings of need for others that they've repressed.[6] Although the quality of day care may affect the infant's trust and sense of well-being, studies show that a mother's sensitivity to her infant has a lot more to do with attachment security than to whether an infant is in alternative care. Moreover, under some circumstances high-quality day care appears to counteract the negative effects of bad parenting.[7]

There is still debate about the impact of day care on child development, and some traditionalists blame working parents and day care for belligerent and aggressive children, juvenile obesity, psychoactive drug use, and teenage sex, among other problems.[8] However, in her presidential address to the American Psychological Association in 2005, the psychologist Diane F. Halpern stated that "there is an emerging consensus that effects are more likely to be negative when the work schedules of the caretaking parents (usually the mother) [are] erratic and unpredictable; the hours are long and she faces other significant stressors, such as poor health, poverty, and little control over work-related events. In other words, children, families, and work suffer when the parent has few sources of support and stress is high."[9] Professor Halpern believes that it's time to end the "mommy wars" and "games of mother blame" and focus on basing policy on the best evidence of what benefits children and families.

We fully agree.

## AUTONOMY VERSUS SHAME AND DOUBT

About the age of 2, children want to act on their own, and they show rebelliousness to adult authority, the start to achieving a sense of autonomy. Kids want to do things for themselves, express themselves without losing loving support from parents. By this self-expression, children try to avoid the shame of being seen as babies who can't control their bodily functions, dress themselves, or handle a fork and spoon. They want to be able to feel good about themselves. Parents should treat this rebelliousness by setting limits and giving reasons why.

But not all parents respond this way. In the bureaucratic family, some parents impose overly strict demands, such as too-early toilet training. The danger is that the child will avoid humiliating shame by obsessively complying, becoming the uptight, super clean, and humorless anal character described by Freud. Alternatively, the child is plagued by doubt and needs constant reassurance that he or she is doing the right thing. But all shaming isn't bad. Although extreme shaming of a child at this age can cause deep hurt and anger, without some homeopathic shaming, children don't learn to conform to social expectations and are vulnerable to more serious humiliations later in life.

The child in an interactive family may have to deal with various parenting figures, less consistency, and less certainty. Sensing the parents' insecurity about standards and their guilt about not being around when needed, a 2-year-old may begin to negotiate with parents for more freedom, playthings, or a later bedtime.

Many interactive children seem to have responded to parental indecision with a loss of respect for adults. According to an Associated Press–Ipsos poll in the fall of 2005, "nearly 70 percent of Americans said they believed that people are ruder now than they were 20 or 30 years ago and that children are among the worst offenders." In 2002, according to surveys by Public Agenda, only 9 percent of adults saw children as "respectful toward adults."[10]

According to Dan Kindlon, a Harvard University child psychologist, although most parents would like their children to be polite, considerate, and well-behaved, they're too tired, worn down by work, and personally needy to demand proper behavior. "'We use kids like Prozac,' he said. 'People don't necessarily feel great about their spouse or their job but the kids are the bright spot in their day... They don't want to feel bad. They want to get satisfaction from their kids. They're so precious to us. What gets thrown out the window is limits. It's a lot easier to pick their towel up off the floor than to get them away from the PlayStation to do it.'"[11]

So, as on the TV show Nanny 911, unbridled nagging children run family dictatorships where mom and dad are there to serve them at all times. Some parents have become so disempowered that they need help from experts like Brian Orr, a pediatrician and author, who runs workshops north of Boston on how to say "no" to children. Think of the future transference to bosses when these kids get to the workplace. They won't idealize bosses, and they may shy away from becoming a parental-type boss. Who wants to deal with a bunch of demanding kids?

Although parents of Interactives often let their kids disempower them, they do teach their children to compete for success, whatever it takes. When it's about achievement, these parents get serious and take charge. Kindlon also said, "We're insane about achievement... Schoolwork is up 50 percent since 1981, and we're so obsessed with our kids getting into the right school, getting the right grades, we let a lot of things slide.'"[12]

And that brings us to the next two stages.

## INITIATIVE VERSUS GUILT AND ANXIETY

This is the stage where kids take the initiative and start to play together. Traditionally, preschool boys and girls play separately, boys being more aggressive and girls focused more on creating group harmony.[13] This is the stage at which kids also start comparing themselves, forming an identity based on being smarter, cuter, a better athlete, and so on.

In the traditional family, children up to age 5 or 6 are still essentially egocentric and see things only from their own point of view. Although they may rebel against adult commands, the grown-ups rule and other kids are rivals for the authority's love and approval.[14]

When this pattern is reproduced in bureaucracies, it causes childlike emotions in employees who compete for the boss's favor. In the traditional family, rebellion against authority is resolved when boys identify with father and his outlook on life (what Freud called the resolution of the Oedipus complex) while girls identify with mother and take on her values. Going against these internalized parents (the superego) causes feelings of guilt. In bureaucracies, when subordinates identify with the CEO, even copying his dress and mannerisms, they no longer feel childlike with the boss; rather, they feel just like the boss, especially when dealing with their own subordinates.

Being less emotionally dependent on adults, children of interactive families are quicker to forge ties with other kids. While the psychological pitfall for the bureaucratic character was fear of parents' disapproval, which becomes internalized as crippling guilt, for the interactive character it's anxiety about not being in with the group.[15] This anxiety can drive kids into over conformity in their urgency to be accepted. Alternatively, children may totally reject the group and form alliances with other "outcasts" whose resentment curdles into fantasies of revenge.

Of course, most kids do learn to fit in. But while normal bureaucratic conformity results from identification with older role models, the interactive child becomes increasingly alert and responsive to changing fads and fashions among peers. The author of the 1950 book, *The Lonely Crowd,* David Riesman was the first sociologist to see that the traditional obsessive and inner-directed American, whose internal gyroscope determined right and wrong, was being challenged by a new type, who was other-directed and whose interpersonal radar signaled the appropriate way to act.¹⁶ By the start of the 21st century, other-direction combined with peer transferences was becoming the dominant form of social control for the interactive social character.

By the end of this stage, bureaucratic children cooperate at play to work out conflicts with authority in central-person games like hide-and-seek, where the group bands together to escape "It," the oppressive authority, or Simon Says, where the way to win is to follow Simon's directions, and Simon can penalize you for failing to comply. In contrast, interactive children are much further along in forming relationships at play and on the Internet. They are more concerned with getting grown-ups to serve them than with escaping from authority.

## INDUSTRY VERSUS INFERIORITY

When children reach the age of 6 or 7, they are ready to become workers. But their first work depends on the mode of production in their culture. In peasant villages, boys follow their fathers to the fields and girls help their mothers with cows, pigs, and chickens; caring for younger siblings; and cooking, washing, and cleaning. They are identifying with their parents and becoming much like them.

In the bureaucratic world, the main work for children at this stage is schoolwork, and the tools kids must master are those used for reading and understanding, writing clearly, and solving abstract problems. The bureaucratic child learns internal discipline, to sit still for long periods and concentrate, and to memorize concepts and formulas, construct arguments, and take tests.

In the bureaucratic world, boys begin to play team sports where they develop a capacity for reciprocity—the ability to not only understand and follow fair rules, but also design them.¹⁷ In these games, kids learn not only to play by the rules, but also to put themselves in another person's role; not only to play, but also to execute plays that require cooperation, like the double play in baseball, the power sweep in football, and the pick-and-roll in basketball. Reciprocity expressed as fairness tempers both egocentric competition and authoritarian hierarchy.

Overly bureaucratic managers don't make use of reciprocity. They divide to conquer and provoke egocentric rivalry. Even in the most cooperative organizations, there will still be conflict about whether to be a team player or strive for individual distinction In professional sports, this tension is resolved by evaluating players on both individual statistics and contribution to the team.

To succeed in the interactive world, a child's industry is essential, but so are her talents. As factory jobs and, increasingly, knowledge work moves offshore, and transactional jobs (those traditionally handled by operators, bank clerks, and salespeople) are automated, the jobs that remain are low-paying service jobs (maintenance, fast-food sales and prep), better paying service positions (in teaching, healthcare, transportation, hospitality), or high-salaried knowledge work (consultants, lawyers, doctors, engineers, managers). Unlike jobs that require formulaic intelligence, manual dexterity, or muscle power, the jobs that increasingly will be available call for analytic reasoning, imagination and creativity, people skills, and emotional intelligence.[18] Of course, construction workers, electricians, carpenters, and plumbers will continue to be needed, and many of these skilled craftspeople will do well economically, but the gap in wages and wealth between knowledge workers and those who hold other types of jobs has been growing.[19]

A troubling finding from social psychologists is that while upper-middle-class parents have become career directors for children age 7 and younger, working-class parents are much less involved in their children's lives — and their success. The richer parents know what's coming for their children, and their anxiety about their kids' future ability to maintain their status drives parents to drive the kids to take part in a host of after-school activities, from supervised educational experiences to Little League games.

Sociologist Annette Lareau, who has been observing parents and children for more than 20 years, finds that the upper-middle-class kids are prepared to succeed in the world of knowledge work by parents who are facilitators and coaches, who allow kids to talk back and express their negative feelings (as long as they do their homework), shine on stage, and show that they can make a good impression at an interview to get accepted into a program of their choice. Although working-class parents are more likely to give orders and demand respect, they also let their kids play freely. There is less anxiety, less manipulation, more autonomy. But Lareau writes that the anxious, driven kids become successful professionals, while the working-class kids don't.[20]

The knowledge mode of production demands continual learning and collaboration, and traditional forms of schooling that may have served for the bureaucratic era are now found wanting. There's been a lot of debate about the best way to prepare children to succeed in the knowledge economy, much too much to summarize here. What we can say, however, is that the debate between the proponents of rigorous "teaching to the test" versus those who favor "learning to learn" falsely opposes the need for kids to master the fundamentals of learning— memorize and practice basic arithmetic, language, scientific facts, historical events, and so on — to the need to develop critical thinking, communication skills, and the motivation to learn. Some progressive educators can be compared to piano teachers who ask pupils to express emotion in their playing before they've mastered the keys and learned the scales, while some conservative educators can be likened to piano teachers who never inspire their pupils to put their heart into their art.

Kids benefit from teachers who combine discipline with challenge, rigor with fun, respect for precision with creativity, and accountability with collaboration. This is especially true for disadvantaged children in the inner cities whose future opportunities depend on good schooling. Kids also benefit from learning via technology. Many students are now being directed to online resources to teach them such skills as algebra, so their teachers can spend more time in class helping them practice problem-solving.

Schooling not only teaches children skills. It also shapes their social character. The education offered by charter schools like KIPP (Knowledge Is Power Program) and Success Academy addresses the need to mold a productive social character. Many of their students are from disadvantaged families, and have been brought up in a culture of welfare, crime, and fatalism. Unlike children brought up in affluent families with a culture that emphasizes learning, disadvantaged children need stricter, more disciplined schooling with longer classroom hours. Their parents need to commit themselves to collaborate with their teachers.

In 2015 KIPP had 183 schools in 20 states and the District of Columbia. The organization has served 70,000 children, 95 percent of whom are African-American or Latino. About 94 percent of KIPP middle school graduates have gone on to high school, and 82 percent of these students have entered college. I have visited KIPP schools in three states and have been extremely impressed by the ability of the teachers to engage these children in learning and creative expression.

College is not the best path for everyone. Apprenticeship programs and schools that prepare high-school students for craft and service occupations are good alternatives. With the rising cost of college tuition, some young people find that becoming a plumber, electrician, bricklayer, chef, or truck driver avoids the student-debt trap and can lead to a lucrative and fulfilling career.

Some private schools are focused on preparing children for what they believe will gain them success in the interactive economy. One such school is St John's School and Community College in Marlborough, Wiltshire, England. Patrick Hazlewood, the headmaster, says, "The national curriculum kills learning stone dead by compartmentalizing subjects as if they have no relation to each other."[21] The school bases teaching around five competencies for business proposed by the Royal Society for the Encouragement of Arts, Manufactures and Commerce: learning, citizenship (ethics and society), relating to other people, managing situations, and managing information (critical thinking and finding things out).

Industrious children raised as Bureaucrats risked becoming narrowly focused and unimaginative. Now industrious interactive children risk becoming glib and shallow if they think knowledge is just a click of a mouse away. In the bureaucratic classroom, the unsuccessful child would lose self-confidence and self-esteem, triggering a vicious cycle of poor performance. Although this could also happen to the interactive child, denial of failure is supported by the anti-bureaucratic popular culture and pop psychology, which inflate the self and put down authority. Defending against the loss of self-esteem, these children overestimate their capabilities and become impervious to coaching and 360-degree feedback.[22] Good teachers help these children understand that the discipline required for learning and self-expression makes a huge difference in their future ability to learn and to play a productive role in the interactive society.

Aside from making it easy to gather information, the Internet has a profound influence on shaping the interactive social character and facilitating interaction, especially when combined with mobile devices. The first thing that many 10-, 11-, or 12-year-olds do after school is use their apps to connect with correspondents all over the world to play games. For these kids, global networking comes naturally.

There has been concern about the effects of game playing on kids. Some games are extremely violent. Are they making kids aggressive? Do games detach kids from reality? Can they train kids to kill? So far, according to a report in *The Economist*, the evidence is inconclusive.[23] Kids who tend toward violence may be pushed over the edge by violent games like *Grand Theft Auto*.[24] These games, however, also require players to learn a great deal. They must construct hypotheses about the intra-game world and test them. They learn the game rules through trial and error, solve problems and puzzles, develop strategies, and get help from other connected players or look up "cheat codes" when they're stuck. They also learn to share leadership roles.

Whereas the bureaucratic child played at different roles and identities — being a grown-up, a policeman, firefighter, model, nurse, doctor, and so on — the interactive gamester moves in alternative realities and takes on alternative personalities. The ability to do so can be a strength, but only as long as game players know the difference between the game and reality. Interactives may be surprised to find that when the "game" is over in business, it's not so easy to change identities — and there aren't any super powers hidden in virtual bushes or lockboxes. And that takes us to the next developmental stage.

## IDENTITY VERSUS ROLE CONFUSION

Youth is the time between childhood and adulthood, By this time, individuals should have gained basic skills for work and relationships. But during puberty and adolescence, rapid body growth and genital maturity cause confusion about identity. Youths struggle with the physiological revolution inside them and the grown-up tasks ahead of them. Who are they becoming? How do others view them? How should they connect the roles and skills they have practiced with the occupational prototypes that appeal to them? How will they decide on a vocation?

Youth is a time of exuberance and experimentation, sometimes-grandiose fantasies and ambitions, and daredevil risk taking — what I've called a "narcissistic moment."[25] This is a time of freedom, when children feel the whole world is open to them and they can do anything they put their minds to. They think of themselves as invulnerable. For the bureaucratic personality, it may mean rejecting father's or mother's plans for them — their parents' ideas of what they should do for a living — or rebelling against the tyranny of the peer group. When bureaucratic teenagers imagine adult life, they often think in narcissistic terms, turning jobs that require years of rote study and training, such as doctor or lawyer, into heroic, high-wire acts: They'll become a world-famous surgeon, or a lawyer who overwhelms the Supreme Court with brilliant arguments.

For interactive youth, fantasies often include getting rich, but they are also more likely than bureaucratic youth to envision being part of a great team: a new Apple, Google, Dust Brothers, Facebook, or Dreamworks.[26] Ultimately, however, the inner discipline and real-world skills formed in earlier stages make the difference between fantasy and reality, success and failure. Few people ride the narcissistic moment into a lifetime adventure by creating a world-class career or a great company that changes the world.

A challenge of youth is to integrate all the pieces of identity that make up a self-concept. We all have attachments — to family, nation, a religious group, even teams — with which we identify. But for adolescents, the roles and identities of the child at home and the youth outside can clash. Erikson wrote that the main psychological danger of this stage was role confusion, not only between home and the peer group, but also possibly about sexual identity. Erikson saw falling in love at this stage as an attempt to gain a sense of identity by being defined and affirmed in a passionate relationship.

He wrote that "young people can also be remarkably clannish, and cruel in their exclusion of all those who are 'different,' in skin color or cultural background, in tastes and gifts, and often in such petty aspects of dress and gesture as have been temporarily selected as the sign of an in-grouper or out-grouper."[27] He saw this intolerance as the dark side of defense against identity confusion and as a way of testing loyalty and trust.

Erikson also described youth as a time of idealism, of committing oneself to an ideology or religion. Soon after he wrote this, in the 1960s, the enlarged cohort of baby-boomer youth began to undermine the bureaucratic social character. They attacked "dehumanizing" bureaucratic rules, roles, and technology with an ideology of libertarianism. The youth that survived this self-indulgent orgy were somehow able to combine pleasure seeking with pragmatism. The losers were the ideological extremists, revolutionaries who became disillusioned cynics, tribalistic cultists, and drug addicts.

In contrast to Europeans whose identities are more tightly tied to social class and place of birth, Americans have had more freedom in shaping their identity, as exemplified by two American icons. Robert Frost, born in San Francisco and educated at Dartmouth and Harvard, failed as a farmer in New Hampshire and went to England, where he recast himself as the craggy prototype of the rural New Hampshire farmer-poet. Robert Allen Zimmerman, a middle-class Jewish musician from Duluth and Hibbing, Minnesota, became Bob Dylan, the folk-rock balladeer and figurehead of the 1960s.[28]

Interactives have a protean ability to take on and shed identities that serve their needs, just like the characters in video games or screen avatars on social networking sites. Madonna has been a prototype, continuously reinventing herself to fit, or sometimes lead, the fashions of the times. Furthermore, Interactives often mix their idealism with self-interest as they join identity groups based on occupation, politics, business, race, religion, disabilities, or sexual orientation.

Whereas the challenge for the bureaucratic social character was to construct an individual identity and not just put on an identity laid out by parents and other authorities, the challenge for Interactives is to find meaning. In large part, this has to do with finding a vocation, work that engages talents and values, but many Interactives feel a need for more than a vocation to provide a sense of meaning. The UCLA Higher Education Research Institute reports that in 2004, three-quarters of 112,000 students from 236 colleges indicated that they were "searching for meaning and purpose in life."[29] That's why many Interactives seek help from therapists, Eastern spiritual disciplines like Yoga, or religions. That's why Rick Warren's *The Purpose-Driven Life: What on Earth Am I Here For?* sold millions of copies.[30]

Finding a meaningful purpose, a center to anchor changing identities and role taking can become a platform for the next stage. For most people, however, by the end of this stage, personality, including social character, has fully formed. How that personality develops depends on the next stages.

## INTIMACY VERSUS ISOLATION

The challenge for younger adults, from age 20 to 40, is to achieve an intimate, trusting relationship. To do this they have to be able to trust themselves as much as they trust the other person. This is not just a matter of faithfulness. Without a firm identity, intimacy is threatening: Someone can be taken over by another person, losing identity as well as freedom. For most people, establishing a loving relationship, overcoming loneliness, and creating a family are essential to becoming a mature person.

Ideally, a family supports the positive development of all its members. By development we mean the increased capability to both determine and satisfy the needs that strengthen us — the need to know and understand, to create, and to love. In contrast, compulsive or addictive needs enslave us, making us dependent not only on drugs or sex, but also on constant reassurance from others, protection against potential risks, or the adrenaline rush of taking risks. Achieving maturity means becoming more aware of our needs, able to reinforce those that are developmental, and frustrate those that are addictive, making choices that strengthen us.[31] It means developing and practicing a healthy philosophy of life.

In the bureaucratic era, the goal of this stage was forming a unit for mutual care and success, with clearly differentiated male and female roles. The danger was that this intimate family might isolate itself and become a tribalistic haven, held together by narcissistic self-inflation ("We're better than everyone else").

At its best, the interactive family avoids this pitfall and builds a network that reaches beyond blood ties to connect with others who share its developmental values. But there are two kinds of pitfalls for Interactives. One is the inability to fully commit and fully trust. This may be caused by lack of identity integration. On a deeper level, it may stem from early attachment issues. Detached, avoidant adults repress strong needs for mothering, but are driven by these needs into relationships and then repelled by infantile yearnings and behavior — either their own or the other person's. This cycle of attraction and repulsion can result in superficial coupling and frequent break-ups.

The second pitfall has to do with the pressure that two careers put on a relationship. Interactives who are economically independent won't stay in a bad relationship. In the past, dependence on a sole breadwinner might have kept a spouse from leaving. Not now. So if both partners are economically independent, mature understanding and compromise are urgently needed if they are to sustain their relationship, especially when either one or both of them feel career pressures.

Freud described psychological health as *lieben und arbeiten,* to love and to work. This is a formula that fits any social character, but it seems essential for interactive well-being. Interactives want to love their work but many of them need to work at love. As Erich Fromm wrote in *The Art of Loving,* there is little education or understanding about the kind of love that strengthens self and other and deepens trust.[32] Relationships built on narcissistic love, the projection of one's ideal onto the other, collapse when the mutual illusion fades, and then the prince and princess become frogs in each other's eyes. Love as infatuation is different from love as agape, deep knowledge and care about what's best for the other person.

Trust is strengthened not only by affirmation but also by the kind of love that refuses to ignore danger when the other person strays from the path that both believe is best for his or her well-being.

During this stage young people are also establishing themselves at work. In the bureaucratic era, the ideal was to move up corporate or government hierarchies, make partner in a law or accounting firm, or establish a professional practice. Interactives still want status and power, but they are now more likely to view corporations and government as postgraduate training for more freewheeling careers. Like professional athletes, they see themselves as assets that can be leased but not owned by companies, and their commitment is to meaningful projects and teams, not to powerful organizations.

## GENERATIVITY VERSUS STAGNATION

The next stage is when individuals, having achieved a productive role at work and sustainable intimate relationships, face the challenge of generativity, bringing along the next generation as parents, teachers, coaches, or institution builders who articulate and defend good values — possibly as the kind of leader we need. This is the time when a person's philosophy of life should be conscious and clarified, and the personality fully developed.

Erikson first thought this period lasted from about age 40 to 65, but that was when he was in his 40s. When he was in his 80s and still active, he realized that people could stay generative for a longer time. The generative role was clearer in the bureaucratic era, however, especially for men who could move up the hierarchy and mentor promising younger men who, in turn, were attracted to them as father figures. The productive bureaucrat who identified with father figures took pride in being an expert who could teach the younger generation. Mentor and mentee enjoyed the transferential relationship and helped each other succeed. When women first took management roles, the ones able to simulate father-daughter relationships were best able to find mentors.

The traditional bureaucracies allowed, even encouraged, middle managers to be mentors, both at work and in volunteer organizations. There was less pressure, more time for bonding. In contrast, in companies today there is little time and even less energy for these forms of sociability. And even when there is time, the new social character is uneasy in the role of mentor or protective authority. Other than success, Interactives' highest value is tolerance in terms of race, religion, sexual orientation, and ideology. Their moral code is akin to "Live and let live" or "Judge not, that you be not judged." And they don't think they should have to defend organizational values they didn't have a say in framing, saying, "Those are not my values and I'm not the police." But on a team or task force, they aren't tolerant of poor performance that affects them. One value everyone shares is results.

The most generative of the Interactives may take leadership roles as facilitators or bridge-builders, preferably for a project. They want it to be clear they are adding value for others, not trying to dominate them. They don't want to seem power hungry, but they are learning that a leader needs the power to get things done. Ideally, that power can be gained by engaging rather than commanding followers.

Ultimately, both Bureaucratics and Interactives who fail to become generative stagnate. Bureaucrats take on the traits of their narrow roles, like a character in one of Franz Kafka's novels or Max Weber's "specialists without spirit."[33] Underdeveloped Interactives never deepen their knowledge or commit themselves to others. They have nothing to teach and no one wants anything from them. Keep in mind that we all need to feel needed, and a person who feels needed by no one will likely feel like a total failure.

And this is more than a personal failure. The more Interactives fail the test of generativity, the more our society suffers. We need generative leaders who defend the values that support a free, productive, and environmentally sustainable society. The well-being of the next generation depends on whether Interactives understand and accept the challenge of generativity and whether enough of them are willing to become the leaders we need.

## EGO INTEGRITY VERSUS DESPAIR

Erikson first wrote about the final stage of life when he was in his 40s and revised his ideas when he was in his 80s and then again, shortly before his death, when he was in his early 90s. That's when he wrote, "Lacking a culturally viable ideal of old age, our civilization does not really harbor a concept of the whole life."[34] He thought that elders in our society (now called seniors) are no longer seen as bearers of wisdom, but as embodiments of shame.

Writing this at age 84, I can testify that that's not always the case. Erikson himself contradicted the statement by his continued generativity. Another example was W. Edwards Deming, the statistician who brought total quality management first to Japan and then to the United States; he was still teaching at age 90. At that time, he invited me to discuss leadership with him. We met periodically over a three-year period, and each time he took notes (as did I); he was still learning. John Gielgud, the great English director and actor, was still acting in films at age 95. Peter Drucker, the expert on organization and management, was active when he died at age 96. At age 93, his wife, Doris, was running the company she started at age 80. Sidney Harman was leading Harman International at age 88. Warren Buffet remains an active and influential investor and businessman at age 86. Charles Handy in his book *The Second Curve*[35] wrote that his friends who, like him were in their 80s, were either still working or dead. Surely, people working in their 80s have the luck of good genes, but staying engaged has helped keep them from the physical and mental collapse common to old age.

It's too early to see how the Interactives will deal with old age. However, populations in the advanced economies are aging, and people who used to retire at age 65 or earlier may remain in the workforce until and beyond age 70. In 2014 almost 35 percent of adults age 65 to 69 were either still working or looking for work.[36] Furthermore, companies are offering part-time projects to valuable employees this old and even older.[37] And, of course, a number of people in their 60s, 70s, and 80s do volunteer work for charities and nonprofits, demonstrating that generativity doesn't necessarily stop with retirement from paid work. Programs like Civic Ventures' Experience Corps, which has assigned 1,800 tutors and mentors to children, connect seniors with good work where they're needed.

This is all to the good. Research indicates that working during retirement, together with exercise and diet, can help us live longer and healthier.[38] And there's evidence that retirement without active engagement can cause the despair Erikson wrote about. A study of retired people by psychologist Ken Dychtwald emphasizes the benefits of "reinventing" one's life after retirement. He writes, "Having a vision for the future and planning for that vision are as important as money in achieving a fulfilling retirement."[39]

Erikson focused on how people might view themselves at the end of life. Having a sense of integrity means that one's purpose and values have not been betrayed, or that they've been reaffirmed and reclaimed if they had, at some point, been lost. Despair means losing one's way and, what is more devastating, any hope of regaining it. Those who have betrayed themselves live with self-disgust, and the rationalizations they devise don't overcome their depression when they have lost their love of life.

In contrast, a sense of ego integrity is gained by mature realism, understanding what has been possible to do, given one's opportunities and abilities, and always taking luck into account. This includes remaining engaged and generative as long as physically possible, concerned and hopeful about the future, and related to what is alive and needs protection — especially children and the environment that sustains us — as opposed to resigning from the present and retreating into the past. Many people talk about never retiring. For some, this stems from a love for the work they do; for others, there is an economic necessity. Working past the normal retirement age can be a source of fulfillment and pride, or a deepening despair and struggle against the potential inability to support oneself.

Maintaining the ego integrity of the bureaucrat required playing his role with dignity and effectiveness, resisting illegitimate commands and corrupting pressures. After retirement, it required continued learning, reading, traveling, and volunteer activities. For most women, it meant providing care and emotional support while staying sharp through volunteer and cultural activities.

The despairing bureaucrat was like Tolstoy's Ivan Ilyich, who realizes only on his deathbed that he has never stood up for what he thought was right and never really been himself, only what others expected him to be. Tolstoy wrote:

> *His mental sufferings were due to the fact that that night, as he looked at Gerásim's sleepy, good natured face with its prominent cheek-bones, the question suddenly occurred to him: "What if my whole life has really been wrong?"*
>
> *It occurred to him that what appeared perfectly impossible before, namely that he had not spent his life as he should have done, might after all be true. It occurred to him that his scarcely perceptible attempts to struggle against what was considered good by the most highly placed people, those scarcely noticeable impulses which he*

*had immediately suppressed, might have been the real thing, and all the rest false. And his professional duties and the whole arrangement of his life and of his family, and all his social and official interests, might all have been false. He tried to defend all those things to himself and suddenly felt the weakness of what he was defending. There was nothing to defend.*

*"But if that is so," he said to himself, "and I am leaving this life with the consciousness that I have lost all that was given me and it is impossible to rectify it — what then?"*

Perhaps the despairing interactive character will be more like Ibsen's Peer Gynt, a seemingly free spirit who confuses self-indulgence with self-actualization and self-marketing with intimacy, and ends up alone and burned out. Acting out all his greedy impulses and betraying people who trusted him, Peer Gynt mistakenly believes he's being true to himself. In the end, "the button-maker" who comes for his soul tells Peer Gynt that he has no self. By never committing himself to anyone or anything and never responding with his heart, Peer Gynt has become a blank. He has failed the challenge of ego integrity.

Maintaining integrity in the market-dominated world calls for principled pragmatism — continually testing one's purpose and values in terms of results. For those who've been engaged in the complex market world, it means living with contradictions and uncertainty without losing hope. This requires a faith that gives meaning to creative engagement with one's community, which in the interactive age may include people throughout the world who share a common purpose: to protect the environment, keep destructive extremists in check, and work to improve the quality of life for all.

Ego integrity alone, however, does not guarantee happiness. A seventy-five year longitudinal study of Harvard graduates reported that the only correlation with happiness was sustaining loving relationships.[40] The next chapter describes the kinds of leaders we need for effective organizations that will support the development of the interactive social character.

CHAPTER 8

# Leaders for Knowledge Work

THE LEADER WE WANT is not always the leader we need. This has been true throughout history. Getting the leader that people wanted (rather than needed) has sometimes led to the fall of nations and collapse of companies. Despite warnings from the biblical judge Samuel, the Israelites insisted on a king, got one, and were sorry later. In our time, boards of directors have hired dominating, charismatic CEOs who turned out to be costly busts. The world over, people continue to elect inept and corrupt leaders. Some of these leaders have satisfied the unconscious and irrational transferential needs of their followers.

The bureaucratic social character is drawn to father-figure leaders—tall, commanding, and confident. But Interactives want to be collaborators, not followers. They'd most like to join a band of brothers and sisters. If they want a leader at all, they'll opt for someone who'll provide a service for them. But just because they know what they want doesn't guarantee they'll get the leader they need.

This chapter describes the kinds of leaders needed in the knowledge organizations we've worked with, studied, or learned about from other researchers. In this age of turmoil and transformation, we demand more of our organizations than ever before. We want companies to continually innovate, producing ever better products at lower costs. We want to travel farther and faster. We want more energy for light, heat, and air-conditioning but fearful of the effects of climate change, we want companies and government to give us clean, cheap solutions. As brilliant technicians automate away jobs and companies send work overseas, we want our schools to educate the young—not just the elite, but everyone—to fill the roles in knowledge organizations. And as our aspirations for a longer and healthier life grow, we want healthcare organizations to do what once would have been thought miraculous.

A new kind of leadership is required to organize knowledge workers to meet these demands.

A challenge for leaders is to transform bureaucracies where individuals comfortably play autonomous roles into collaborative learning communities. To meet this challenge, leaders need to understand their collaborators and help their collaborators to understand them. Just as Bureaucrats limit themselves by serving as childlike followers to a daddy figure leader, Interactives risk disillusionment by searching for a leader who makes no demands.

Rowena Davis, an undergraduate at Balliol College, Oxford University, won a prize for her essay on leadership in 2005 by describing people with leadership qualities that appeal to Interactives.[1] Jonathan (she doesn't tell us her subjects' last names) connects people who want to collaborate and then gets out of their way; Nita, another admired leader, builds networks for change. Davis says that these leaders "create space and opportunity for action." And they listen to the people they serve. They aren't full of themselves, they don't act superior, and they treat people equally.

Dee Hock, who built the nonhierarchical Visa network,[2] is one such leader. Pierre M. Omidyar, founder of eBay, is another. But these leaders didn't just create space and opportunity for action. They each had a vision and partnered with others to build the processes that businesses and customers could use. In fact, they're more like the two types of good leaders described to me by Bryan Huang, an entrepreneurial Interactive from Beijing. "One is the emergent leader who facilitates the flow," said Huang.[3] Examples would include the network leaders who are needed to gain collaboration across organizational boundaries. The other is the executive leader "who has a vision people want to follow and can show how to make it happen."[4] Huang is describing two of the types of leaders needed in knowledge organizations.

A danger for Interactives is insisting on filling leadership roles with non-leaders, people no one follows. In 1990, the sociologist David Riesman, based on his study of the process to select university presidents, observed that many of the selection processes resulted in choosing a president who satisfied all constituencies: faculty, alumni (for fund-raising), football boosters, and diversity groups. Such an individual might be a good facilitator or mediator and even a network leader, but not a visionary with strong views.[5] In some cases visionaries who made it through the university president selection process, such as Larry Summers at Harvard and Ed Hundert at Case Western Reserve, provoked faculty censure and didn't last long in their jobs.

In this time of profound change, even the most effective network leaders are not the only kind of leaders we need. Such leaders won't stretch us out of our comfort zones or inspire us to tackle the big problems facing our country. They won't transform bureaucratic organizations for the knowledge age, and they won't make the tough decisions that have to be made when there's no consensus. For that, we need different types of leaders who collaborate with each other. Knowledge-age organizations need a leadership system rather than a bureaucratic management structure.

In the age of knowledge work, leadership has become more essential than ever, as well as more complex. In previous chapters, we have shown that farmers and craftspeople work alone or in a master-apprentice relationship, and that a bureaucratic manager controls a hierarchy of people with autonomous objectives and formatted tasks. In both these modes of production, the social character supported strong parental transferences that bound followers to leaders. In both, leaders knew their followers' work better than the followers themselves did.

Knowledge workers, however, are specialists challenged to collaborate across boundaries. They usually know their work better than their bosses do, and their closest ties may be to colleagues. We saw in Chapter 2 that these Interactives don't want to follow bureaucratic bosses, and may even rebel against them. In a meeting I attended, Paul Adler, a professor at the University of Southern California Marshall School of Business, described a group of interactive software developers who flat-out refused to follow a bureaucratic manager, even though they recognized his technical expertise. They thought they'd function better as a collaborative heterarchy, in which leadership would shift according to which specialist had the relevant knowledge for the task at hand.[6] Teams like these need leaders, not managers, to set and interactively communicate a meaningful purpose, and place people in roles that fit their abilities. The team can pretty much manage itself.

Clearly, business leads government and not-for-profits in designing organizations, strategies, and styles of leadership for knowledge work. That's because business must continually compete to survive. The leaders who make use of the best ideas succeed, so they continually scan the business world to find out what works.

132  *The Leaders We Need*

But business by itself can't solve the needs we have for healthcare, education, a sustainable environment, energy independence, and national security. That takes a combination of policy, programs, and organizations in both the public and private sectors, working together.

## THE KNOWLEDGE WORKPLACE

To understand the kinds of leaders needed for knowledge work, consider the existing jobs in the United States. About 80 percent of them are labeled service work by the U.S. Department of Labor. We can plot these jobs in terms of a national employment on a graph bordered by a horizontal axis of service work and a vertical axis of knowledge work as shown in Figure 8-1. Each axis goes from low- to high-paid jobs. Low-paid service jobs include janitors, hotel workers, waiters, maids, security guards, and cleaners, jobs that do not require years of study. High-paid service would be international fashion models and professional athletes who

**FIGURE 8-1**

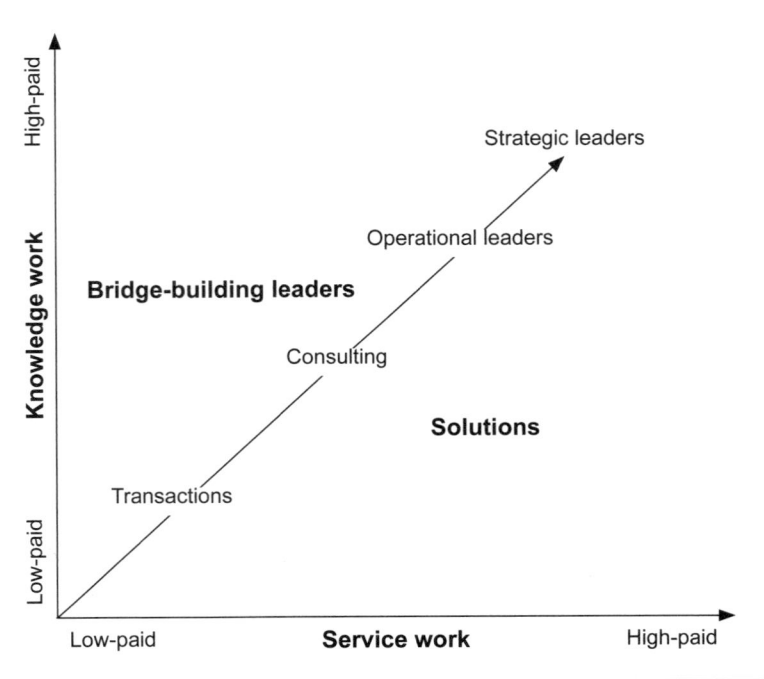

**The Need for Leaders**

are entertainers, jobs that demand knowledge not formally taught in institutions of higher education. Low-paid knowledge work includes that done by lab technicians, accountants, and simple programmers; high-paid knowledge work includes that done by marketing experts, scientists, mathematicians, economists, financial analysts, product developers, and inventors. Bisecting the knowledge-service space in Figure 8-1 is a vector of solutions—the application of knowledge so that it becomes a service. This vector rises from handling simple transactions like sales to teaching and the various types of consulting (medical, legal, financial, etc.) and continues to the strategic, operational and network leaders needed to give purpose to, integrate, and operationalize knowledge work. The contents of the space shown in Figure 8.1 is constantly changing as inventors and programmers on the vertical axis automate transactional and, increasingly, professional and consulting work. Telephone operators disappear, ATMs replace transactional bank tellers, buyers and sellers connect via the Internet and displace middlemen. But these knowledge workers don't just destroy jobs. They can also create new jobs in renewable energy, healthcare, nanotechnology, and so on. To do so, however, requires leaders.

**FIGURE 8-2**

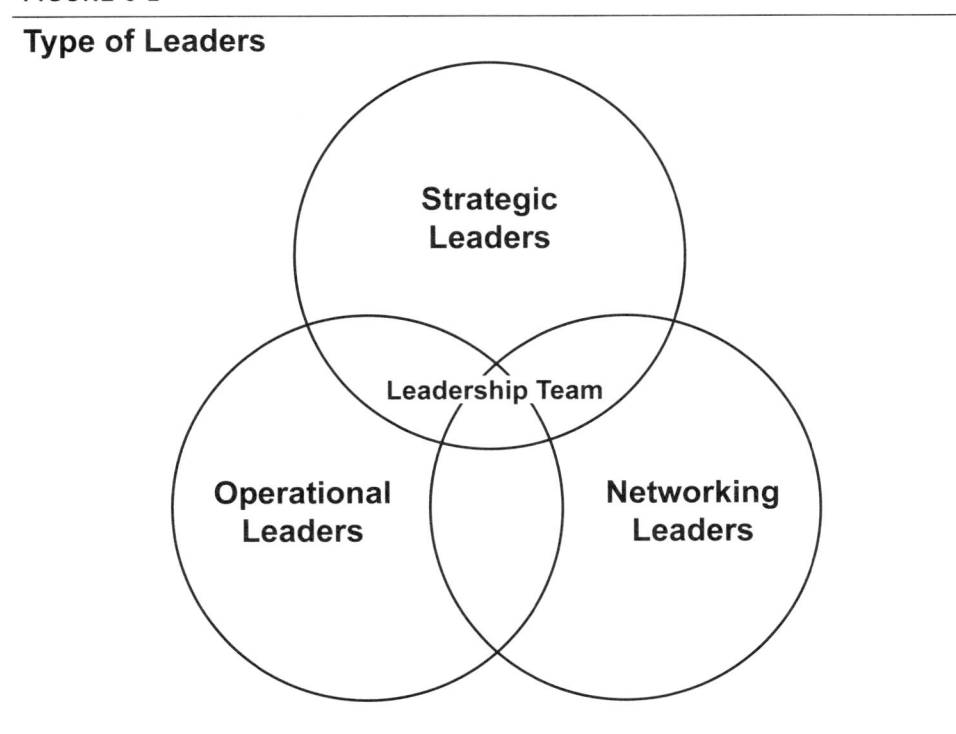

**Type of Leaders**

Figure 8.2 depicts the three types of leaders needed to run a knowledge-creating organization.[7]

1. *Strategic visionaries*: Envisaging the need for a new strategy and organizational transformation, these leaders prod, push, and persuade others to follow. They are often productive narcissists, bold innovators with red or red-blend motivational value systems like Steve Jobs, Larry Ellison, Bill Gates, Jeff Bezos, and Elon Musk. But they can also be more collaborative marketing types like Bob Iger of Disney who was smart enough to buy Pixar, thus getting John Lasseter's creativity for great animation films like Toy Story, as well as Steve Jobs as a board member in his final years. The collaborative strategist seeks to build an organizational vision through discussion with collaborators rather than authoritative pronouncements from on high. The history of IBM sharply illustrates the contrast between the industrial and knowledge modes. When Thomas J. Watson, CEO of IBM from 1914-1956, a productive narcissist, wanted to establish the values for IBM to live by, he wrote them down, published them, and continually repeated them. But when Samuel J. Palmisano CEO of IBM from 2002-2011, a more interactive marketing type, wanted to transform IBM for the knowledge age, he opened the company's intranet to all employees for frank, freewheeling "jams" in which he participated as an equal, and from which new values and ideas emerged.

2. *Operational implementers*: These essential organizational leaders are frequently exacting, green motivational value system types. They make sure the strategy is implemented, turning shared purpose into results. There have been a number of successful partnerships between obsessive operational leaders and narcissistic visionaries, including Herb Kelleher and Colleen Barrett of Southwest Airlines, Andy Grove and Craig Barrett of Intel, and Bill Gates and Steve Ballmer of Microsoft. Indeed, many narcissistic visionaries, like Don Quixote, would survive only if partnered with a down-to-earth exacting Sancho Panza. Operational types sometimes design the processes that sustain a system, but in a collaborative knowledge mode, opting for process alignment and cross-boundary conversation over tight controls and reliance on organizational charts. To transform resisters into collaborators, they need to be interactive "doctors" rather than dictators.

3. *Networkers*: Advanced solutions companies need network leaders with the ability to develop trusting relationships across organizational boundaries. These leaders—usually a combination of blue-caring and hub-adaptive personalities, but sometimes with a strong dose of red-ambition to transform things—may do more than sustain networks. They may build bridges, not only across corporate departments, but also between companies and different national cultures.

In 2005 Lynda Applegate, a professor at Harvard Business School, facilitated the Global Healthcare Exchange, combining companies to cut transaction costs and gain stronger bargaining power with suppliers. DAI, an international development consulting firm, used the bridge-building leadership of Joan Parker to bring together pharmaceutical companies with development consultants and national governments to address the problem of HIV/AIDS in African communities. Captain Linda Lewandowski of the U.S. Navy was put in charge of the Sense and Respond Logistics (SARL) project in the Pentagon's Office of Force Transformation to facilitate the rapid delivery of weapons and ammunition to battlefield units during the Iraq War. To achieve her objective, she enlisted different types of services in the U.S. military and its allies to participate in a network of communication and response, a dramatic change from the old way of negotiation between bureaucratic service hierarchies.

Of course, this role is more easily assumed by a person with an interactive social character who is used to bringing people together to solve problems than by a bureaucratic expert who is used to directing people to follow instructions. In fact, network leaders individually may have little formal power; their power comes from their skill in creating consensus. An interactive network leader once told me that she saw her role as getting people to understand each other. "People allow me to take this role," she said. She believed she had more authority because it had been freely given to her than if she had been given a formal supervisory role. Having had this kind of role myself at AT&T where I was charged with getting union and management to transform a rigid bureaucracy into a learning organization, I can testify that network leaders don't need a formal managerial role, but they do need support from the top. Moreover, having a formal role can actually limit effectiveness by identifying the bridge-builder with the interests of a particular unit.

It takes these three kinds of leaders, working together, to achieve a common purpose, especially in complex knowledge companies. Whatever their style, effective leaders infuse energy into an organization with their passion and conviction. As they insist on results, they encourage people to perform beyond their comfort zones.

## LEADERS FOR SOLUTIONS

Although traditional leaders may view Interactives as hard to lead and as having an anarchic ideal of leadership, Interactives better fit the needs of many companies moving away from product-based business models to knowledge work, particularly solution strategies. To avoid narrowing profit margins on products that are becoming commodities, companies like IBM and GE have been wrapping products in services that require employees to work collaboratively with customers.

In the late 1990s, I was a consultant to ABB (Asea Brown Boveri) in Canada at a time when the company's electrical products were becoming commodities and margins were disappearing. To boost profits, we explored the potential of doing business with large customers like Cominco, a zinc mining and smelting company, that proposed partnering with ABB rather than merely buying equipment from ABB to increase energy efficiency and decrease environmental pollution.[8] To pursue this opportunity, ABB had to pull technical people together from its different business units to collaborate with Cominco's engineers, and this called for network leadership. ABB management included Borje Fredriksson, a productive marketing type with an interactive social character.

Fredriksson had to persuade traditional bureaucratic ABB managers that other large customers from paper and pulp companies and utilities really wanted to buy solutions rather than products. He did this by bringing the customers to management meetings and letting ABB's managers question them directly. Fredriksson and I then interviewed managers to determine the organizational changes that would be needed to realize the new solutions strategy. When it came time to design the new system, we again brought the key managers together in an interactive process. Recognizing that they would have to communicate the results to their own teams, these managers decided to continue the interactive process, and they defined it as follows:

- Dialogue—meeting of the minds
- Constructive engagement
- Seeking logic
- Full trust—openness
- Understanding each other
- Common language
- Openness to different perspectives

They also noted that it was not:

- Telling people
- Explaining to your staff
- Just listening

After using an interactive process to design the structure, processes, and measurements needed to implement a solutions strategy, they answered a question they asked me at the start: Why use the interactivity process?

- Interactivity is the glue that makes the whole bigger than the sum of its parts.
- Interactivity is essential for understanding the new strategy.
- Interactivity will continuously develop and improve the strategy itself.

In many companies, employees with the bureaucratic social character are much more comfortable with a clear line of authority than with collaboration. But companies that are shifting from selling products to coproducing solutions with their customers recognize the need to move away from traditional hierarchical bureaucracies. They need to redesign processes and change measurements and incentives, and they need network leaders like Fredriksson. Jay Galbraith has written about efforts to make this sort of shift and about the network leadership sought at such companies as Nestlé, Nokia, and Citibank. He describes the shift in terms of forming cross-boundary networks that require leaders who can build trusting relationships to facilitate consensus-based decision-making. He reinforces the point that the best network leaders don't need formal authority, and adds that formal authority without talent, which includes Personality Intelligence, won't lead to success.[10] Network leaders succeed only when the operational collaborators grant them authority to convene people and the visionaries make clear that they are helping to implement the organization's strategy.

CHAPTER 9

# Becoming a Leader We Need

IN THESE TUMULTUOUS TIMES, we urgently need leaders who will mobilize people for the common good. The turmoil of transformation in technology and global markets, shifts in offerings from products to solutions, demand for better education and health care, and threats to our security all call for leadership that creates collaboration and responds to human needs. In this new context — the age of knowledge work — would-be leaders can't get people to follow them by relying solely on techniques that worked in the past. That's because historic changes in culture are forming a social character in the advanced globalized economy that is more interactive and less bureaucratic. Whereas father transferences once linked followers to leaders, now sibling and peer transferences undermine hierarchical authority. Interactives may reluctantly follow a leader because they feel they have to, but they'll want to follow a leader who makes them respected collaborators.

Although Interactives fit the needs of flatter, networked businesses, to be most effective these organizations need a combination of leadership types—transformational visionaries, exacting operational leaders, trust-creating network leaders—reflecting the different styles and psychological profiles that have been described in this book.

Yet basic questions about leadership remain. Why do people become leaders? Are leaders born or made? What are the qualities of mind and heart that will enable our needed leaders to gain willing collaborators? And how can these qualities be developed? How can you become a leader we need?

## WHY PEOPLE BECOME LEADERS

Clearly, genetic qualities like curiosity, conscientiousness, agreeableness, and emotional stability make a positive difference in developing leadership ability. Schooling, sports, and other activities provide opportunities to practice leadership and strengthen those qualities. Natural leaders seem to be able to get people to follow them from an early age, but in different ways. Some operational types are like Mark Twain's character, Tom Sawyer, who cleverly got Ben, Billy, and Johnny to pay him for the chance to whitewash Aunt Polly's fence by pretending the work was fun. Other operational types have a commanding presence, like George Washington, whose height, strength, and courage attracted followers early on. As a farmer, general, and president, Washington was a great operational leader. He was essential to implementing Alexander Hamilton's strategic vision for the new nation.

Strategic visionaries may not show their abilities right away. Some show their leadership qualities only by responding courageously to a difficult challenge, like Martin Luther King, Jr., who stood up against racial discrimination in the United States and created a visionary movement, or Mohandas Gandhi, who started out as a barrister and responded to British discrimination in South Africa and India by leading a revolution. Business leaders with visions of new products that change the way we work and live—and the strategic skills to turn their vision into a successful enterprise—may emerge when young, like Bill Gates, or when older, like Henry Ford.

Networking leaders typically are less commanding than the other two types, but they are natural facilitators and mediators. We recognize them as people who want to help people and who are good at building consensus and resolving conflicts.

Among our chimpanzee cousins, natural leaders emerge and force others to follow. What differentiates us from other primates is that we humans have reasons for becoming leaders. As discussed in Chapter 4, these reasons or purposes can be for personal power or for the common good. Some individuals have tried to satisfy their thirst for power and glory by becoming leaders, and people have followed them, either seduced by promises or out of fear. Almost everyone who has worked in a bureaucratic organization has at one time or another suffered under a dictatorial boss.

Power and glory, however, are not the driving motives of the leaders we need. We need leaders who care about people, their well-being and development — like Moses, who became a leader by reacting to the injustice of Egyptian slave masters and developing slaves into free people; like Abraham Lincoln, who became a leader by challenging the injustice of slavery in America and freeing the slaves; like Mahatma Gandhi, Martin Luther King, Jr., and Nelson Mandela, who became leaders by opposing the injustices of racial segregation and oppression and working to bring people together; like Dorothy Day and Mother Teresa, who became leaders by caring for helpless outcasts.

Many good leaders find meaning in making organizations work well and bringing out the best in people. But what most inspires the leaders we need and their collaborators is the vision of furthering the common good, whether by empowering people (Bill Gates of Microsoft, Steve Jobs of Apple, and Larry Page and Sergey Brin of Google), educating disadvantaged people (Mike Feinberg and David Levin of KIPP), or improving the environment (Jeff Immelt of GE and Elon Musk of Tesla Motors).

Written 2,500 years ago, the following description of a leader by the Taoist Chinese philosopher Lao Tzu explains that an ideal leader doesn't need to be idolized but strengthens others so they become independent and empowered.

> *The best of all leaders are the ones who help people so that eventually they don't need them.*
>
> *Then come the ones the people love and admire.*
>
> *Then come the ones they fear.*
>
> *The worst let people push them around (and, therefore, aren't leaders at all).*
>
> *People won't trust leaders who don't trust them.*
>
> *The best leaders say little, but what they say is fully credible.*
>
> *And when they're finished with their work, the people say we did it ourselves.*[1]

Lao Tzu and Confucius gave their advice about ideal leadership in the context of ancient China that was different from modern democratic societies These two philosophers were trying to make Chinese rulers with unquestioned authority act with benevolence toward their subjects. But even in this context, these philosophers described the leadership wisdom of knowing and trusting followers, understanding their needs, helping them to meet those needs, and empowering them.

I am the Strategic Leadership advisor for Our Little Brothers and Sisters (NPH), an organization that includes homes, schools, and healthcare facilities for at-risk children in 9 countries in Latin America and the Caribbean (Mexico, Guatemala, El Salvador, Honduras, Nicaragua, Peru, Bolivia, Haiti, Dominican Republic). Leaders of this organization either grew up in NPH homes, graduated from universities and returned to serve, or they were volunteers from Europe and the USA who stayed as leaders. When I recently asked some of them to reflect on the qualities essential for their leadership, they said that above all is an attitude of caring for the children, responding to their needs. NPH leadership also requires understanding, communicating and practicing the philosophy of NPH's founder, Father William Wasson. This philosophy includes the following principles:

- Children should feel secure, not only because they are cared for, but also because they receive education that prepares them for a productive life in their countries.

- Children should also contribute to the NPH family by working according to their abilities. This strengthens both their self-esteem and a productive mindset.

- Children should be brought up to share what they have with others and to care for people in need.

- They should learn to take responsibility, individually and collectively, for doing the right thing rather than just obeying bureaucratic rules.

This philosophy has helped NPH leaders to improve the lives of more than 18,000 children in over 60 years.

## The Qualities of a Leader We Need

Although there are different types of leaders, the best share these qualities: purpose, passion, ethics, and courage. Without a purpose, a reason for asking others to follow or collaborate with them, they would not be leaders. Without passion to achieve that purpose, they would not be convincing; effective leaders energize an organization with their passion. Without ethics, they can't be trusted. And without courage, they would not overcome resistance, nor would they be trusted to defend their organizations and the people who join them.

People who lack these qualities will not become leaders by going through leadership training. Those who do have these qualities can become more effective leaders by understanding the people they want to lead and by developing Strategic Intelligence.

## UNDERSTANDING PEOPLE—A HEART THAT LISTENS

We often hear that global competitiveness calls for more and better training in science and technology, but it depends as much or more on leaders who understand the people they want to lead. Management researchers estimate that virtual teamwork in global technology companies is 90 percent about people and 10 percent about technology.[2]

While understanding people has become more important, it has also become more difficult than in the past. In traditional villages, everyone shares the same social character, and a variation from the norm stands out like a sore thumb.[3] Peasants observe each other closely, catching expressions of jealousy, envy, greed, or anger. Their gossip mill grinds relentlessly, spreading news about neighbors. They have a sour view of human nature and are suspicious of each other. A Mexican villager who worked with a neighbor for more than 25 years told me he didn't trust his *compadre*. Why not? In a dream, this man had knifed him. Was the dream acutely sensing a potential attack? Or was it more likely expressing distrust of anyone not part of the villager's immediate family? Another interpretation might be that the dreamer was thinking about cheating his neighbor and feared revenge.

For historic reasons, peasants have reason to distrust people who don't belong to their village. They have had little experience with outsiders, and they've been taken in by slick politicians and salespeople over the years. Suspiciousness doesn't hamper farm work, and it's effective in protecting against getting fleeced. The gossip network informs everyone about each other so that fear of public disapproval and shaming keeps villagers on the straight and narrow.

In the industrial age, managers of bureaucracies avoided having to understand individuals by using formulas to control behavior. Individual jobs were formatted, results were measured, and incentives — the carrots in carrot-and-stick organizational models — were used to motivate people who were ranked according to their results and how well they served the boss. Incentives reinforced strong father transferences that made subordinates want to follow the boss.

Yet, at IBM, AT&T, and the other large companies that I studied in the 1970s, few managers could describe the personalities of their bosses or peers. Furthermore, top managers often asserted their superiority over subordinates with humiliating teasing, put-downs, and ridicule. Such behavior would be considered abusive in the diverse workforce of the knowledge era, and maybe even grounds for a lawsuit. But at the time, workers swallowed these insults with forced smiles. This behavior was an accepted part of the corporate culture, solidifying the hierarchy.

In the knowledge age, there are still many bureaucratic organizations, but as firms become more like collaborative communities, there is a mix of transferential feelings. To gain a following, leaders must be "doctors" and "role models" rather than "parents." Furthermore, the interactive social character doesn't take kindly to abusive bosses, and that accounts for the popularity of emotional intelligence (EI). As detailed by Daniel Goleman in the 1990s, EI includes such qualities as empathy and self-control. Managers with EI communicate more effectively and have smoother relationships with subordinates than those who lack it. EI is especially important for operational and network leaders and matters less for strategic leaders. Some of the most successful strategic visionaries — Bill Gates, Steve Jobs, Jeff Bezos, Elon Musk, and Larry Ellison, to name the most well-known — have been reported by subordinates as losing their temper in meetings and ridiculing people for ideas they call stupid. Even those productive narcissists who are gifted with empathy aren't particularly self-aware or caring with their underlings. Leaders can tactically use empathy to seduce people into thinking that they understand them and sympathize with their plight. But when leaders say they feel your pain, it doesn't necessarily mean that they care about you or even understand you.[4]

Although EI is a significant element in understanding people, it's only a part of Personality Intelligence. To understand people means to understand how they think and what motivates them — their personality. This understanding is intellectual as well as emotional. Some people are gifted with this kind of understanding. Great novelists and playwrights create believable personalities, some of whom become prototypes for how we view people, for we don't recognize anything we can't name or categorize. For example, the Sami people in the north of Scandinavia see and name different colors of reindeer skin that others see only as a kind of yellow-brown, and the trained botanist sees variations in plants and flowers that don't register for the rest of us. So it is with personality. By describing characters, their personality, and passions, Shakespeare, perhaps the greatest writer in terms of Personality Intelligence, teaches us to see some of the personalities we meet in our own lives: the Hamlets and Horatios, Othellos and Iagos, Romeos and Juliets, Macbeths and Lady Macbeths. Freud, who often cited Shakespeare and other great writers, developed a list of personality types that systematically describe a universal cast of characters.

From antiquity to the present, the most astute monarchs, presidents, and generals have tried to understand personality in order to predict the behavior of key lieutenants or adversaries. For them, knowing the people they must fight and those they depend on was a matter of life and death. Some used astrology, which offered an elaborate set of personality descriptions based on date and time of birth. Now, organizational leaders use personality questionnaires, like SDI, that boast test validity.[5] Still, people can game these paper-and-pencil tests. They can consciously or unconsciously give answers they think put them in the best light. A good theory of personality types and knowledge of social character, cultural values, and identities are essential for understanding people, but Personality Intelligence also requires the ability to directly experience another person's emotional attitudes.

Can anyone fully understand another person? Heraclitus, the pre-Socratic philosopher, wrote, "You could not in your going find the ends of the soul, though you traveled the whole way: so deep is its law."[6] Even though we may never fully know another person, to begin to know others in their uniqueness, understand their psyches, and have some sense of how they see the world requires a combination of a good theory and experiential capability, qualities of both head and heart.

In traditional thinking about wisdom, the heart is a metaphor for the kind of experiential knowledge that should combine with conceptual knowledge to develop Personality Intelligence. In the Bible, King Solomon dreams that God asks him, "What shall I give thee?" and he answers, "Give thy servant, therefore, a heart with skill to listen, so that I may govern thy people justly and distinguish good from evil."[7]

People think that qualities of the heart are opposite to those of the head; that heart means softness, sentiment, and generosity, while head means tough-minded, realistic thought.[8] But in pre-Cartesian thought, the heart was the true seat of intelligence and the brain the instrument of logic and calculation. The head alone can decipher codes, solve technical problems, and keep accounts, but it can't resolve emotional doubt about what is true, good, or beautiful. The head alone can't give emotional weight to knowledge and, therefore, can't fire up courage based on knowledge of what is right to do. The root of the English word "courage" is the Latin *cor*, meaning "heart." Historically, the heart was the seat of intelligence and feeling. Today, we know that the head can be smart and score well on an IQ test, but without emotion it cannot be wise, and certainly not about people. That takes a heart that listens.[9]

Intellectually, it's possible to observe patterns of behavior that fit the SDI personality types — for example, the exacting green's neatness and methodical moves, the caring blue's pleasure at giving help and receiving affirmation, the red visionary's self-involvement and bias toward action, and the adaptive hub person's flexibility and sensitivity to interpersonal cues.[10] Even body language can express type of personality, as in the exacting person's tight lips, elbows close to the body, or finger wagging for emphasis. But recognizing personality types can't help us to know that a person is sad, happy, loving, angry, resentful, envious, doubtful, or insincere. Yes, to a certain extent, we can recognize emotions like anger and fear from facial expressions and body language. Indeed, Paul Ekman, a professor of psychology at the University of California Medical School, San Francisco, teaches people to recognize at least seven facial expressions: sadness, anger, fear, surprise, disgust, contempt, and happiness.[11] But it's only when we can experience those feelings directly in others, just as in ourselves, that we can be sure about what we see. That takes a developed heart.

Intellect organizes data from and about other people, but it doesn't experience them. Knowledge from the head alone is devoid of emotion. The more we experience what we observe, the more information we have to understand others. We use our heads fully to reason and affirm only when our hearts are engaged. Of course, the term "heart" doesn't just mean the organ that pumps blood. Rather it's a figure of speech (like all hands on deck) to represent one of our body parts focused on experiencing and understanding not only others but also ourselves. Describing recent research on mirror neurons, which allow us to experience another's emotions, Goleman cites Giacomo Rizzolatti, the Italian neuroscientist who discovered them. According to Rizzolatti, these systems "allow us to grasp the minds of others not through conceptual reasoning but through direct simulation; by feeling, not by thinking."[12]

But knowledge of the heart also refers to self-understanding. With a detached heart, we remain unaware of our own feelings. I've had patients who, when asked what they are feeling, say, "I'm feeling fine," even though I (through my mirror neurons) experience directly their sadness or anger. This repression of feeling leaves them anesthetized, half asleep.

When both head and heart develop together, the result is heightened experiential perception and expanded understanding of others, enhanced awareness of truth versus sham, and increased energy and courage to act on convictions.

Developing both head and heart doesn't guarantee always being right about people. We can be fooled by another's charm or our own wishful thinking. However, the opposite of doubt isn't certainty but, rather, faith in our ability to get to the truth and our willingness to risk being wrong or gullible, because we know we can learn from our errors. Similarly, Personality Intelligence doesn't guarantee doing what's right. There will always be ethical dilemmas to consider, even for someone with the clearest vision and highest moral values.

When executives are asked to list the competencies of an effective leader, they mention skills like good decision making, strategic thinking, coaching, team building, communicating complex messages, and selecting and developing talent. Although all these skills can be learned to some degree, how well they're executed depends on intellectual and emotional qualities, a person's brains and personality.

We've discussed the kind of personalities that fit the three types of leadership roles needed in the knowledge workplace. And we've mentioned the new kinds of intelligence — strategic and personality — that equip leaders for the challenges of our time. Let's now consider how to develop these intellectual abilities.

## DEVELOPING PERSONALITY INTELLIGENCE

Personality and Strategic Intelligence are the new leadership qualities for the age of knowledge work. Although both require analytic and practical intelligence, Personality Intelligence builds more on Emotional Intelligence; Strategic Intelligence, more on systems thinking and practical intelligence.[13] Rather than expecting all leaders, even the best ones, to score at the top range in both types of intelligence, we can also think of a leadership team in which different members contribute different qualities of intelligence. Of course, to make this work, the whole team needs to understand these qualities and why they are essential to strategy and visioning on the one hand, and to improving relationships, dissolving distorting transferences, selecting talent, and motivating and partnering effectively on the other. Even though some members of a team will excel over others, everyone can improve both Personality and Strategic Intelligence.

In Chapter 5 and Chapter 6 we've described how to recognize different types of personality and how to make use of that knowledge. But to develop Personality Intelligence you must also develop your heart. The heart is a muscle. Figuratively and literally, without exercise it won't get strong. Overly protected, it's easily hurt. There's a term for a person with a weak heart and a strong sense of guilt: a bleeding heart, typically a caring personality with liberal beliefs who may not understand the people they want to help. When the object of these good intentions isn't grateful, the bleeding heart feels taken in.

All social characters and personality types can develop their hearts, but there are typical differences in the attitudes of different personality types when fully experiencing self and others. Brought up in a more or less close-knit nuclear family, the bureaucratic social character typically has strong emotional ties that cause strong transferences. To avoid feeling vulnerable or being misled by their emotions, bureaucrats sometimes build a shell around their hearts. For example, one such CEO said, "If I opened myself up to people, they would eat me alive." Another said, "I've a shell around my heart, and even my children feel and resent it." But the lack of Personality Intelligence resulting from an overprotected heart diminished their effectiveness. It made these two executives vulnerable to counter-transferences whereby they overvalued inadequate but admiring subordinates. Self-protectiveness leaves the unexercised heart flabby and causes managers to obsess over decisions when they need to take action.

In contrast, Interactives tend to be more detached. At an early age, they don't expect parents to always be there for them, and they become emotionally independent. It's easier for them to break off unsatisfying relationships, but it's also harder to commit themselves to others. Although they may have radar-like interpersonal intelligence, they use their gut rather than their heart in deciding about people. This leads to overvaluing people's appearance — whether or not they look good, present themselves well, or seem confident. Unresolved doubt often underlies these quick judgments. Interactives, especially marketing types, know who's on their side only as long as they're on the same team. Yet, the most productive Interactives are self-developers, and just as they recognize the need to keep mind and body up to speed, so they may grasp the benefit of developing the heart.

Of course, some people don't just protect a tender heart, but also harden it in pursuit of power, revenge, or an ideology, including one that may justify terrorism. These are the most dangerous leaders, those unmoved by the feelings of others. An example is Fidel Castro, who was "remorseless and unforgiving of his perceived enemies," and wrote from prison, "I have a heart of steel."[14]

Developing the heart means exercising it, being willing to experience strong and even painful feelings. It means leaders should not ignore the guilt they may feel when making an unpopular decision, firing people, or otherwise causing grief in order to further the common good, and they should not ignore the anger of those who are hurt. No muscle gets strengthened without exercise.

Just as there are disciplines to develop the intellect, such as mathematics, logic, and science, so there are disciplines to develop the heart.[15] They are: clearing the mind to see things as they are, listening to ourselves, and listening and responding to others.

*Clearing The Mind*

Heraclitus wrote that when we dream we are in different worlds, but awake, we are in the same reality. Only when we are fully awake do we see things as they are. Yet, many people go through life half-asleep because they repress uncomfortable perceptions and feelings.

Clearing the mind to see things as they are means frustrating, rather than repressing, the cravings that cloud the mind and avoiding fantasy and all other forms of escapism. We can't see people as they are when our minds are clouded by emotions like lust, anger, or jealousy. For example, a glutton isn't the best judge of gourmet cooking.

To see things as they are, we have to practice frustrating the fantasies and passions that keep us from being clear-eyed and fully awake. At an early age, we naturally repress thoughts and impulses that make us feel crazy or could get us into trouble. But the habit of repression can spread, blocking self-awareness.

*Listening to Ourselves*

Listening to ourselves means experiencing what we would feel and think if we weren't defending ourselves from unpleasant feelings and thoughts. Freud's motto, taken from the poet Terrance, was "Nothing human is alien to me." We have within us all the human potentialities and passions, creative and destructive. If we were fully in touch with ourselves, we'd experience murderous madness and dark despair, but also transcendent love and cosmic consciousness.

Great mystics like Meister Eckhardt, St. John of the Cross, and the Buddhist masters journey to the depths of the soul to free the self from enslaving needs and affirm the human capacity to find transcendent relatedness to the universe, to overcome the illusion, as Einstein put it, that we are isolated beings. In the Judeo-Christian tradition, the goal is oneness with God. In the nontheistic Buddhist tradition, it's enlightenment — being fully awake and present. An essential function of religious and philosophical thinking is to contain and give meaning to what we can experience when we become aware of powerful and troubling repressed feelings. Freud tried to substitute a psychoanalytic framework, but I think his insights need to be understood within a more spiritual context. This is what Erich Fromm did in his humanistic psychoanalysis.

Although there's a limit to how much we can, at the same time, function in the rough and tumble world and also explore the depths of our psyches, we can practice getting in touch with what we really experience with other people and not repress uncomfortable thoughts and feelings. In his book *Blink*, Malcolm Gladwell cites studies showing that first reactions are often more accurate than studied evaluations.[16] We sometimes repress our first negative perceptions of people. As we saw in Chapter 3, unconscious transference projections can cover the real personalities of bosses or subordinates. Of course, sometimes it's inconvenient to admit to ourselves what we really feel about the people we need to get along with. But we can't do anything about improving bad relationships if we don't see people as they are.

Getting in touch with oneself, self-awareness, is a goal of psychoanalysis, especially uncovering transferences that distort how we see others. But analysis is a costly process, and unless a person is suffering from psychological causes, it's not practical for most people. Furthermore, when I taught and supervised analysts, very few showed the talent for or interest in exploring the unconscious any more than was necessary to alleviate a patient's anxiety or depression. And even while undergoing deep analysis with Erich Fromm for eight years, I still found it helpful to practice a Zen Buddhist form of daily meditation to get in touch with myself. Besides Zen, there are other forms of meditation and prayer that help to connect us to our feelings and silence the noise that muffles the small voice of truth that's in all of us, but is often ignored.

This is one of the strongest arguments for using a personality assessment that is based on psychoanalytic theory and practice. Tools like the SDI build on the solid foundation established by Freud and Fromm, but go further by making the benefits of these insights available in the form of assessment results (rather than through weekly therapy sessions). In some ways, the person conducting the assessment plays the role of the analyst: listening (by way of standardized questions), evaluating the responses, classifying them according to a personality typology, and presenting the results to guide the learner in a process of self-discovery. This gives leaders a framework for listening to themselves, and a common language for communicating with others.

*Listening and Responding to Others*

Listening and responding to others when we have cleared the mind and are awake frees us from the obsession with self, so we can see others more clearly. This kind of listening is active, reaching out with head and heart to understand what we are hearing. Paradoxically, when we obsess about what others think of us, we reinforce our egocentrism. That just keeps us in ourselves. We overcome egocentrism only when we get out of ourselves to see things from another's point of view. That doesn't mean assuming that others feel what we'd feel in their place. Rather, we need to make an effort to understand how others view things through their own lenses, even experience directly what they experience — an effort of both head and heart. Beyond understanding is service — reaching out to others, and responding with intelligence and passion to those who need our help.

By practicing these disciplines, we not only strengthen our ability to understand and act. As Albert Schweitzer wrote, only those who have sought and found how to serve well will be truly happy.[17] By realizing a vocation of service, we strengthen our hearts, bring joy and fulfillment to our lives, and attract others who find meaning in the same missions.

## DEVELOPING STRATEGIC INTELLIGENCE

In my earlier study of narcissistic leaders, I found that the most successful strategic visionaries demonstrate Strategic Intelligence (SI),[18] a mix of analytic, practical, and creative elements.[19] Now, when we need visionaries and their leadership teams to take on the challenges of economic development, health care, education, alternative energy, environmental protection, and national security, these leaders should be able to anticipate future trends, think systemically, design effective social systems, communicate meaning and purpose to motivate and educate collaborators, and partner with other types of leaders who complement their strengths.

The largest gap in the intellectual ability needed for effective leadership in the knowledge age is systems thinking. Without it, leaders can't understand the relation of global forces to local pressures, macro policy to micro implementation, and social character to individual personality. Without it, their organizational vision lacks coherence. When linear thinkers connect the dots, they draw straight lines rather than create the dynamic interactive force field that represents a knowledge-age organization.

After I first wrote about SI, a group of consultants joined me to interview more than 30 top executives about it.[20] These leaders agreed that the elements of Strategic Intelligence were essential for a CEO's effectiveness. They told us that a major part of the CEO's role was to think about the future, and all of them worked on their foresight, using tools like scenario planning. In one way or another, all these executives scanned the relevant business environment. At large companies and government agencies alike, they were taught "what-if" thinking. U.S. naval officers were even graded on their foresight.

But with few exceptions, these executives told us that of all the elements of SI, they were weakest on systems thinking. Their knee-jerk approach to a problem was to attack and analyze, to break it into clearly manageable pieces — stacked rather than integrated — and to manage the various parts of their organization rather than the interactions among them.

Why is systems thinking so hard for many executives? And can it be taught?

Some people are natural systems thinkers, while others think in terms of clearly definable details and simple cause-and-effect relationships.[21] Visionaries tend to be systems thinkers while exacting types are more inclined to make lists. Contrast Freud, the visionary, who conceived of behavior as resulting from the interaction of passions (id), conscience (superego), and self-interest (ego), with research psychologists who list behavior traits they can measure but that have no obvious relationship to each other. Some of the great business entrepreneurs have been systems thinkers, like Henry Ford, who designed the model system for the industrial age, and Toyota's Taiichi Ohno, who transformed Ford's system of pushing out a standardized product to a pull system of lean production and just-in-time delivery of varied products demanded by customers. Some business leaders have failed because they lacked systems thinking.[22]

Some of the most creative leaders I've known or studied have designed social systems with a distinct purpose: the well-being of the people they served. Each of their organizations became collaborative cultures based on shared values and principles, with processes and measures that reinforced the purpose. Sure, they still needed some bureaucratic-type rules, but these were kept to a minimum. One of the leaders' primary roles was to educate and persuade people to internalize their core principles so rules wouldn't be needed.

One way to learn systems thinking is to study the experiences of other organizations. Corporate executives who are trying to transform bureaucracies, to twist silos into networks, can learn much from the Mayo Clinic. Designed by William Mayo, the organization's culture can be more effective than formal rules in strengthening the role of network leaders. When patients arrive at Mayo, internists are assigned as the network leaders of their care. In complex cases, these doctors bring together the specialists who decide and integrate treatment. They form an effective team not because the internist-leader has any power over them, but because they believe that working together is the best way to achieve the Mayo Clinic's purpose of high-quality patient care.

For car companies, the Toyota system has become the gold standard, the model most others have tried to copy.[23] Toyota is an exceptional example of an advanced industrial company that employs and teaches systems thinking. Recently, I asked the chief engineer at a supplier to several auto companies whether there was any difference in how Toyota related to his firm, compared to other car companies. There was. When the supplier had a quality problem, other customers just told the supplier to fix it. "Toyota," the chief engineer said, "is deeply involved. They won't relent until they understand how the system is causing the problem. The other companies just want the problem to go away. We sometimes work around the problem and that adds cost. Toyota partners with us. Their system solutions improve quality and cut costs."

In the knowledge age, there is no best way to organize work. Organizations can learn from, but should not copy, each other. To enable others to learn from the best cases of effective organizational systems, case writers at business schools should be systems thinkers who are sensitive to the interaction of roles, processes, competencies, operating principles, and values and who are able to evaluate all these elements in terms of how well they work together to further the system's purpose. Few business school accounts of the cases I've worked on within a company or government agency meet this test.

Toyota tries to teach systems thinking to its suppliers in their kaizen workshops. The chief engineer of the auto supply company I visited said, "Getting people to learn systems thinking is hard. In the workshop, they may suddenly get it. But when they go back to their factory and try it out, sometimes they can't do it, or it doesn't work right and the other managers discount it. You can't develop and use it without top management support."

One way top management can develop systems thinking in their company is by organizing workshops where teams made up of managers from different divisions apply systems thinking in creating a new offering or business. With Russ Ackoff, who taught participants the principles of systems thinking, I've led workshops like these to focus on the kinds of leadership that encourage the collaboration needed to design and implement innovative visions. More recently, I've led these workshops with Tim Scudder.

The most direct way to educate managers about social systems is to get them to take part in transforming their own organizations. I've facilitated this process in a few companies, including the MITRE Corporation, which does technical consulting and R&D for the U.S. military and the Federal Aviation Administration. Faced with increased competition and complaints from MITRE's clients, in 1990, Barry Horowitz, CEO at the time, recognized the need for change and asked me to help. In the past, clients that had purchased new technology from MITRE sometimes had trouble using it. They wanted business solutions integrating the technology, and that called for better understanding and collaboration, both with clients and within MITRE.

The essential story is that Horowitz and the MITRE vice presidents redesigned the organization to achieve the new purpose. This called for creating new client relationships, adapting the organizational structure, evaluating MITRE professionals on marketing and leadership as well as on technical skills, and instituting supportive training programs. MITRE had the advantage of a tradition of working with technical systems, so it was relatively easy to get managers to understand social systems. Furthermore, some MITRE executives — like Jack Fearnsides, who was trying to transform the air-traffic control system, and Lydia Thomas, who became president and CEO of the company's Mitretek Systems spin-off — also learned to apply knowledge of personality and social character in placing managers and coaching them to collaborate.

An essential quality for leaders in the knowledge age is the ability to keep learning and, specifically, to keep developing and employing their Personality and Strategic Intelligence. Change — whether in the form of new technologies, competition, or political and environmental dangers — is continual and a leader will always have to work with new people. The time is long past when executives preside over smoothly running, stable bureaucracies, or when national leaders can ignore the larger world. However there are many people with leadership qualities ready and willing to respond to the challenges of our time, to become the leaders we need. Those of us who study and teach leadership have the challenge of helping them to succeed.

As much as leaders might want simple formulas for dealing with people, they won't be helped by them. Some will need help to understand and change mindsets formed in the bureaucratic-industrial era. Others, such as the technical professionals who chose careers in technology to escape the messy world of people, will need help to move out of their comfort zones to connect with the human side, to know themselves.

To become a leader we need, keep in mind that the people who will help you succeed aren't all just like you. Increasing numbers of them won't follow the good parent model of leadership. To make them willing collaborators, especially the Interactives, you'll need to develop and communicate a vision and an organizational philosophy, including the purpose of your work together, that inspires them. You need to be consistent, and sometimes that means being tough. By understanding your collaborators and helping them find roles in which they can demonstrate and develop their strengths, you'll gain their respect, maybe even their trust. And then, you will have become a leader we need.

# Notes

*Preface*

1. John W. Gardner, On Leadership (New York: The Free Press, 1990).
2. For example, John P. Kotter, "What Leaders Really Do," Harvard Business Review, May–June 1990, 103–112.
3. James McGregor Burns, Leadership (New York: Harper & Row, 1978).
4. After the publication of this book, I learned that Peter Drucker gave this same definition in an interview with Gerhard Friedberg.
5. Knowledge worker is a term coined by Peter Drucker in 1959 as a person who works primarily with information or someone who uses or develops knowledge in the workplace.
6. Written with Clifford L. Norman, C. Jane Norman, and Richard Margolies (Jossey-Bass, 2013)
7. (Oxford University Press, 2013)
8. (Harvard Business School Press, 2007), first published as The Productive Narcissist (Broadway Books, 2003)

*Chapter 1*

1. Jack Weatherford, Genghis Khan and the Making of the Modern World (New York: Crown, 2004).
2. For example, a survey by the National Opinion Research Center, University of Chicago conducted between August 2004 and January 2005 found only 22 percent of the public expressed a "great deal of confidence" in the executive branch of the federal government, 29 percent in banks and financial institutions and 25 percent in leaders of organized religion. Reported in the New York Times Magazine, December 11, 2005, 25. In the United Kingdom, less than 20 percent of the public expressed either "a fair amount" or "a great deal" of trust in the heads of large companies and even less in labor government ministers and senior civil servants ("Trust Me, I'm a Judge," The Economist, U.S. edition, May 5, 2007, 71).
3. The socio-psychoanalytic concept of social character was conceived by Erich Fromm (1900–1980). Fromm saw personality as the human equivalent of animal instinct. Another way of putting it is that personality shapes our instincts. To some extent, this is true of other mammals. But it is even more so for us humans, with our larger brains, longer period of dependency, and greater need for learning. If humans had to decide each action, we'd be overwhelmed by the choices. Personality structures our attitudes to work and how we relate to others, what we find most satisfying and dissatisfying

and what we expect from others in our culture. While part of our personality is genetically determined, particularly temperament, character can be considered the part that is learned. The social character is that learned part of our personality we share with others in our culture or subculture.

4. Bureau of Labor Statistics report: Employment Characteristic of Families—2004, Table 4, "Families with own children: Employment status of parents by age of youngest child and family type, 2003-2004 annual averages" Father employed, not mother (married-couple families): 7,867, Families maintained by women: 8,161 (numbers in thousands).

5. Erich Fromm and Michael Maccoby, Social Character in a Mexican Village (Englewood Cliffs, NJ: Prentice-Hall, 1970; reprinted with new introduction by Michael Maccoby [New Brunswick, NJ: Transaction Publishers, 1996]

6. Of the fifty most generous philanthropists in 2005, fifteen, including these innovators, support new schools. BusinessWeek, November 28, 2005, 61.

7. Sigmund Freud, The Dynamics of Transference, vol. XII, The Standard Edition of the Complete Psychological Works of Sigmund Freud (London: The Hogarth Press, 1958), 97–109 (orig. pub. 1912); Michael Maccoby, "Why People Follow the Leader: The Power of Transference," Harvard Business Review, September 2004, 76–85.

8. In The Moral Basis of a Backward Society (Glencoe, IL: The Free Press, 1958), Edward Banfield describes similar dynamics in Southern Italian peasant families

9. Michael Maccoby, The Leader: A New Face for American Management (New York: Simon & Schuster, 1981).

10. Michael Maccoby, The Gamesman: The New Corporate Leaders (New York: Simon and Schuster, 1976).

11. Michael Maccoby, The Productive Narcissist: The Promise and Peril of Visionary Leadership (New York: Broadway Books, 2003), released in paperback edition with a new preface by author as Narcissistic Leaders: Who Succeeds and Who Fails, (Boston: Harvard Business School Press, 2007).

12. Michael Maccoby, Why Work: Leading the New Generation (New York: Simon and Schuster, 1988; 2nd ed. Why Work? Motivating the New Workforce [Alexandria, VA: Miles River Press, 1995]); Charles C. Heckscher et al., Agents of Change: Crossing the Post-Industrial Divide (Oxford: Oxford University Press, 2003).

13. Charles Heckscher and Paul S. Adler, eds., The Firm as a Collaborative Community: The Reconstruction of Trust in the Knowledge Economy (Oxford: Oxford University Press, 2005).

14. Rakesh Khurana, Searching for a Corporate Savior: The Irrational Quest for Charismatic CEOs (Princeton, NJ: Princeton University Press, 2002).

15. Erich Fromm, Escape from Freedom (New York: Rinehart: 1941).

16. Erich Fromm, The Working Class in Weimar Germany: A Psychological and Sociological Study; trans. Barbara Weinberger, ed. Wolfgang Bonss (Cambridge, MA: Harvard University Press, 1984); see also Richard J. Evans, The Third Reich in Power, 1922–1939 (London: Penguin, 2005).

17. In "Employees Want to Hear It 'Straight' from the Boss's Mouth," Financial Times, December 1, 2006, Alison Maitland reports: "What employees really want, according to a new survey, are straight-talkers who keep them up to date with bad, as well as good news instead of putting on a performance or preaching through PowerPoint."

## Chapter 2

1. These qualities were cited by CEOs and other leaders in speeches given at The World Business Forum in New York, September 13–14, 2005.

2. Thomas H. Davenport, Thinking for a Living: How to Get Better Performance and Results from Knowledge Workers. Boston: Harvard Business School Press, 2005.

3. Betsy Morris, "Genentech: The Best Place to Work Now," Fortune, January 11, 2006, 79-86.

4. See, for example, Donald Roy, "Quota Restrictions and Goldbricking in a Machine Shop," American Journal of Sociology, March 1952, 427-442.

5. Elton Mayo, The Problems of an Industrialized Civilization. Boston: Division of Research, Harvard Business

School, 1933. F. J. Roethlisberger and William J. Dickson, Management and the Worker: An Account of a Research Program Conducted by the Western Electric Company, Hawthorne Works. Cambridge, MA: Harvard University Press, 1939.

6. See the description of my work at AT&T in Chapter 2 of Charles C. Heckscher et al., Agents of Change: Crossing the Post-Industrial Divide. New York: Oxford University Press, 2003.

7. Richard Gillespie, Manufacturing Knowledge: A History of the Hawthorne Experiments. Cambridge, UK: Cambridge University Press, 1991, p. 79. In his fascinating history of the Hawthorne studies, Gillespie goes back to the original field notes and memos and finds that the researchers differed among themselves about the findings and the workers argued about the conclusions.

8. Douglas McGregor, The Human Side of Enterprise. New York: McGraw-Hill, 1960. Abraham Maslow, Motivation and Personality. New York: Harper, 1954.

9. Abraham Maslow, Eupsychian Management. Homewood, IL: R.D. Irwin, 1965, p. 36. Maslow's examples of evolved versus unevolved people compare Americans to people from the third world. For example, referring to Peter Drucker's elaboration of Theory Y, management by objectives, he writes, "Where we have fairly evolved human beings able to grow, eager to grow, then Drucker's management principles seem to be fine. They will work, but only at the top of the hierarchy of human development. They assume ideally a person who has been satisfied in his basic needs in the past, while he was growing up, and who is now being satisfied in his life situation. He was and now is safety-need gratified (not anxious, not fearful). He was and is belongingness-need satisfied (he does not feel alienated, ostracized, orphaned, outside the group; he fits into the family, the team, the society; he is not an unwelcome intruder). He was and is love-need gratified (he has enough friends and enough good ones, a reasonable family life; he feels worthy of being loved and wanted and able to give love—this means much more than romantic love, especially in the industrial situation). He was and is respect-need gratified (he feels respect-worthy, needed, important, etc.; he feels he gets enough praise and expects to get whatever praise and reward he deserves). He was and is self-esteem-need satisfied. As a matter of fact, this doesn't happen often enough in our society; most people on unconscious levels do not have enough feelings of self-love, self-respect. But in any case, the American citizen is far better off here, let's say, than the Mexican citizen is" (p. 15).

10. Michael Maccoby, The Leader: A New Face for American Management. New York: Simon & Schuster, 1981, p. 75.

11. Michael Maccoby, The Leader: A New Face for American Management. New York: Simon & Schuster, 1981, p. 166. See also Heckscher et al., Agents of Change, chapter 2.

12. Anabel Quan-Haase and Barry Wellman, "Hyperconnected Network." In Charles Heckscher and Paul S. Adler (eds.), The Firm as Collaborative Community. New York: Oxford University Press, 2006, p. 314.

13. Edward E. Lawler III, Motivation in Work Organizations. San Francisco: Jossey-Bass, 1993, p. 43.

14. Viktor E. Frankl, Man's Search for Meaning. Boston, MA: Beacon Press, 2006.

15. See Michael Maccoby, Why Work? Motivating the New Workforce, 2nd ed. Alexandria, VA: Miles River Press, 1995.

16. Jean Piaget, The Moral Judgment of the Child. New York: The Free Press, 1965; orig. pub. 1932. Jean Piaget, Play, Dreams and Imitation in Childhood. New York: Norton, 1951.

17. For a fuller description of Kohlberg's stages of moral reasoning and other views on the subject, see Daniel K. Lapsley, Moral Psychology. Boulder, CO: Westview Press, 1996.

18. It is dedicated to Lorenzo de' Medici, Duke of Urbino (1492–1519). This was not Lorenzo the Magnificent of Florence, the great patron of the arts who died in 1492, but a grandson who ruled as a dictator and whose claim to fame is his tomb in Florence, sculpted by Michelangelo. By dedicating his book to Lorenzo, Machiavelli hoped, vainly as it turned out, that the duke would revive his political career and end his exile.

19. Niccolò Machiavelli, The Prince, trans. Harvey C. Mansfield, Jr. Chicago: University of Chicago Press, 1985, p. 69.

20. Niccolò Machiavelli, The Discourses, Book 3, Chapter 20. London: Penguin Classics, 1984, However, Machiavelli writes that for a republic, it's better to have a harsh commander like Manlius because he reinforces Republican values of discipline and justice without regard for rank or riches. Valerius's method is harmful, he writes,

because it prepares the way for tyranny. How so? What Machiavelli doesn't mention but history tells us is that Valerius Corvinus, though originally a Republican, went over to join Octavian (who became Emperor Augustus) to destroy the Republic. This message may be that a considerate general can become a popular politician (think of Dwight D. "Ike" Eisenhower) and might become a dictator while a tough general (think of George Patton) sticks to the military and is no such threat.

21. Niccolò Machiavelli, The Discourses, Book 3. London: Penguin Classics, 1984, p. 468.

22. Niccolò Machiavelli, The Prince, Chapter XXV, trans. Harvey C. Mansfield, Jr. Chicago: University of Chicago Press, 1985.

23. Michael Maccoby, "Trust Trumps Love and Fear," MIT Sloan Management Review, 45(2), Winter 2004, pp. 14-16.

24. Alan Deutschman, "Psychopathic Bosses," Fast Company, July 2005, 44-51.

25. Jim Collins, Good to Great. New York: Harper Collins Business, 2001, p. 127.

26. Jim Collins, Good to Great. New York: Harper Collins Business, 2001, p. 27.

27. Michael Maccoby, Narcissistic Leaders: Who Succeeds and Who Fails. Boston: Harvard Business School Press, 2007. Neither Collins nor Jack Welch mentioned the other personality types I've observed: the caring and marketing types. I'll discuss these types in Chapter 5.

28. Jack Welch with Suzy Welch, Winning. New York: Harper Business, 2005, pp.181-184.

29. This research on professional football players was done on the San Diego Chargers by Dr. Arnold T. Mandell, then chairman of the Department of Psychiatry, University of California, San Diego. "A Psychiatric Study of Professional Football," Saturday Review, October 5, 1974, pp. 12-16.

30. Michael Maccoby, The Gamesman: The New Corporate Leaders. New York: Simon and Schuster, 1976, Chapter 6.

31. Andrew Pollack, "Hewlett's 'Consummate Strategist,'" The New York Times, March 10, 1992.

32. Personal communication from Martin C. Faga, CEO of MITRE in McLean, Virginia, June 22, 2006.

33. Leonard Shapiro, "NFL Coaches Take a Gentler Approach," The Washington Post, November 6, 2005.

34. Carol Hymowitz, "Two Football Coaches Have a Lot to Teach Screaming Managers," The Wall Street Journal, January 29, 2007.

35. John Brauch, "NBC Gives Barber the Ball and He Runs with It," The New York Times, February 14, 2007.

36. Reported by Jena McGregor, "Game Plan: First Find the Leaders," BusinessWeek, August 21-28, 2006.

## Chapter 3

1. This chapter builds on my article, "Why People Follow the Leader: The Power of Transference," Harvard Business Review, September 2004, pp. 76-85.

2. Sigmund Freud, Character and Anal Eroticism, vol. IX, The Standard Edition of the Complete Psychological Works of Sigmund Freud. London: Hogarth Press, 1958, pp. 167-177 (orig. pub. 1908).

3. Sigmund Freud, Observations on Transference Love, vol. XII, The Standard Edition of the Complete Psychological Works of Sigmund Freud. London: Hogarth Press, 1958, p. 168 (orig. pub. 1915).

4. http://www.cps-ltd.co.uk, February 2005.

5. Michael Maccoby, "Achieving Good Governance for Psychoanalytic Societies," American Psychoanalyst, Winter/Spring 2004, 9, 13.

6. Lydia Thomas, interview with author, August 5, 2004.

7. I've disguised all names and possible identifying aspects of my clients.

8. Sigmund Freud, Observations on Transference Love, vol. XII, The Standard Edition of the Complete Psychological Works of Sigmund Freud. London: Hogarth Press, 1958, p. 196 (orig. pub. 1915).

9. This thesis of the increase of sibling transferences linked to the changing family structure is based on my experience and that of colleagues, including academic researchers and psychotherapists, who report that their patients from these family backgrounds express these transferences in therapy.

10. Along with the emphasis on protecting Americans from terrorists were ads projecting a paternal image of George W. Bush. One widely broadcast TV ad was "Ashley's Story," in which Bush comforts a teenage girl who lost her mother in the 9/11 attacks. The transferential appeal reaches its peak when Ashley says about Bush, "He's the most powerful man in the world, and all he wants to do is make sure I'm safe, that I'm OK." Cited by Kevin Lanning, "The Social Psychology of the 2004 U.S. Presidential Election," Analyses of Social Issues and Public Policy, 5(1), 2005, p. 150.

11. Michael Maccoby, Narcissistic Leaders: Who Succeeds and Who Fails. Boston: Harvard Business School Press, 2007. Michael Maccoby, Clifford L. Norman, C. Jane Norman, and Richard Margolies, Transforming Health Care Leadership: A Systems Guide to Improve Patient Care, Decrease Costs, and Improve Population Health. San Francisco: Jossey-Bass Publishing, 2013. Michael Maccoby, Strategic Intelligence: Conceptual Tools for Leading Change. Oxford, UK: Oxford University Press, 2015.

## Chapter 4

1. Michael Maccoby, Narcissistic Leaders: Who Succeeds and Who Fails. Boston: Harvard Business School Press, 2007. In the village, the entrepreneurs bought the land these people had been given after the revolution in order to build weekend houses for rich people from Mexico City. Left landless, these villagers soon used up the money and were forced to become day laborers.

2. Alexis de Tocqueville, Democracy in America. New York: Vintage Books, 1958, p. 330.

3. Peter F. Drucker, "Management and the World's Work," Harvard Business Review, September-October 1988, p. 75.

4. Charles Dickens, Little Dorrit. New York: The Modern Library, 2002, p. 114 (orig. pub. 1857).

5. "Public officers in the United States are not separate from the mass of citizens; they have neither palaces nor ceremonial costumes. This simple exterior of persons in authority is connected not only with the peculiarities of the American character, but with the fundamental principles of society . . . A public officer in the United States is uniformly simple in his manners, accessible to all the world, attentive to all requests, and obliging in his replies. I was pleased by these characteristics of a democratic government; I admired the manly independence that respects the office more than the officer and thinks less of the emblems of authority than of the man who bears them." Alexis de Tocqueville, Democracy in America. New York: Vintage Books, 1958, pp. 214-215.

6. Max Weber, The Protestant Ethic and the Spirit of Capitalism. New York: Scribner, 1958, p. 182 (orig. pub. 1904-1905).

7. Cited by Robert K. Merton, "Bureaucratic Structure and Personality," in K. Kluckhohn and H. A. Murray (eds.), Personality in Nature, Society, and Culture. New York: Alfred A. Knopf, 1961, p. 378.

8. Erich Fromm, The Anatomy of Human Destructiveness. New York: Harper and Row, 1970, p. 294.

9. Cited by Robert K. Merton, "Bureaucratic Structure and Personality," in K. Kluckhohn and H. A. Murray (eds.), Personality in Nature, Society, and Culture. New York: Alfred A. Knopf, 1961, pp. 363-376.

10. Cited by Robert K. Merton, "Bureaucratic Structure and Personality," in K. Kluckhohn and H. A. Murray (eds.), Personality in Nature, Society, and Culture. New York: Alfred A. Knopf, 1961, pp. 363-376.

11. Peter F. Drucker, "Management and the World's Work," Harvard Business Review, September-October 1988, p. 75.

12. Michael Maccoby, Why Work? Motivating the New Workforce. Alexandria, VA: Miles River Press, 1995.

13. In Melvin L. Kohn and Carmi Schooler's Work and Personality (Norwood, NJ: Ablex Publishing, 1983), a massive study of 3,100 men at all levels of corporations and government, the authors found that the ideal job for these bureaucrats is one that allows autonomy. Notably, labor unions in the United States bargained to give workers the right to ownership of their jobs, in effect giving them a certain autonomy and protection from arbitrary authority. In contrast, European unions tended to bargain for influence at the executive level while allowing management more flexibility in running the shop floor. As a result, American industry suffered from elaborate contracts that detailed a worker's job and made clear that the worker could not be asked to do anything else. This led to the

ridiculous and costly situation in American industries like steel, where one electrician work on a wall only up to a certain height while above that a different electrician owned the job.

14. Kenneth Blanchard and Spencer Johnson, The One Minute Manager: Increase Productivity, Profits, and Your Own Prosperity. New York: William Morrow and Company, 1982.

15. According to 2003 U.S. Census statistics, 67 percent of Americans work in private service industries, 17 percent in government, and 11 percent in manufacturing. That's a lot of organizations.

16. Michael Maccoby, The Gamesman: The New Corporate Leaders. New York: Simon & Schuster, 1976.

17. William H. Whyte, Jr., The Organization Man. New York: Simon & Schuster, 1956.

18. Michael Maccoby, The Gamesman: The New Corporate Leaders. New York: Simon & Schuster, 1976, p. 120.

19. Jack Welch with Suzy Welch, Winning. New York: Harper Business, 2005.

20. Among AT&T's well-known bad decisions were giving up cellular telephony after inventing it, trying to compete in computers, buying NCR, and deciding the Internet was a fad.

21. Michael Maccoby, Why Work? Motivating the New Workforce. Alexandria, VA: Miles River Press, 1995.

22. John C. Beck and Mitchell Wade, Got Game: How the Gamer Generation Is Reshaping Business Forever. Boston: Harvard Business School Press, 2004. In a private talk, Beck said that 100 percent of Harvard undergraduates were video gamers.

23. But these gamesters can lose touch with reality. A research laboratory director told me that one of them she directed kept playing with the data until he got the "right" result. When she questioned its accuracy, he said, "But that's the result you asked for."

24. John C. Beck and Mitchell Wade, Got Game: How the Gamer Generation Is Reshaping Business Forever. Boston: Harvard Business School Press, 2004, p. 154. Surveys of video gamers show a drop-off in play as the gamers age and have to focus more on work and family. It remains to be studied whether these attitudes toward work and leadership are sustained; see Nick Wingfield, "Game Companies Worry as Players Grow Up, Grow Bored," The Wall Street Journal, February 14, 2007.

25. John C. Beck and Mitchell Wade, Got Game: How the Gamer Generation Is Reshaping Business Forever. Boston: Harvard Business School Press, 2004, pp.121-122.

26. I've found that they do appreciate, even enjoy, the kind of co-coaching designed by Marshall Goldsmith, where neither person is superior to the other. See, for example, Marshall Goldsmith, "Try Feedforward Instead of Feedback," http://www.marshallgoldsmithlibrary.com.

27. Gary Hamel, "First Let's Fire All The Managers," Harvard Business Review, December, 2011.

## Chapter 5

1. Although few managers have advanced very far in understanding people, almost all have taken and discussed the Myers-Briggs Type Indicator test, which is based on the theories of Carl G. Jung, the Swiss psychoanalyst. However, test-retest studies of the Myers-Briggs don't show high reliability. Even so, since introversion-extraversion is genetically determined, Myers-Briggs taps into a valid trait. See, for example, Leslie A. Thomas and Robert J. Harvey, "Improving Measurement Precision of the Myers-Briggs Type Indicator" (paper presented at the Annual Conference of the Society for Industrial and Organizational Psychology, Orlando, FL, May 1995).

2. This is the questionnaire in chapter 1 of Narcissistic Leaders: Who Succeeds and Who Fails. Boston: Harvard Business School Press, 2007.

3. "Expanding the Innovation Horizon, the Global CEO Study 2006," IBM Business Consulting Services.

4. For examples of types of collaboration in the knowledge workplace, see Charles Heckscher and Paul S. Adler, eds., The Firm as Collaborative Community: The Reconstruction of Trust in the Knowledge Economy. Oxford, UK: Oxford University Press, 2006. Also by Heckscher, The Collaborative Enterprise: Managing Speed and Complexity in Knowledge-Based Businesses New Haven, CT: Yale University Press, 2007.

5. Lynda M. Applegate et al., "IBM: Uniting Vision and Values," Case 9-805-116. Boston: Harvard Business School, 2006.

6. This research finding by Mitzi Montoya-Weiss of NC State University and Anne P. Massey of Indiana University was reported in CIMS Technology Management Report, Winter, 2006-2007. NC State University Center for Innovation Management Studies.

7. Allison Maitland, "Le Patron, der Chef and the Boss," Financial Times, January 9, 2006.

8. These were Thailand, Taiwan, South Korea, China, Hong Kong (then independent), Malaysia, Singapore, Indonesia, and the Philippines. When Lindahl first asked me to go to these countries, I wasn't sure that Asians would be open with me. I said I'd test my ability by trying Thailand and Taiwan. Before leaving, I read as much as I could about the culture and history of these countries. I went first to Bangkok and was pleasantly surprised by how open the Thai managers were, giving frank opinions about the expats. I remarked on this to one Thai manager who said, "Most foreigners come and just tell us what they want us to do. You understood how important to us is Buddhism, and you listened."

9. The Chinese government has recently become more favorable to Confucius as a means of indoctrinating respect for their authority. Richard McGregor, "The Pursuit of Harmony—Why Fast-Changing China Is Turning Back to Confucius," Financial Times, April 12, 2007, p.11.

10. Geert Hofstede, "Cultural Constraints in Management Theory," in Robert P. Vecchio (ed.) Leadership: Understanding the Dynamics of Power and Influence in Organizations. Notre Dame, IN: University of Notre Dame Press, 1997), p. 479.

11. Marcus Buckingham and Donald O. Clifton, Now Discover Your Strengths. New York: The Free Press, 2001.

12. Adapted from P. T. Costa Jr. and R. McCrae, "Trait Psychology Comes of Age," in Theo B. Sonderegger (ed.), Psychology and Aging, vol. 39 of Nebraska Symposium on Motivation, 1991. Lincoln, NE: University of Nebraska Press, 1992, pp. 169-204.

13. There still remains strong debate about whether personality traits combine to form factors, or whether these factors are the primary drivers, which produce traits. David C. Funder, "Personality." Annual Review of Psychology, 52 (2001), pp. 197-221.

14. Wilt, Joshua, David M Condon, Ashley Brown-Riddell, and William Revelle, "Fundamental Questions in Personality." European Journal of Personality, 26 (2012), pp. 629-31.

15. Richard Olivier uses this theory in his mythodramas (www.oliviermythodrama.com), as does Carol Pearson in her books and seminars (www.herewithin.com).

16. Michael Maccoby, Narcissistic Leaders: Who Succeeds and Who Fails. Boston: Harvard Business School Press, 2007.

17. Descriptions of the mixed types can be found in the appendix of Narcissistic Leaders: Who Succeeds and Who Fails. Boston: Harvard Business School Press, 2007.

18. Sigmund Freud, Libidinal Types, vol. XXI, The Standard Edition of the Complete Psychological Works of Sigmund Freud. London: Hogarth Press, 1961(orig. pub. 1931), pp. 215-220.

19. Sigmund Freud, Libidinal Types, vol. XXI, The Standard Edition of the Complete Psychological Works of Sigmund Freud. London: Hogarth Press, 1961(orig. pub. 1931), pp. 215-220.

20. The questionnaire is published in Chapter 1 of Narcissistic Leaders: Who Succeeds and Who Fails (Boston: Harvard Business School Press, 2007). Richard Margolies used the questionnaire in leadership workshops with the U.S. Army Corps of Engineers. Most of the business media managers at VNU have marketing personalities. Matt Downs and Michael Anderson, while students at Stanford Business School under the direction of Charles O'Reilly, gave the questionnaire to executives of Bay Area businesses. Nine of ten high-tech entrepreneurs were narcissists and six of seven manufacturers were obsessives.

21. Tony Barclay, interview with author, March 9, 2007.

22. Kwame Anthony Appiah, The Ethics of Identity (Princeton, NJ: Princeton University Press, 2005, p.117). Appiah goes on to write: "The social identities that clamor for recognition are extremely multifarious. Some groups have the names of the earlier ethnicities: Italian, Jewish, Polish. Some correspond to the old races (black, Asian, Indian); or to religions (Baptist, Catholic, Jewish). Some are basically regional (Southern, Western, Puerto Rican). Yet others are new groups that meld together people of particular geographic origins (Hispanic, Asian American) or are social categories (woman, gay, bisexual, disabled, Deaf ) that are none of these. And, nowadays,

we are not the slightest bit surprised when someone remarks upon the 'culture' of such groups. Gay culture, Deaf culture, Chicano culture, Jewish culture: see how these phrases trip off the tongue. But if you ask what distinctively marks off gay people or Deaf people or Jews from others, it is not obviously the fact that to each identity there corresponds a distinct culture. 'Hispanic' sounds like the name of a cultural group defined by sharing the cultural trait of speaking Spanish; but, as I've already pointed out, half the second-generation Hispanics in California don't speak Spanish fluently, and in the next generation the proportion will fall. 'Hispanic' is, of course, a category that's as made-in-the-U.S.A. as black and white, a product of immigration, an artifact of the U.S. census. Whatever 'culture' Guatemalan peasants and Cuban professionals have in common, the loss of Spanish confirms that Hispanic, as a category, is thinning out culturally in the way that white ethnicity has already done."

## Chapter 6

1. Salvatore R. Maddi, 1996. Personality Theories. Sixth ed. Long Grove, IL: Waveland Press.
2. Sigmund Freud, Libidinal Types, vol. XXI, The Standard Edition of the Complete Psychological Works of Sigmund Freud (1931; London: Hogarth Press, 1961), 215–220.
3. Fromm, Erich. 1947. Man for Himself. New York: Rinehart.
4. Michael Maccoby, Narcissistic Leaders: Who Succeeds and Who Fails (Boston: Harvard Business School Press, 2007).
5. Porter, Elias H. 1976. "On the Development of Relationship Awareness Theory: A personal note." Group & Organization Management 1 (3):302-309.
6. Scudder, Tim, Debra LaCroix, and Simon Gallon. 2014. Working with SDI, 2nd Edition. Carlsbad, CA: Personal Strengths Publishing.
7. Porter, Elias H., and Tim Scudder. 1973, 2015. Strength Deployment Inventory, Self Edition. Carlsbad, CA: Personal Strengths.
8. B.W. Tuckman. 1965. Developmental Sequence in Small Groups. (Psychological Bulletin, Vol 63(6), 1965), 384-399.
9. Deci, Edward. 1995. Why We Do What We Do: Understanding the psychology of self-motivation. New York, NY: Penguin Books: Koestenbaum, Peter, and Peter Block. 2001. Freedom and Accountability at Work. San Francisco, CA: Jossey-Bass/Pfieffer.
10. Porter, Elias H., Tim Scudder, and Simon Gallon., 2015. Strengths Portrait, Self Edition. Carlsbad, CA: Personal Strengths.
11. Tim Scudder, Michael Patterson, and Kent Mitchell, Have a Nice Conflict (San Francisco, CA: Jossey Bass, 2012).
12. Cloke, Kenneth, and Joan Goldsmith. 2005. Resolving Conflicts at Work. Revised ed. San Francisco, CA: Jossey-Bass.
13. Murray, Henry A, and Clyde Kluckhohn. 1948. "Outline of a Conception of Personality." In Personality in Nature, Society, and Culture, edited by Clyde Kluckhohn and Henry A Murray, 3-32. New York, NY: Alfred A Knopf.
14. Harry McCracken, "Satya Nadella Rewrites Microsoft's Code," Fast Company, October 2017, p. 55

## Chapter 7

1. Erik H. Erikson, Childhood and Society. New York: Norton, 1950.
2. See Betty Friedan, The Feminine Mystique. New York: Dell, 1964. Margaret Henning and Anne Jardim found that women who succeeded in management in the 1970s were almost invariably close to their fathers (Margaret Henning and Anne Jardim, The Managerial Woman. New York: Anchor/Doubleday, 1978). The father-daughter transference often went both ways, as father-fixated women became the protégés of paternalistic bosses.
3. Carol K. Sigelman and Elizabeth A. Rider, Life-Span Human Development, 4th ed. Belmont, CA: Thomas-Wadsworth, 2003.

4. Lynda Laughlin, Employment History of Women Before First Birth: 1961–1965 to 2004–2008, U.S. Census Bureau, October 2011, pp. 12-13.

5. "Employment Characteristics of Families in 2014," BLS report, http://www.bls.gov/news.release/famee.toc.htm.

6. Mauricio Cortina and Mario Marrone, eds., Attachment Theory and the Psychoanalytic Process. London: Whurr Publishers Ltd., 2003.

7. Carol K. Sigelman and Elizabeth A. Rider, Life-Span Human Development, 4th ed. Belmont, CA: Thomas-Wadsworth, 2003, p. 382. According to Department of Labor Statistics, about 30 percent of infants of working mothers are cared for by their parents, 30 percent by a relative, 20 percent in family day-care homes (typically run by a woman in her own home), 10 percent in large day-care centers, and a small percentage with hired nannies.

8. Mary Eberstadt, Home-Alone America: The Hidden Toll of Day Care, Behavioral Drugs and Other Parent Substitutes. New York: Sentinal, 2004.

9. "Psychology at the Intersection of Work and Family," American Psychologist 60(5), 2003, p. 400.

10. Judith Warner, "Kids Gone Wild," The New York Times, November 27, 2005.

11. Judith Warner, "Kids Gone Wild," The New York Times, November 27, 2005.

12. Judith Warner, "Kids Gone Wild," The New York Times, November 27, 2005.

13. E. E. Maccoby, The Two Sexes: Growing Up Apart, Coming Together. Cambridge, MA: Harvard University Press, 1999.

14. Jean Piaget, The Moral Judgment of the Child. New York: The Free Press, 1965. (Orig. Le Jugement Moral Chez l'Enfant. Neuchâtel, Switzerland: Editions Delachaux & Niestlé, 1932).

15. Sigelman and Rider, Life-Span Human Development, p. 382.

16. David Riesman, The Lonely Crowd. New Haven, CT: Yale University Press, 1950.

17. Jean Piaget, The Moral Judgment of the Child. New York: The Free Press, 1965. (Orig. Le Jugement Moral Chez l'Enfant. Neuchâtel, Switzerland: Editions Delachaux & Niestlé, 1932).

18. W. Michael Cox, Richard Alan, and Nigel Homes, "Where the Jobs Are," The New York Times, May 12, 2004. These knowledge worker jobs include financial service sales, recreation workers, nurses, lawyers, teachers and counselors, actors and directors, architects, designers, photographers, hair stylists and cosmetologists, legal assistants, medical scientists, and electronic engineers.

19. Bradford C. Johnson, James M. Manyika, and Lareina A. Yee, "The Next Revolution in Interactions," McKinsey Quarterly, 4, 2005.

20. Annette Lareau, Unequal Childhoods: Class, Race, and Family Life. Berkeley: University of California Press, 2003.

21. The New School in Alternative Learning," Financial Times. November 7, 2005, http://search.ft.com/nonFtArticle?id=051107000791.

22. Kenneth M. Nowack and Sandra Mashihi, "Evidence-Based Answers to 15 Questions About Leveraging 360-Degree Feedback," Consulting Psychology Journal: Practice and Research, 64(3), 2012 pp. 157-182.

23. "Breeding Evil?" The Economist, August 4, 2005.

24. An example was Devon Moore of Fayette, Alabama, a teenage minor who killed three policemen in a way that seemed to mimic what he did in the game. After his capture, Moore reportedly told the police, "Life is like a video game. Everybody's got to die sometime." However, Moore, who was brought up by various foster parents and was a poor student, had the risk factors that predict criminal behavior. 60 Minutes, March 6, 2005.

25. Michael Maccoby, Narcissistic Leaders: Who Succeeds and Who Fails. Boston: Harvard Business School Press, 2007.

26. According to a survey of Washington, D.C.- area teens, 60 percent of whites and 81 percent of African-Americans say it's likely that they'll someday be rich. Richard Morin, "What Teens Really Think," Washington Post Magazine, October 23, 2005.

27. Erik H. Erikson, Childhood and Society. New York: Norton, 1950.

28. "One thing for sure," writes Dylan, "if I wanted to compose folksongs I would need some kind of new template, some philosophical identity that wouldn't burn out." Bob Dylan, Chronicles, Vol. 1. New York: Simon & Schuster, 2004, p. 73.

29. "Spirituality in Higher Education: A National Study of College Students' Search for Meaning and Purpose (2004–2005)," www.spirituality.ucla.edu/reports.

30. Rick Warren, The Purpose-Driven Life: What on Earth Am I Here For? Grand Rapids, MI: Zondervan, 2002.

31. Michael Maccoby, Why Work? Motivating the New Workforce, 2nd ed. Alexandria, VA: Miles River Press, 1995.

32. Eric Fromm, The Art of Loving. New York: Bantam Books, 1963. (Orig. pub. 1956.)

33. Max Weber, The Protestant Ethic and the Spirit of Capitalism. New York: Scribner, 1958, p. 182.

34. Erik H. Erikson, The Life Cycle Completed. New York: Norton, 1998, p. 114.

35. Charles Handy, The Second Curve. London: Random House Books, 2015, p. 216.

36. Laura Mullane and Mary Beth Lakin, "Redefining the Golden Years," American Council on Education, January 29, 2007, http://www.acenet.edu.

37. Sue Shellenbarger, "Gray Is Good," Wall Street Journal, December 2, 2005. This fits with the findings of the Harvard study. See George E. Vaillant, Aging Well: Surprising Guideposts to a Happier Life. Boston: Little, Brown, 2002.

38. Business Week, June 27, 2005, p. 84.

39. Bureau of Labor Statistics "Labor Force Statistics from the Current Population Survey. Household Data, Annual Averages. Chart 3. Employment status of the civilian noninstitutional population by age, sex, and race. http://www.bls.gov/cps/cpsaat03.htm (8/5/15).

40. George E. Valliant in his book Triumphs of Experience (Cambridge: Harvard University Press, 2012) writes "There are two pillars of happiness revealed in seventy-five-year old Grant Study (of Harvard graduates). One is love. The other is finding a way of coping with life that does not push love away." p. 50.

## Chapter 8

1. Stefan Stern writes "When 50 executive MBA students at a leading international business school were asked recently what word they would use to describe themselves, they opted for labels such as 'catalyst', 'change-agent', 'consultant' and 'leader.' None of them wanted to be thought of as a 'manager.' " Financial Times, December 19, 2006.

2. Dee Hock, One from Many: VISA and the Rise of the Chaordic Organization (San Francisco: Berrett-Koehler, 2005).

3. Bryan Huang, interview with author, August 1, 2005

4. Bryan Huang, interview with author, August 1, 2005.

5. Judith Block McLaughlin and David Riesman, Choosing a College President, Opportunities and Constraints (Princeton, NJ: The Carnegie Foundation for the Advancement of Teaching, 1990).

6. Paul S. Adler, "Beyond Hacker Idiocy: The Changing Nature of Software Community and Identity," in The Firm as Collaborative Community: The Reconstruction of Trust in the Knowledge Economy, ed. Charles Heckscher and Paul S. Adler (Oxford: Oxford University Press, 2006), 179–198.

7. These concepts are further developed in Michael Maccoby, Strategic Intelligence, Conceptual Tools for Leading Change, Oxford: Oxford University Press, 2015. That book includes exercises for developing leadership for change.

8. Michael Maccoby, "Learning to Partner and Partnering to Learn," Research Technology Management 40, no. 3 (May–June 1997): 55–57.

9. For a description of the process of change, see M. Maccoby, Strategic Intelligence, Conceptual Tools for Leading Change, Oxford University Press, 2015.

10. Jay R. Galbraith, "Mastering the Law of Requisite Variety with Differentiated Networks," in Heckscher and Adler, The Firm as Collaborative Community, 179–198.

## Chapter 9

1. My adaptation, from Lao Tzu, Tao Te Ching, XVII, trans. D. C. Lau (New York: Penguin Books, 1963).
2. Gale Cutler, "Mike Leads His First Virtual Team," Research Technology Management (January–February 2007): 67.
3. In the Mexican village Fromm and Maccoby studied, however, there were three types of social character: descendants of free farmers, descendants of hacienda peons, and a small group of entrepreneurs.
4. Missing from descriptions of EI is a quality we do find in some narcissists who are neither particularly empathic nor self-aware. That's a sense of humor, the emotional equivalent of a cognitive sense of reality. Life is often absurd and, as noted in chapter 9, some of the most effective leaders bring people down to earth, defuse tense situations, even puncture their own self-importance with humor. We should be wary of humorless would-be leaders. They tend to be the rigid ideologues or holier-than-thou moralists.
5. Some questionnaires probe for behavioral strengths. Both SDI and the questionnaire Maccoby designed are based on psychoanalytic types, dynamic styles of relatedness that underlie both strengths and weaknesses. See Marcus Buckingham and Donald O. Clifton, Now Discover Your Strengths (New York: The Free Press, 2001) and Michael Maccoby, Narcissistic Leaders: Who Succeeds and Who Fails (Boston: Harvard Business School Press, 2007), chapter 2.
6. Kathleen Freeman, Ancilla to the Pre-Socratic Philosophers (Oxford: Basil Blackwell, 1947), 27.
7. 1 Kings 3:5-15 (New English Bible).
8. Michael Maccoby first presented this discussion of head and heart in The Gamesman (New York: Simon & Schuster, 1976), chapter 7.
9. As a result of King Solomon's asking God for a heart that listens, "all the world courted him, to hear the wisdom which God had put in his heart" (1 Kings 10:24, New English Bible).
10. Recent research suggests females are more observant of facial expressions than males, and that this difference is hardwired in the brain. See Louann Brizandine, "The Female Brain," New York Times, September 10, 2006.
11. Paul Ekman, Emotions Revealed: Recognizing Faces and Feelings to Improve Communication and Emotional Life (New York: Times Books, 2003).
12. Daniel Goleman, Social Intelligence: The New Science of Human Relationships (New York: Bantam Dell, 2006), 43.
13. For a description of the difference between analytic, practical, and creative intelligence, see Robert J. Sternberg, The Triarchic Mind: A New Theory of Human Intelligence (New York: Viking, 1988) and Successful Intelligence: How Practical and Creative Intelligence Determine Success in Life (New York: Plume, 1997).
14. Ann Louise Bardach, "Letters from Prison: Castro Revealed," Washington Post, February 25, 2007, Outlook, 5.
15. Michael Maccoby first learned of this reading the Muqaddimah of Ibn Khaldûn, the 14th-century Moroccan philosopher and social historian (trans. Franz Rosenthal, Bollinger Series XLIII, Princeton, NJ: Princeton University Press, 1958). I have taken off from his theory to develop my own interpretation of the discipline of the heart.
16. Malcolm Gladwell, Blink: The Power of Thinking Without Thinking (New York: Little, Brown and Company, 2005).
17. Albert Schweitzer, Reverence for Life (New York: Philosophical Library, 1965), 34 and throughout the book
18. This concept is developed in Transforming Health Care Leadership by Michael Maccoby , Clifford L. Norman, C. Jane Norman, and Richard Margolies (San Francisco:Jossey Bass Publishing, 2013) and Strategic Intelligence by Michael Maccoby (Oxford: Oxford University Press, 2015).
19. Michael Maccoby, Narcissistic Leaders: Who Succeeds and Who Fails (Boston: Harvard Business School Press, 2007).
20. They included: Richard Greene, Richard Margolies, Edith Onderick-Harvey, Mark Paulson, Mark Paulson, Jr., and Gary Wolford.

21. Michael Maccoby first discovered this when he gave Rorschach tests to corporate managers for the study that became The Gamesman: The New Corporate Leaders (New York: Simon and Schuster, 1976). The systems thinkers saw ink blots as a whole, rather than as clearly distinct but unrelated parts. The most creative systems thinkers described action, a story about how the parts were interacting.

22. See examples in Michael Maccoby, Narcissistic Leaders: Who Succeeds and Who Fails (Boston: Harvard Business School Press, 2007).

23. Honda is an exception with a culture that emphasizes cross-functional teamwork. Many of the attempts to copy the Toyota system have been partially successful at best, because the copiers have focused only on the economic and technical elements of the system and ignored the social and human element. See Michael Maccoby, "Is There a Best Way to Build a Car?" Harvard Business Review, November-December 1997, 161-171.

# Index

ABB (Asea Brown Boveri), 71, 73, 75, 76, 138
accountability, 96, 97, 119
achievement, parental emphasis on, 115
Ackoff, Russ, 156
Adams, Scott, 24
Adler, Paul, 133
affluent families, 119
agape, 125
agreeableness, 79, 142
agreement, inability to reach, 75
Ahlstrom Corporation, 77
Airbnb, 66
Allen, Woody, 60
American Psychological Association (APA), 114
antibureaucratic leadership, 33
anxiety
   about future, in affluent families, 118
   initiative versus guilt and anxiety, 111, 116
   persistence of, 4, 48
Appiah, Kwame Anthony, 84
Apple Computer, 122, 143
Applegate, Lynda, 137
apprentice(ships), 15, 119, 133
archetypes of personality, 79
Aristotle, 26
Art of Loving, The (Fromm), 124
Asea Brown Boveri, (see ABB)

Asia(n), 61, 74, 76, 77
astrology, 147
AT&T, 5, 7, 12, 17, 19-25, 33, 40, 46, 59, 63, 77, 137, 146
attachment(s), 13, 81, 113, 114, 122, 124
authority
   formal, 27, 33, 57, 59, 104
   paternal, 6
   rebellion against, 48
   shared, 4, 23, 34, 65
autocratic, 10, 28, 35, 74, 85
autonomy
   of child in interactive family, 9, 63
   sought by bureaucratic personality, 33, 60, 61, 63
autonomy versus shame and doubt, 111-114

Bachelor, The, 65
Ballmer, Steve, 105, 16, 136
Barber, Tiki, 35
Barclay, Tony, 83
Barret, Collen, 136
Barret, Craig, 136
Bartleby the Scrivener (Melville), 57
Beck, John, 63, 64
behavior patterns, 79
Belichick, Bill, 34
Bell System (AT&T), 7, 40, 59, 63

benevolent despot, xiii, 69, 76
Bethlehem Steel, 18
big five personality traits, 79
Blink (Gladwell), 152
body language, 148
Boeing, 42
brainstorming, 94, 95
bridge-building leaders, xiv, 134, 137
Brin, Sergey, 32, 66, 143
Broad, Eli, 6
Brunell, Mark, 35
Bureaucracies, 57
   identification with CEO of, 116
   in post-Civil War (U.S.) period, 56, 58
   transforming into collaborative communities, 2, 25, 72, 85, 132, 155
bureaucrat(s)
   integrity versus despair, 128
   negative image of, 57, 58
   as poor leaders, 11
   public-spirited, 58, 59
bureaucratic conformity, 116
bureaucratic family
   intimacy stage in, 124, 125
   over-strict demands in, 114
   rebellion against authority, 121
bureaucratic followers, 13, 53
bureaucratic managers
   control of workers, 69, 133, 146
   in industrial mode of production, 59, 65, 70
   as obstacles, 37-38
   qualities of, 16, 93
   subordinate types and, 53-54, 70
bureaucratic paternalism, 13, 34
bureaucratic personality, 7, 56
   caricatured, 57, 60
   father transferences and, 38
   hierarchical motivational patterns and, 59
   social character and, 56
   stereotyping of, 58
bureaucratic social character, 7-8, 15, 54
   comfort with line of authority, 139
   development pattern of, 59
   interactive social character and, 60-66
   motivated by challenge, 8

   negative life cycle development of, 111
   obsessive, 33, 34
   in period of transition, 35, 54
   positive life-cycle development of, 110
   sense of identity, 65, 84
   social scientists' views of, 58, 59
   transferences and, 44-47, 69, 87
bureaucratic theory of leadership, 3
Burns, James McGregor, xii
Bush, George W., 48

Calian, Samuel Carnegie, 10
Carnegie, Andrew, 6
Camp, Garret, 66
Case Western Reserve, 133
Castro, Fidel, 12, 151
Center for Advanced Study in the Behavioral Sciences (Stanford), 61
challenge, as motivator, 8, 76, 94, 141
changing context, xiii-xv, 1-6
charter schools, 119
Cheske, Brian, 66
Chicago Bears, 35
Chicago Board of Trade, 105
Chicago Mercantile Exchange, 105
children
   of affluent families, 112
   development of, 109-121
   effects of video games on, 63, 64, 123
   rudeness of, 115
China, 1, 7, 57, 144
Churchill, Winston, xiii, 18
Cincinnatus, 69
Cirovski, Sasho, 35
Citibank, 140
CME Group, 105
Civic Ventures, 127
Civil War, 58, 83, 84
clearing the mind, 151
Clinton, Hillary Rodham, 44
Clinton, William Jefferson, 47-49
coaches
   executive coaches, 37, 47, 50, 103
   football coaches, 33-35

managers as, 22, 23, 26, 45, 64, 149
  parents as, 118
cognitive style, 62, 83
collaboration
  attitudes of, in football coaching, 35
  cultural variation in social character and, 60, 65, 71, 75, 139
  facilitating, 34
  in knowledge mode of production, 15, 118
  meanings of, 71
  sibling leaders and, 42
collaborative heterarchy, 133
collaborators
  followers as, xiii, 50, 51
  interactives as, 131, 132
Collins, Jim, 31, 32
Cominco, 138
competition, spirit of, 9
conflict
  avoidance, 80
  conflict sequence, 90, 91, 100, 102
  motives in, 99
  organizational, 73, 74, 76, 100-104
Confucius, 17, 18, 144
conscientiousness, 79, 142
conscious self-interest, 7
context
  Cultural, (see cultural context)
  ignored by Theory Y, 21, 22
  of leadership, xi-xv, 15-16
contextual leadership, 30
countertransference, 41
courage, 14, 141, 145, 148, 149
Crichton, Michael, 41
cult-like organizations, 9
Cultor, 77
cultural change, 1-3
cultural context
  of leadership, xiii, 3, 15
  of personality development, 82, 110
  variation in social character and, 73-76
culture
  common, of global business, 72, 141
  human nature shaped by, 3
  Organizational, 24, 45, 46, 72

  variations in social character, 59, 73, 82
Cummins Engine Company, 23

DAI, 83
Davenport, Thomas H., 17
Davis, Rowena, 132
day care, 113, 114
Dell, Michael, 6
Deming, W. Edwards, 23, 127
Deming Prize, 24
democracy, cultural context of, 56
Department of Labor, U.S., 134
Dewey, John, 58
Dickens, Charles, 57
dictator(ships), 1, 11, 15, 69, 115, 136
Dilbert cartoons, 24
Disclosure (Crichton), 41
dominant mode of production, 5, 67
dot-com bubble, 32
Dreamworks, 122
Drucker, Peter, 34, 56, 59, 60, 127
Dust Brothers, 122
Dweck, Carol, viii
Dychtwald, Ken, 127
Dylan, Bob, 123

eBay, 92, 93, 132
Ebbers, Bernie, 32
Eckhardt, Meister, 152
École Nationale d'Administration, 76
Economist, The, 120
ego integrity versus despair, 111, 112, 126
Einstein, Albert, 152
Ekman, Paul, 148
Ellison, Larry, 9, 31, 136, 146
emotional intelligence, 19, 150
  popularity of, 71, 146
  in understanding people, 45, 72, 118
emotional stability, 79, 142
entrepreneurs, xiii, 5-7, 12, 65, 66, 82, 155
Erikson, Erik H., viii, 112. 122, 125-128
  theory of personality formation, 109
Escape from Freedom (Fromm), 12

Ethics, Nicomachean (Aristotle), 26
Europe(an), 1, 4, 19, 56, 75, 77, 122
European Union, 84
Evans, B.O., 70
executive coaches, 50
executive teams, 50, 71, 82
Experience Corps, 127

family(ies)
    affluent, 119
    bureaucratic (see bureaucratic family)
    changing structure of, 4, 38, 43, 61
    close ties with, 37, 42
    identity and, 122, 123
    in industrial-bureaucratic age, 59, 61, 84
    interactive (see interactive family)
    positive development and, 110, 123, 124
    relationships, social change and, 51
    sense of self rooted in, 55
    social character and, 53
farming-craft social character, 6, 7
father transference, 45-47
    emphasized in psychoanalysis, 38
    in Europe and Asia, 29
    in traditional organizations, 13
fear of boss (leader),28, 29, 31, 34
Fearnsides, Jack, 157
Federal Aviation Administration (FAA), 157
Feinberg, Mike, 143
Financial Times, 75
Finland, 77
Florida Power and Light, 24
followers
    changes in attitudes of, 3
    as collaborators, 17
    motivations of, 26, 38, 68
    reasons for following, 8, 12, 16
    relations to leaders, 1, 10, 67-69
    social character of, 5, 11
    studies of, 5
    types of bureaucratic managers and, 33, 34
    unwilling, 17, 68
followership, 5, 17, 39, 43

football coaches, 33-35
Ford, Henry, 6, 12, 32, 70, 142, 155
Ford Motor Company, 70, 155
foresight, 154
formal authority, 140
Foster, George M., 7
France, 68, 75, 76
Fredriksson, Borje, 138, 140
Freud, Sigmund, viii, ix, xv, 4, 39, 41, 42, 47, 50, 79-82, 90, 91, 114, 116, 124, 147, 152, 153, 155
Freudian, 38
Fromm, Erich, viii, ix, xiv, 5, 6, 12, 13, 17, 55, 58, 64, 79-82, 90-92, 124, 152, 153
Frost, Robert, 122

Galbraith, Jay, 140
Gallup Organization, 78, 81
gamesman, 63
Gamesman, The (Maccoby), 33, 62
Gandhi, Mohandas, 142, 143
Gates, Bill, 6, 9, 31, 49, 105, 136, 142-146
Gebbia, Joe, 66
GEI Consultants, 94
Genentech, 17
generativity versus stagnation, 111, 112, 125
George III, King of England, 58
Germany, 56, 71, 73, 75
    Hitler's role in, 12
    Weimar Republic, 12
Gengis Khan, 1
Gibbs, Joe, 34, 35
Gil, Phupinder, 105
Gillespie, Richard, 20
Gillette, 31
Gladwell, Malcolm, 152
Goleman, Daniel, 146, 149
Good to Great (Collins), 31, 32
Google, 25, 43, 66, 122, 143
Got Game (Beack and Wade), 63
Grand Theft Auto (video game), 120
Grove, Andy, 136

Hackborn, Dick, 33, 34
Halpern, Diane F., 114
Hamilton, Alexander, 142
Hanson, (Lord) James, 49
Harman, Sidney, 127
Harman International Industries, 5, 7, 8, 22
Harry Potter (Rowling), 48
Harvard Business Review, 41, 65
Harvard Business School, 19, 137
Harvard Program on Technology and Society, 61
Harvard University, 115
Hawthorne effect, 19, 20
Hazlewood, Patrick, 120
heart
    clearing the mind and, 151
    deep listening and, 86, 145, 152
    developing, 148, 149
    listening and responding to others, 150, 153
    qualities of, 148, 150
    self-understanding and, 149
Heraclitus, 30, 147, 151
Herzberg, Frederick, 8
Hewlett-Packard (HP), 9, 12, 33, 69
hierarchical motivational patterns, 59
hierarchy of human needs, 21
Higher Education Research Institute (UCLA), 123
historical context of leadership, 15-35 (see also leadership context)
    ancient Rome, 11, 29
    Hawthorne Studies, 19, 20
    Machiavelli, 2, 17, 28-32, 69, 82, 107
    manager as educator
    Taylorism, 18-23, 28
    Theory X and theory Y, 21, 22, 26
Hitler, Adolf, xii, 12, 13, 28, 32, 68, 81
Hock, Dee, 132
Hofstede, Geert, 77, 78
Horowitz, Barry, 157
HP, (see Hewlett-Packard)
Huang, Bryan, 132
human relations training, 19
Hundert, Ed, 133
Hurd, Mark, 69
Hussein, Saddam, 12, 28, 69

IBEW (International Brotherhood of Electrical Workers), 24
IBM, 9, 33, 46, 70-72, 76, 77, 84, 136, 138, 146
Ibsen, Henrik, 129
idealism, in adolescence, 122
identity(ies), 55, 83-86
    attitude of basic trust and, 113
    kinds of, 121
    as motivators, 85
    national identity, 83, 84
    shifting, changing, 55, 64
identity groups, 84, 85, 123
identity versus role confusion, 111, 112, 121
Iger, Bob, 136
Immelt, Jeff, 143
independence, 55, 63, 64, 81, 134
industrial bureaucracy, 18
industrial-bureaucratic age
    family in, 109, 110
    generativity in, 125
    identification with organization in, 84
    leadership in, 146
    Taylorism and, 20
    TQM and, 23
industrial bureaucratic social character, 7
industrial engineers, 19-21
industrial mode of production, 15
industry versus inferiority, 111, 112, 117
initiative versus guilt and anxiety, 111, 116
innovators, 6, 80, 136
integrity, sense of, 16, 17, 38, 46
Intel, 33, 136
intellectual skills, xiv, 73, 86, 89
interactive family
anxiety and over-conformity in, 111, 116
    autonomy of child in, 114, 118
    child development in, 113, 115, 124
    intimacy stage in 123-125
interactive personality, 39, 60
interactive process, in system design, 139
interactive
    comfort with global management, 70, 71, 77
    desire to be collaborators, 16, 131
    distrust of parental relationships, 113
    gamer attitudes of, 63, 64

ideal leaders for, 70, 76, 77, 93, 143
inability to commit in, 65, 151
old age and, 127
as reluctant followers, 17, 68
for solution strategies, 138
strengths and weaknesses of, 63
tolerance of, 126
interactive social character
    bridge building and, 126, 134, 137, 138
    bureaucratic social character and, 61
    dislike of abusive bosses, 146
    fit with projects and teams, 63
    internet and, 9, 10, 77
    in knowledge work, 63
    negative life-cycle development of, 111
    in periods of transition, 35
    positive life-cycle development of, 110
    sense of identity, 55, 65
    sibling transference and, 54
International Brotherhood of Electrical Workers, (see IBEW)
interpersonal radar, 116
intimacy versus isolation, 111, 112, 123
introspection, 49, 104
Italy, 29, 30, 84

jams (IBM), 72, 136
Japan, 8, 23, 24, 57, 127
Jethro (father-in-law of Moses), 10
Jobs, Steve, 9, 78, 136, 143, 146
Johnson, Lyndon Baines, 47
Jung, Carl, 79

Kafka, Franz, 59, 126
kaizen workshops, 156
Kalanick, Travis, 66
Kegan, Robert, ix
Kelleher, Herb, 136
Kerry, John F., 48
Khurana, Rakesh, 11
Kindlon, Daniel, 115
King, Martin Luther, Jr., 142, 143
KIPP (Knowledge is Power Program), 119, 143

knowledge mode of production, 15, 118
knowledge organizations
    Personality types in, 3
    Strategic visionaries for, 136, 142, 146, 154
knowledge work
    Design of, 24
    Empowerment in, 17
    Leaders for, 15, 16, 86
    No need for leaders in, 25
    Productivity in, 24
    Social character and, 9, 109
knowledge workers
    Empowered by expertise, 25
    Jobs created and destroyed by, 118
knowledge workplace
    Intellectual skills needed in, 86
    Leader-follower relationship in, 70
    As social system, 71
Kohlberg, Lawrence, 27

Lao Tzu, 17, 143, 144
Lareau, Annette, 118
Lasseter, John, 136
Lawler, Edward E., III, 27
leader(s)
    Ability to attract followers, 38
    autocratic, 10, 28, 35, 74, 85
    bridge-builders, 126, 134, 137, 138
    changing views of, 2-5
    defined, vii, xi
    development of, 141
    dictators, 1, 11, 15, 69, 115, 136
    as entrepreneurs, xiii, 5-7, 12, 65, 66, 82, 155
    fear of boss, 28, 29, 31, 34
    ideal, description of, 70, 76, 77, 93, 143
    networking leaders, 135, 142
    operational leaders, 135, 141
    personality of (see personality)
    sibling leaders, collaboration and, 42
    types of, 135-138
    visionary (see visionary leaders)
    wrong leader for situation, 11
The Leader (Maccoby), 10
leader, becoming, 141

    developing personality intelligence, 67
    developing strategic intelligence, 154
    reasons for, 142
leadership
    antibureaucratic, 33
    avoiding challenge of, 69
    farming-craft social character and, 6-7
    importance of understanding people, 13
    in industrial-bureaucratic age
    industrial-bureaucratic social character and, 7-8
    inspirational, need for, 23
    kinds of, 10
    knowledge work, social character of, 9
    literature on, 38
    moral values of organization and, 28
    paternalistic, 15, 21, 34, 39, 43, 46
    power as motive for, 67
    support for wrong leadership, 5, 11
    in work of knowledge workers, 53
leadership context (see also historical context
        of leaderships)
    change in, xiii
    changing, 1-5
    modes of production and, 15
leadership philosophy, vii, 70, 92, 102, 104
leadership system, 133
leadership teams, 93, 94, 135, 150, 154
Lee Kwan Yu, xiii
levels of moral reasoning, 27
Levinson, Art, 17
liberty, xiii, 31, 56-60
life cycle, 110
Lincoln, Abraham, xiii, 18, 143
Lindahl, Göran, 71, 76
linear thinkers, 154
Linna, Väinö, 77
listening
    active, understanding and, 18, 35, 107
    deep listening, 151, 152
    heart that listens, 86, 145
    and responding to others, 151, 153
Lombardi, Vince, 34
Lonely Crowd, The (Riesman), 116
Long, Huey, 12

Machiavelli, Niccolò, 2, 17, 28-32, 69, 82, 107
Madonna, 123
management by objectives, 60
Manlius Torquatus, 29
Margolies, Richard, viii
Maslow, Abraham, 8, 21, 22, 25-28
massively multiplayer online role-playing games
        (MMORPGs), 37, 64
maternal attachment, 113
Mayo, Elton, 19
Mayo, William, 155
Mayo Clinic, 155
MBO (Management by Objectives), 60
McGregor, Douglas, 21, 22, 25, 27, 28
meaning, in life, 16, 27, 54, 84, 85, 123, 129, 152, 154
meaning, in work, 10, 13, 16, 23, 59, 64
meditation and prayer, 153
Melville, Herman, 57
Merton, Robert, 59
Messier, Jean-Marie, 32
Mexican Revolution of 1910-1920, 7, 55
Microsoft, 105, 136, 143
MITRE Corporation, 34, 157
Mitretek Systems, 44, 157
modes of production, 15, 82, 133
    industrial mode, 15
    knowledge mode (see knowledge
        mode of production)
    manufacturing mode, 60
money, as incentive, 8, 19, 26, 38, 127
monotonous work, 18
moral reasoning, development of, 27
moral values, 28, 149
Morning Star Company, 65
Moses, 10, 11, 143
Mother Teresa, 143
mother transference, 44, 105
motivation(s)
    academic theories of, 8, 18, 19, 79
    of followers, 38, 39, 49
    Hawthorne, studies of (see Hawthorne effect)
    hierarchical patterns of, 59
    improvement of common good, xiii, 4, 28, 67
    power as, for leaders, 68
motivational value system, 54, 78, 90, 91

multiple transferential relationships, 42
Musk, Elon, 31, 136, 143, 146

Nadella, Satya, 105, 106
Nanny 911, 115
Napoleon Bonaparte, xiii, 32, 68, 81
Narcissistic Leaders (Maccoby), xv, 50, 79, 154
narcissistic love, 124
national identity, 83, 84
natural leaders, 8, 142
negative transferences, 49
Nelson, Bill
Nestlé, 140
networking leaders, 135, 142
New England Patriots, 34
New York Giants, 35
NOAA Fisheries (National Oceanic and Atmospheric Administration), 98
nontraditional families, 4
Nuestros Pequeños Hermanos (NPH), 144
NYMEX (New York Mercantile Exchange), 105

Obama, Barack, 48
objectivity, cultural value of, 74
Oedipus complex. 116
Ohno, Taiichi, 155
Olson, Jim. 19, 21
Omidyar, Pierre M., 132
One Minute Manager, The (Blanchard and Johnson), 60
openness, 13, 79, 139
operational leaders, xiv, 134–136, 141
organization(s)
    demands upon, 22, 85, 118, 132
    identification with, 84
    moral values of, 28
organizational stress, 40
Organization Man, The (Whyte), 60, 62
Orr, Brian, 115
Oxford University, viii, 37, 76, 132

Page, Larry, 32, 66, 143
Palmisano, Sam, 72, 136
Parker, Joan, 137
Parson, Richard, 67
participation, as motivation, 20, 27
partnering, 30, 150
paternal transferences, 46, 51, 77, 87
pay incentives, as motivation, 20
PayPal, 92, 93
Pendleton Civil Service Reform Act of 1883, 58
Pentagon, 137
Perón, Juan, 12
personality
    big five factors, 79
    efforts to understand, 83, 86
    Erikson's theory of personality formation, 109
    fit to managerial role, xiv, 30–32,
    of leader, 3, 30
    Machiavelli on, 28-30
    uniqueness of, 50, 79, 106
personality intelligence
    conceptual variables in, 73
    conflict, 99-101
    developing, 67
    emotional intelligence as part of, 72
    to gain collaborative partners, 70
    identities in, 73
    importance of, 13, 67
personality types
    comparative typologies, table of, 90
    genetically influenced traits, 3, 81
    in knowledge organizations, 81
    understanding strengths of, 78
    view of organizational purpose, 92
    viewed through social character, 26, 28, 54, 78, 81, 82
Philadelphia Eagles, 34
Piaget, Jean, 27
Pittsburgh Theological Seminary, 10
Pixar Studios, 136
place, identity and, 83
Porter, Elias, 64, 79, 80, 90, 91, 100
post-Civil War (U.S.) period, 58
power, as motive for leadership, 67, 68

pragmatism, 122, 129
Prince, The (Machiavelli), 28-30
Procter & Gamble, 23
productivity, 18-22, 27, 40
psychoanalysis, 5, 38-40, 90, 152, 153
psychological health, 124
Purpose Driven Life, The (Warren), 123

Quan-Haase, Anabel, 25, 26
questionnaires, 12, 147

rate busters, 19
Reagan, Nancy, 45
Reagan, Ronald, 45, 47
rebellion against authority, 116
reciprocity, 117
regional identities, 84
Reid, Andy, 34
relationship awareness, 90
religion
    eastern spiritual disciplines, 123, 153
    identity and, 83, 84, 122
repression, 149, 152
research studies
    of followers and leaders, 5, 7, 18, 19
    of people creating new technology, 5, 21,
        25, 61, 63, 145
    surveys, 78
Riesman, David, 116, 132
Rizzolatti, Giacomo, 149
Rockefeller, John D., 6, 32
Roethlisberger, Fritz, 19
role confusion, 111, 112, 121
Roosevelt, Franklin Delano, 18, 47, 79
Rorschach test, 62
Rowling, J. K., 48
Russia, 57

Säid Business School (Oxford), 76
St. John of the Cross, 152
St John's School and Community College, 120
Samuel (leader of Israelites), 131

SARL (Sense and Respond Logistics), 137
Schneider, Stephen, 41
Schweitzer, Albert, 154
self-awareness, 89, 152, 153
self-esteem, 2, 85, 120, 144
self-expression, 3, 114, 120
self-interest, conscious, vii, 7, 69, 84, 100, 123, 155
self-understanding, 149
sense of purpose, xiv, 24
sense of self, 12, 54, 55, 86
service work, 134
SDI (see Strength Deployment Inventory)
Shakespeare, William, 2, 17, 147
sibling transferences, 39, 42, 48, 49, 77
Singapore, xiii, 69, 76
situational management, 30
Six Sigma, 23
Smith, Ken, 101
Smith, Lovie, 34, 35
Smith College, 111
sociability, cultural value of, 74, 126
social change, 2, 31, 50
social character, xiv, 2, 53
    bureaucratic (see bureaucratic social character)
    bureaucratic personality and, 56
    from bureaucratic to interactive, 54, 60, 141
    collaborative, 34
    cultural variations in, 73, 74
    development of, 6, 11, 65, 109
    dominant mode of production and, 5
    family and, 38
    farming-craft (see farming craft social character)
    followers, leadership and, 4, 5, 13, 43
    generational differences, versus, 54
    ideals of, 61
    industrial-bureaucratic, 7
    influence of, 3
    interactive (see interactive social character)
    of interactive versus bureaucratic followers, 9, 10, 61, 84
    knowledge work and, 9, 16
    national variations in, 71, 74-77, 85
    needs and, 26
    in personality intelligence, 3, 73
    role in leadership, 3

stages of development and, 110, 111
unconscious aspects of, 54
view of personality types through, 26, 28, 54, 78, 81, 82
social selection, 6
social systems, 154-157
Solomon, 14, 148
solution strategies, 138
Sony Corporation, 69
Southwest Airlines, 136
Spain, 84
Speer, Albert, 68
stages of development, Erikson's
approximate ages of, 112
autonomy versus shame and doubt, 114
ego integrity ersus despair, 126
generativity versus stagnation, 125
identity versus role confusion, 121
industry versus inferiority, 117
initiative versus guilt and anxiety, 116
intimacy versus isolation, 123
trust versus mistrust, 113
stakeholders, 28
Stalin, Josef, xii, 12, 28, 69
Stanford University, 61
stereotyping, 40, 50, 74
Stevenson, Adlai, 111
strategic intelligence, 50, 145, 150, 154
strategic leaders, xiv, 134, 135, 144, 146
strategic visionaries, 136, 142, 146, 154
Strauss, Leo, 28
Strengths Portrait, 98
Strength Deployment Inventory (SDI), vii, 32, 43, 50, 82, 90-92, 94, 95, 100-106, 147, 148, 153
stress, 30, 40, 100, 114
Stringer, Howard, 69
Summers, Larry, 133
Survivor, 65
suspiciousness, 79, 145
Sweden, 23, 65, 73
Switzerland, 73
system solutions, 156
systems thinking, 86, 94, 150, 154-156

Taylor, Frederick Winslow, 18-20
Taylorism, 18-23, 28
teams
conflict, 101
dynamics, stages of, 93-95
effective, as social systems, 85, 98, 155, 156
executive (see executive teams)
interactive social character and, 9, 63, 65
leadership (see leadership teams)
level of awareness in, 43, 50, 71, 83
self-managed, 9, 65, 133
virtual teams, 72
team sports, 117
technical professional knowledge workers, 9
technology
leadership and, 9-10, 65, 106
research studies on, 21, 25, 61, 63, 145
Texas Instruments, 9, 33
Theory X, 21
Theory Y, 21, 22, 26
Thomas, Lydia, 44, 157
Time Warner, 69
Tocqueville, Alexis de, 56, 58
Tolstoy, Leo, 128
Total Quality Management (TQM), 23, 24, 127
Toyota, 8, 155, 156
traditional families, 4, 44, 60, 77, 111
transferences,
changing transferences, 42, 43, 141
countertransference, 41
dealing with, 40, 41, 49-51, 105, 150, 153
father transferences (see father transferences)
fear and, 69
Freud's discovery of, 4, 39
mother transference (see mother transferences)
parental (see parental transferences)
power of, 38, 40
sibling transference (see sibling transferences)
social change and, 55, 77, 117, 133
in traditional organizations, 13
unconscious (see unconscious transferences)
transferential veneration, 46
Transforming Health Care Leadership (Maccoby, et. al), xv, 50
Trump, Donald, 49

trust
    identity and, 85
    interactives' distrust of relationships, 64
    intimacy and, 6, 15
trust versus mistrust, 111-113
Tuckman, B.W., 93
Twain, Mark, 141

Uber, 66
unconscious, 147, 153
    aspects of social character, 54
    motivation, 38, 39
    transferences, 13, 16, 20, 42-44, 46, 50, 83, 131
understanding people. (see also personality intelligence)
    identities and, 85
    importance of, 13, 71
    intellectual skills and, 147
    leader-follower relationship in, 70, 106
    listening heart and, 145
unions, 19, 21, 84, 85
United Kingdom, 57, 75, 76
University of Chicago, 28
University of Maryland, 35
University of Toronto, 25
Unknown Soldier, The (Linna), 77

Valerius Corvinus, 29
Veblen, Thorstein, 58
Veterans Administration (VA), 101, 102
virtual teams, 72
Visa Network, 132
visionary leaders, 9, (see also strategic visionaries)
Visioning, xii, 150
Vivendi, 32
vocation of service, 154
Volvo, 7, 23, 65

Wade, Mitchell, 63
Walt Disney Company, 136
Warnotte, Daniel, 58
Warren, Rick, 123

Washington, George, 17, 69, 142
Washington Mutual, 101
Washington Redskins, 34
Wasson, Father William B., 144
Watson, Thomas, Sr., 46, 136
Weber, Max, 58, 126
Weimar Republic, 12
Welch, Jack, 32-34, 42, 62, 82
Wellman, Barry, 25, 26
Western Electric (AT&T), 7, 19
Westinghouse, 12
Whyte, William H. Jr., 62
Wilhelm II, King of Prussia (Kaiser Wilhelm), 12
Winfrey, Oprah, 6
Winning (Welch), 32
World of Warcraft (video game), 79
Worldcom, 32

Yahoo!, xiii, 30
Yang, Jerry, xiii, 30

Zapata, Emiliano, 7
Zimmerman, Robert Allen, 123

# Acknowledgments from the First Edition

This book grew out of two articles, written for different readers. One, "Toward a Science of Social Character," was written for psychoanalysts and psychotherapists, to help them understand the changes they are facing in the personality and problems of their patients. I first tested out the theory of a shift from the bureaucratic to the interactive social character in meetings of the Academy of Psychoanalysis and the International Forum of Psychoanalysis. Mauricio Cortina, a psychiatrist, made valuable contributions to my thinking, especially how changes in psychotherapy were matching the change in social character.

Later, I introduced this theory of a changing social character in a research seminar on collaborative organizations led by Charles Heckscher, a sociologist who has been extremely helpful with his encouragement and criticism of a draft of the first edition of this book. I benefited greatly from the interaction with members of the seminar, whose research enriched my understanding of the changes taking place in the knowledge workplace: Paul S. Adler, Lynda M. Applegate, Mark Bonchek, Nathaniel Foote, Jay R. Galbraith, Robert Howard, John Paul MacDuffie, Saul A. Rubinstein, Charles F. Sabel, and Barry Wellman. Their research and earlier versions of some of the material I've developed in this book were published in *The Firm as Collaborative Community*, edited by Heckscher and Adler.

The second article, "Why People Follow the Leader: The Power of Transference," published in the Harvard Business Review, was written for business leaders to help them understand how to deal with changes in the motivation of their followers. That article describes how the shift in social character requires a revision of Freud's theory of transference—the projection on to others of unconscious emotional attitudes shaped by infantile and childhood relationships. My editor, Diane Coutu, encouraged me to write the article, and as always, she was a brilliant and demanding guide and partner.

Jeff Kehoe at the Harvard Business School Press, read the article and suggested I expand it into a book on leaders and followers. Jeff helped me first to craft a book proposal and then became an indispensable critic and speaking partner as I wrote the book. He has been the kind of editor writers wish for but seldom find, someone who understands and appreciates what the writer is trying to say and challenges him to stretch himself.

The Harvard Business School Press sent a draft of the book to five anonymous reviewers who wrote useful criticism and gave their approval for publication. I thank them for the care they took, and I believe their suggestions improved the book.

The Leaders We Need was selected for the series, Leadership for the Common Good, a partnership between Harvard Business School Press and the Center for Public Leadership at Harvard University's John F. Kennedy School of Government.

I appreciate the time, thought, and useful criticism contributed by Nora Maccoby, Max Maccoby, Erik Berglof, and most of all, Sandylee Maccoby.

Thanks to my assistant, Maria Stroffolino, who prepared the many drafts of this manuscript, and to Monica Jainschigg, a careful and exacting copy editor.

—Michael Maccoby

i. Michael Maccoby, "Toward a Science of Social Character," International Forum of Psychoanalysis 11 (2002): 33–44.

ii. Charles Heckscher and Paul S. Adler, eds., The Firm as Collaborative Community: The Reconstruction of Trust in the Knowledge Economy (New York: Oxford University Press, 2006).

iii. Michael Maccoby, "Why People Follow the Leader: The Power of Transference," Harvard Business Review, September 2004, 76–88.

# About the Authors

***Michael Maccoby*** is a globally recognized expert on leadership who has advised, taught, and studied leaders of companies, unions, governments, healthcare organizations, and universities in 36 countries. His book, *The Gamesman* (1976) was the first bestseller to describe the personalities of leaders in high-tech companies. In his next book, *The Leader* (1981), he proposed as models leaders who developed both their organizations and people. His book *Narcissistic Leaders* (2007) described the strengths and dangers of visionary leaders. In *Transforming Health Care Leadership* (2013), Maccoby and his collaborators show how to improve quality, decrease costs and improve population health. He has authored or coauthored fifteen books, the most recent being *Strategic Intelligence, Conceptual Tools for Leading Change.* (2015). From 1970 to 1990 Maccoby was a research associate and program director at Harvard's Kennedy School of Government. He has taught leadership at Oxford University's Saïd Business School, Sciences Po, and other universities. For his work in Sweden, he was made Commander of the Royal Order of the Polar Star in 2007. In 2016, he received a lifetime achievement award from the Washington School of Psychiatry. His BA and PhD are from Harvard and he is a graduate of the Mexican Institute of Psychoanalysis.

***Tim Scudder*** is a principal at Personal Strengths Publishing (PSP), Inc., where he served as the Chief Executive Officer for over 20 years. He is the author or co-author of several training programs, assessments, and books, including Core Strengths, Results through Relationships, Strength Deployment Inventory, and Have a Nice Conflict. As a consultant and facilitator, Scudder has helped individuals, teams, and organizations reach their potential through improved relationship, teamwork, and strategic skills. His clients have included IBM, CME Group, USC, GEI Consultants, Microsoft, PricewaterhouseCoopers, the US Army, the British Foreign Commonwealth Office, and Twitter. Tim earned his PhD in Human and Organizational Systems from Fielding Graduate University. His research, Personality Types in Relationship Awareness Theory, provided the first empirical validation of Sigmund Freud's views on normal personality types. His Masters degree in Human Development is also from Fielding. He is a fellow of the Institute for Social Innovation and serves on the advisory board at Alliant International University's California School of Management and Leadership. Prior to his career in training and leadership development, he earned a Certified Public Accountancy license and practiced as a CPA, Chief Financial Officer, and financial consultant.